Venice-Abbot Kinney M
Branch Library
501 S. Venice Boulevard
Venice, CA 90291

JUL 16 2014

FROM POMPEII

#40 L.A. PUBLIC LIBRARY — VENICE

JUL 1 6 2014

FROM
POMPEII

The Afterlife of a
Roman Town

INGRID D. ROWLAND

THE BELKNAP PRESS OF
HARVARD UNIVERSITY PRESS
Cambridge, Massachusetts
London, England
2014

937.7
R883

192047556

Copyright © 2014 by the President and Fellows of Harvard College
All rights reserved
Printed in the United States of America

Library of Congress Cataloging-in-Publication Data

Rowland, Ingrid D. (Ingrid Drake)
From Pompeii : the afterlife of a Roman town / Ingrid D. Rowland.
pages   cm
Includes bibliographical references and index.
ISBN 978-0-674-04793-8 (alk. paper)
1. Pompeii (Extinct city)—History.   2. Pompeii (Extinct city)—Civilization.
3. Pompeii (Extinct city)—Social life and customs.   4. Tourism—Italy—
Naples (Province)—History.   I. Title.
DG70.P7R78   2014
937'.72568—dc23   2013037835

To Portia Prebys

Maxima magistra

Contents

Shieldbearer, the sun climbed warring,
and from the depths of the cave a startled bat
hit the light as an arrow hits a shield:
"'Ασίνην τε . . .'Ασίνην τε . . ." If only that could be the
    king of Asini
we've been searching for so carefully on this acropolis
sometimes touching with our fingers his touch upon the stones.

—George Seferis, "The King of Asini"

FROM POMPEII

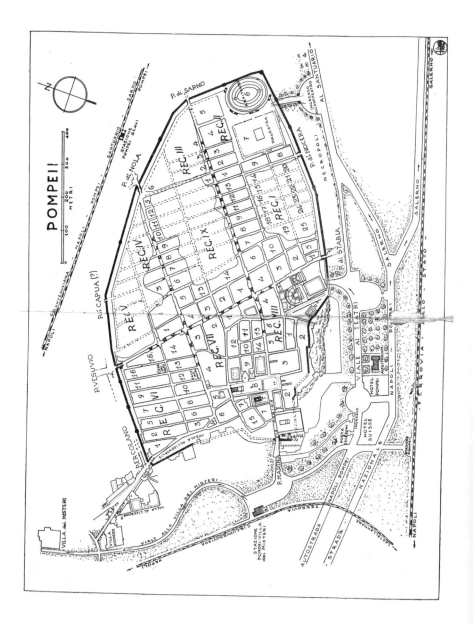

POMPEII

Introduction: Naples, 1962

Shaken by earthquake in A.D. 63, then buried by volcanic ash in A.D. 79, the ancient Roman city of Pompeii was one of the first places in the world to be subjected to systematic archaeological excavation. Since then, the site, because of its exceptional state of preservation, has provided one of our most intimate views into the life of an ancient civilization. With its intact streets, its graffiti, shops, temples, houses, gardens, paintings, statues, mosaics, and its poignant traces of the disaster's victims, human and animal, the buried city has captured the imagination of generations of visitors, readers, and moviegoers. These imagined Pompeiis, however, invariably reflect a particular time and place, a particular interpretation of the city's superabundant archaeological evidence. The history of Pompeii's place in the imagination is by now as complex and as revealing as that of the city itself.

My own experience of Pompeii began in mid-January of 1962, as an eight-year-old fresh off an Italian ocean liner named *Leonardo da Vinci*. My father, a chemist, had won a Guggenheim grant and planned to spend six months in Mainz, Germany, followed by two months in Cambridge, England. But my parents, my brother, and I reached Mainz by sailing from New York to Naples because my parents wanted to see Italy, the land of Sophia Loren, Claudia Cardinale, Marcello Mastroianni, espresso, Leonardo—and Pompeii. We brought a car on board: a boxy red Ford Falcon with a big chrome grille that would draw crowds all the way up the Italian peninsula (along with its very tall occupants). I had already fallen in love with Italian accents: "lahnch is now being ser-ve-dah," "Lay-o-nar-do da Veenci," the new language, and the food. After a night in Naples at the sleek, sixties-modern Hotel Mediterraneo, we took off down the new Autostrada del Sole to see Pompeii, pulling up to the main entrance at Porta Marina with that remarkable car. As we opened its doors, a troop of women swarmed around us, all festooned with wooden trays that hung from straps around their necks piled high with trinkets, chewing gum, and cigarettes. They begged for some of my mother's American cigarettes; Italians in those days were restricted to smoking Italian government brands. The site, as it happened, was closed for its weekly *riposo,* and my parents were unnerved by all these stocky, insistent ladies, so the two of them swept my brother and me across the street into the lobby of the Hotel Vittoria. A desk clerk told us that Herculaneum would be open. Before setting out again (my brother and I were children, after all), we had something to drink at the hotel bar, which gave us a carefully planned view into the vitrines of the hotel's cameo shop. The shop I remember vividly; it boasted both a plaster cast of an ancient Pompeian's body in its own glass cabinet, and a living cameo carver, who showed us how he transformed bits of shell into miniature works of art. We looked without buying (of course I desperately wanted a cameo but kept that desire to myself for several decades); as I would learn years later, my parents could barely afford the coming year abroad, and this was our very first stop. Through a concrete tollbooth that looked like an ancient temple we returned to the Autostrada. A short drive led us to Herculaneum, nestled at the bottom of an enormous square crater that opened out abruptly in the middle of a crowded modern town. A guard in a peaked cap led us down stone-paved streets through the ancient houses, with their miraculously preserved half-timbering, overhanging balconies, and hints of garden, entrancing us, erasing the disappointment of inaccessible Pompeii. My father took two photographs; film, like everything else, was at a premium in those days. In one (Figure I.1), the guard watches carefully over my six-year-old brother, unsteady on his steel leg brace, while I stare out at the camera, my own camera slung around my neck. I am already on a mission.

I plied that little Brownie Starmite camera more eagerly at this ancient site than anywhere else in our eight-month trip, though

I.1   Ingrid Rowland and Jeffrey Rowland in Herculaneum with an unnamed guard, January 1962. Photo: F. Sherwood Rowland.

the photographs reveal more enthusiasm than skill. Afterward, we drove up Vesuvius as far as the road would take us; to my mother's relief, the funicular that led all the way up to the volcano's lip was closed for the winter. Back down the dark, glittering slopes we went, back to Naples and our view across the bay to Capri (which we knew from a popular song as "the Isle of Capree," accented on the final syllable). The English name "Naples" perplexed me; it sounded nothing like beautiful "Napoli." The next morning we set out for what my parents called "Rome," though all the signs pointed to "Roma."

My family's brief tour of the Bay of Naples was the standard mix of buried city, volcano, and metropolis. Until recently, it was impossible to separate a visit to Pompeii or Herculaneum from a trip to Naples, and there is no way to tour any part of the region without coming to terms with Vesuvius. It is also impossible to leave these extraordinary places without extraordinary memories. Because they were formed in childhood, my own first impressions of Naples, Pompeii, and Herculaneum have become a deep stratum in a kind of personal archaeology, but visitors at every age and every stage of life come back from these places changed, sometimes profoundly. This book presents a selection of visitors whose lives were forever altered by their experience of Pompeii, as well as a few who reacted less drastically. It is not an exhaustive list; they have been chosen because their stories are more unusual or more unexpected than most, such as the surprising adventures of Renoir outside France, Freud outside Vienna, Hirohito outside Tokyo, and the spiritual odyssey of a sensitive, driven man named Bartolo Longo, who changed Pompeii at least as much as Pompeii changed him.

The fifty years since my own first trip to Pompeii have brought profound changes to Italy and to public perceptions of its most famous buried city. The most important of these changes may well be the increasing role of international collaboration in every aspect of the site, from understanding the realities of ancient life to preserving its fragile remains. Initially, archaeology, as a discipline of the Enlightenment, tended to serve the ends of that other great Enlightenment invention, the nation-state. Thus Pompeii has served a succession of national governments, from the Kingdom of Naples to the Republic of Italy, to various (and often divergent) patriotic ends. Meanwhile, foreign scholars often looked down on their Italian colleagues, assuming superior knowledge about classical antiquity among many other kinds of superiorities, religious, social, and cultural. In our globalized world, however, where Italy ranks as a world economic power, the buried ancient city has become a model in an entirely different way: as its own version of a recognizably global community, a city that once included Romans, Greeks, Oscans, Etruscans, Samnites, Egyptian immigrants, and a varied population of foreign slaves, incorporating their tastes, languages, and religious predilections with a good deal of success.

At the same time, a radically reshaped Vesuvius, its symmetrical ancient cone blown to pieces in more recent eruptions, stands above Pompeii as a reminder that the city's disastrous end in the early years of the ancient Roman Empire is still a matter of present concern. Seismographers and volcanologists keep the mountain under constant surveillance, but when it decides to erupt again, its power over the human inhabitants of the Bay of Naples will be no less absolute than it was in the reign of the Emperor Titus, nearly two thousand years ago. The beauty of Pompeii's natural setting and the mildness of its climate exert the same potentially fatal attraction for the city's modern settlers as for their ancient predecessors, who repeated stories of long-ago earthquakes and subterranean fires but never expected to endure a calamity at first hand. It is this combination of beauty and danger that gives Pompeii its excitement, and its insistent reminder of our own mortality makes this particular buried city seem so real and so familiar. But there is also an important legacy of experience and inspiration to be found in the stories of visitors to Pompeii who may have lived out the rest of their lives in a different way because of that brief excursion.

Pompeii changes, too, this buried city that has been a blasted plain, a vineyard, a treasure trove, a den of bandits, a carefully managed tourist site, a world-famous ruin threatened by further ruin now that it lies exposed and vulnerable. Pompeii changes, but sometimes it changes slowly. On one of my most recent trips, more than half a century after the first, a vendor called out from her stand at the Porta Marina: "Come and look! I give you a present." She had made the same offer in 1962.

1

Pompeii, May 2013

It is easy to forget how beautiful it is until you are there. Pompeii in May is a perfume of laurel, rosemary, and Spanish broom, *ginestra* (Figure 1.1), the yellow-flowered plant that made the poet Giacomo Leopardi write so movingly about human mortality a few miles from here, in a villa on the lava flows above Torre del Greco:

> Here on the arid back
> Of the dread mountain
> Vesuvius the Exterminator
> Which no other tree or flower cheers
> You spread your solitary sprays
> Fragrant broom . . . lover
> Of somber places cast off by the world,
> The staunch companion of stricken fortunes.
> These fields, spread
> With barren ashes, covered
> In lava petrified

1.1. Spanish broom and poppies, Pompeii, May 2013. Photo by author.

That echoes under travelers' feet,
. . . were famous cities
That the haughty mountain buried in its torrents,
together with their people, blazing lightning
From its fiery mouth. Now ruin enfolds

Everything around
Where you sit, gentle flower, as if
You pity others' doom, and to heaven
You send a perfume of sweetest scent
That soothes the desert.[1]

Leopardi wrote his poem in the latter part of 1836, a few months after a violent March eruption opened a new crater in the cone of Vesuvius the Exterminator and showered the countryside with ash. When the poet called the *ginestra* a desert flower, then, he meant what he said. But now, because Vesuvius has kept silence for nearly seventy years, Leopardi's picture of ashen desolation has turned green; after the heat of a volcano dies down, the soil it deposits is rich with minerals. And so in today's Pompeii, everything is in bloom in May: acanthus, the shiny, spike-leafed plant commemorated on the capitals of Corinthian columns; pomegranates, roses, red poppies. Little chamomile flowers form carpets of miniature daisies inside the ruins. Around the amphitheater in the early morning the only sound is birdsong, carried on the sea breeze that rustles through the trees. Here, in the eastern part of town, hard-packed dirt covers the big gray paving stones as it likely did in ancient times; the wheels of Pompeian carts must have traced their ruts by rolling over soil and mud, not bare rock. Poppies cling to the heaps of unmoved ancient ash. Much of the region around the amphitheater is still unexcavated, and in these wilder places it is easier than it is in the tourist-packed forum to identify with the early visitors to Pompeii, who walked between these umbrella pines when they were saplings, who saw the ancient town peeking forth from farmland. Today much of that farmland is newly planted: in many of these outlying houses, grapevines have been strung in ordered rows between olive trees in backyard gardens, just as Vergil said they should be, writing in the time of Augustus, more than two thousand years ago. Grapes should grow with roses, he said, and so they do, and these are roses bred for their scent as well as their flowers.

At the back of a vineyard near the seaward stretch of the old city wall, a plaque quotes a passage from a letter written in 1863 by the Italian patriot Luigi Settembrini shortly after Pompeii's superintendent, Giuseppe Fiorelli, devised a way to create plaster casts of the eruption's living victims (we shall be hearing about both Settembrini and Fiorelli later on):[2] "They have been dead for eighteen centuries, but they are human creatures seen in their death struggle. This is not art, this is not imitation, these are their bones, the relics of their flesh and their clothing mixed with plaster, and the pain of death that regains substance and form."

Thirteen people died in this little vineyard after taking shelter from the falling volcanic pebbles in a lean-to that may have been a garden shed, an outdoor dining room, or both. They lay there, side by side, buried until 1961.

All of the houses along the empty streets near the amphitheater are closed and locked, and many of the streets are blocked as well, the result of rain damage from the wettest period in recent Italian history (the same rains that have brought the plants into such riotous bloom).[3] Even the Via dell'Abbondanza, the main thoroughfare, running from east to west, is barricaded in many places by improvised wire fences; it is impossible to walk in a straight line from one end of Pompeii to the other without making tortuous detours. A sign on one of the scaffolded houses on Via dell'Abbondanza declares that: "Pompeii is a living city! A city that produces wine from its own fertile vines and food from its own gardens. Pompeii is the daughter and victim of a tragedy; that of its destruction by the eruption of Vesuvius, which took place in 79 A.D. And yet we, moved by the plaster casts of the victims, are happy to be able to observe, admire, and come to know what remains of a Roman city."[4]

In 2011 the building behind this sign was bustling with restorers at work. In 2013 it stands silent and inaccessible. Pompeii is a living city, but much of what lives there is vegetable, reptile, bird, or insect: the bumblebees are huge and fat, jet black or black striped with yellow, the sign of a healthy environment.

The tourist crowds begin where the Via dell'Abbondanza turns into a pedestrian zone—an area the ancient Pompeians marked out for foot traffic only by creating an abrupt step-up in the street's paving blocks, high enough to have stopped any cart or chariot in its tracks. The contrast between the wild Pompeii at the edge of the ancient town and the tourist Pompeii of the forum area is almost as stark as the contrast between centuries and sensibilities that divides modern visitors from the Grand Tourists of the eighteenth century or the resident farmers of every century up to our own. Today most visitors to Pompeii follow a set tour that minimizes the danger of tripping, heart attacks, and casual vandalism by drastically restricting the number of places open for free exploration (and hence the number of guards to pay). By making arrangements in advance, scholars can gain access to many of the closed houses, and with the volumes of people pouring through the forum it is easy, if frustrating, to see why the blockade has been set up. But in my own student days, in the 1970s, Pompeii was a place where anyone could wander and explore freely. Shortly after I received my PhD in 1980, an earthquake rattled Pompeii's tottering ancient walls, and since then nothing has been the same. Once more, the Titans had begun to move beneath the earth. Shifting soil, the first hint of climate change, renewed Pompeii's vows to the law of entropy, the second law of thermodynamics by whose decree all things eventually fall apart. At least entropy should also diminish some of the damage that human folly has inflicted on Pompeii, thanks to bureaucracy, corruption, organized crime, ignorance, and slashed budgets. Between works of thoughtless construction and thoughtless destruction, excesses of attention and excesses of neglect, Pompeii has become its present strange mix of overly packaged Disneyland and idyllic wilderness walk.

A lovely path for cyclists and hikers leads around the city walls, a quiet, contemplative stroll among old (but not ancient) farmhouses, fields of vines and cultivated snapdragons, huge Vergilian pines, oaks, ancient masonry, and, just outside the perimeter fence, along the old railroad track, the intrusive profile of a hideous concrete industrial building under construction, what locals call an "ecomonster" when they do not simply call it a *pugno nell'occhio*, "a punch in the eye."

2

The Blood of San Gennaro
and the Eruption of Vesuvius

Just beyond the main train station of Naples, a broad, dirty boulevard skirts the coastline. Apparently landlocked, it has a strange name: Via del Ponte della Maddalena, the Street of the Bridge of St. Mary Magdalene. Allied bombers pulverized much of the area in 1943 and 1944, destroying the little church of Saint Erasmus (a Roman soldier who was disemboweled for his faith), but the street has somehow survived, and so, remarkably, has the bridge, although the river that flows beneath it into the Bay of Naples was enclosed in a covered channel long ago. Even when it was clean, free, and open to the sky, the River Sebeto was only about ten kilometers long—or, as the ancient Romans would say, ten times one thousand steps *(mille passuum).*[1] And as long as Naples has existed, that is, ever since the sixth century B.C., the River Sebeto has marked the chief border between Neapolis, the "New City," and the rest of the world.

So, too, for many centuries, the Sebeto's later neighbors, the Ponte della Maddalena and the little church of Saint Erasmus, also marked the extreme outskirts of the city; in many ways these ghostly presences still do. The oldest train line in Italy began here in 1839. Now no fewer than three train stations converge in this same area, close to both the port and the vast emporium of Piazza del Mercato: the Central Station with its high-speed line, the underground station of Piazza Garibaldi, and the private railroad called the Circumvesuviana, the oldest train line in Italy. And here, too, since the latter half of the twentieth century and the rise of the automobile, the filthy, graying on-ramp to the A3 autostrada has performed its flying leaps overhead. But before trains and cars came into existence, the now-desolate no-man's land was also the official point where—on many occasions and for a variety of reasons—the people of Naples came out to meet Mount Vesuvius either on foot or riding on the backs of animals, in carts, or in carriages.

Just beyond the Ponte della Maddalena, for untold centuries a broad boulevard has unfurled its straight-arrow course to the south; since World War II, a marble street sign has enshrined it as the Strada Reggia di Ercolano—wrongly: the name should be (and in fact used to be) Strada Regia, the Royal Road. "Reggia" with two *g*'s means a royal palace, and indeed a royal palace sits farther along the Royal Road, just north of Herculaneum in a place called Portici, "the gateways." For the moment, though, we will stop at the end of the Ponte della Maddalena, the time-honored meeting place for a city and an active volcano.

The story of Pompeii, like that of Naples itself, begins with one of those meetings between a human settlement and the mountain that looms as an untamed menace over the entire bay. Today, the ash-black cone of Vesuvius, glittering with volcanic glass, still shows the scars of its last eruption in 1944, and geologists assure us that another event is long overdue.[2] Unlike its larger Sicilian neighbor, Etna, Vesuvius does not enjoy a reputation as a *vulcano buono,* a "good volcano," which spews its steam and lava constantly and hence more gently. Vesuvius is pent up; when it finally explodes, its rage is unrelenting. At times during its long history, however, it has stored up its wrath for so long that plants have grown again on its naked slopes, and the people who live around it have learned to forget its evil temper.

One of those moments of oblivion seems to have occurred in the first years of the Roman Empire. Writing some twenty years before the birth of Christ, the ancient architect Vitruvius, who may have been a native of the region himself, reported stories that "in the old days fires grew up and abounded beneath Mount Vesuvius, and that therefore the mountain vomited forth flames into the fields all around," but it must have been hard to imagine such chaos amid the ordered luxury of the villas on the scenic seaside cliffs of Baiae, Herculaneum, Oplontis, and Pompeii.[3] The pure line of the mountain's beautifully symmetrical cone had been softened by a riotous growth of grapevines, trees, and flowering plants, their branches as full of chattering birds as the bay beneath it was full of fish. Swarms of butterflies were believed to carry the souls of the dead as they flitted over the slopes of Vesuvius on weightless wings. The world's troubles, in these first days of the Roman Empire, seemed to be almost entirely of human making rather than the fault of nature, troubles like the civil war that had ravaged southern Italy for nearly a century or the slaves' revolt, led by a gladiator named Spartacus, who for a time had made his headquarters in the volcano's wooded crater.[4] Now, however, as Vitruvius noted, the firm hand and godlike intelligence of Augustus promised to bring even human events under control.[5]

Eighty years later, in the reign of Emperor Nero, that control had slipped into decadence, and nature began to rumble her displeasure. An earthquake rattled the Bay of Naples in the year 63, striking the port city of Pompeii with particular ferocity. A marble relief carved just afterward shows some of the damage to the city's forum. This carving decorated the *lararium,* or family shrine, of the wealthy Pompeian banker Lucius Caecilius Iucundus, for reasons we may never really know—perhaps Iucundus died in the disaster and his survivors honored their ancestor in his own home. In any case, the frieze shows that when the earth resettled after the commotion, it left the monuments of Pompeii's forum tilted at crazy angles; we can see the Temple of Capitoline Jupiter and the triumphal arch of Augustus as well as several statues listing dangerously. On the right side of the frieze we see preparations for an expensive sacrifice to appease angry Neptune, the Earth Shaker, or to thank him for not making the upheaval even worse.

Ominously, however, the list of forum buildings damaged beyond repair included the temple to the imperial family, which included, of course, the troubling Nero. Pompeii's city fathers moved the paraphernalia for this important cult out of the ruined forum and into the ancient temple of Zeus Meilichios, a structure dating back to Pompeii's years as a Greek colony and consecrated to the "honey-sweet" underworld version of Jupiter, king of the gods. Zeus Meilichios took the form of a snake; the Pompeians must have hoped that he would use his powers of sweet persuasion to placate the angry earth as he slipped into her folds.

A wall painting from another lararium, this one in Pompeii's House of the Centenary (Figure 2.1), shows the cone of Vesuvius rising in the background beneath a beribboned garland, its slopes lush with every kind of vegetation. In front of the mountain, Bacchus himself, dressed in a costume of gigantic grapes, pours out a libation of wine as his pet tiger (adopted when the god and his cult conquered India) playfully tries to snatch a taste of the liquid. The scene seems to echo a line by the Roman poet Martial (although he probably wrote it a few years later): "Bacchus loves these slopes more than the hills of his native land."[6] A sparrow—usually a symbol of love—flies off to the right, and beneath the god and the mountain we see a magnificent serpent rearing gracefully before a low altar. This is every Roman lararium's traditional good luck

2.1.   Bacchus Standing before Vesuvius, from the House of the Centenary, Pompeii, Fourth Style, 1st century A.D. (fresco). Museo Archeologico Nazionale, Naples, Italy / The Bridgeman Art Library.

symbol, but the resemblance of this particular lucky snake to Zeus Meilichios is unmistakable.

As events would show, honey-sweet Zeus seemed to have his own definite ideas about how to solve Pompeii's problems. Within five years (in the year 68), Nero would be driven from Rome and forced to commit suicide by rebellious elements of the Roman army; his eventual successor, the popular general Vespasian (the fourth emperor to reign in what is now known as the Year of the Four Emperors) introduced a welcome element of sanity into government, the Colosseum into Rome, and public toilets into the design of cities. Once again, by the early 70s, human reason seemed capable of making up for the extravagance of human folly. When Vespasian died in 79, the succession went naturally to his eldest son, Titus, famous for having conquered Jerusalem for Rome nine years before and for depositing the treasures of Solomon's Temple in his father's own Temple of Peace, which adjoined the Roman Forum.

Yet it was during the auspicious reign of Titus, probably on August 24 of A.D. 79, though some scholars think it may have been on November 24, that Mount Vesuvius exploded, burying Pompeii in a shower of volcanic pebbles known as lapilli (Latin for "little stones") and the neighboring town of Herculaneum in a succession of the terrible, fiery torrents known as *pyroclastic flows*. These are quick-moving rivers made up of solid particles—pieces of rock and ash—suspended in white-hot gas. The whole deadly mass spreads like a liquid, but much more quickly, reaching speeds of up to several hundred kilometers an hour and killing virtually every form of life in its path; when it settles, it hardens into a nearly impenetrable solid.[7]

As the sky turned black and the sun red, the admiral in charge of the local Roman fleet, the amateur naturalist Gaius Plinius Secundus (Pliny the Elder), took charge with magnificent efficiency. After setting up plans for evacuating the residents around the Bay of Naples, he set forth in his flagship and commanded his oarsmen to head straight for the coastline beneath the spewing mountain. For all his energy, however, Pliny was a portly, asthmatic man; shortly after the ship landed in Stabiae, the heat, the effort, and the fumes of the pyroclastic flows proved too much for his overburdened heart and lungs. He died that evening on the beach at today's Castellamare di Stabia, as we know from a pair of letters written a quarter of a century later by his nephew, also named Gaius Plinius Secundus (Pliny the Younger).

The younger Pliny had seen the eruption, too, but had decided to stay home and study rather than take to the sea with his uncle for a closer look. This same instinct for self-preservation may well have saved the nephew's life a second time fifteen years later, when he evaded the paranoid clutches of the tyrannical Emperor Domitian, and thus lived to tell the tale of Pompeii for posterity.[8] A dutiful Roman of the senatorial class, Pliny the Younger had acquired his famous uncle's habits of observation, adding to them a literary sensibility the elder Pliny lacked altogether (characteristically, the elder Pliny's *Natural History* discusses marble sculpture as part of a chapter on stone and artistic bronze work in the chapter on metals). But the younger Pliny had good reason to pay attention to his Latin style, for he wrote his two letters about the eruption of Vesuvius in answer to a request from a great writer, the historian Tacitus, who asked his friend for more information about the disaster. Pliny's account, although written from memory, is both a gripping human story and a remarkably informative description of the geological events, enlivened by the ancient Roman habit of describing dramatic situations in the present tense, as if they are happening before our own eyes:

> The cloud was rising from a mountain—at such a distance we couldn't tell which one, but afterwards we learned that it was Vesuvius. I can best describe its shape by likening it to

an umbrella pine. It rose into the sky on a very long "trunk" from which spread some "branches." I imagine it had been raised by a sudden blast, which then weakened, leaving the cloud unsupported so that its own weight caused it to spread sideways. Some of the cloud was white, in other parts there were dark patches of dirt and ash. . . . Ash was falling . . . now, darker and denser. . . . Now it was bits of pumice, and rocks that were blackened and burned and shattered by the fire. Now the sea is shoal; debris from the mountain blocks the shore.[9]

Archaeologists have recovered traces of more than a thousand victims of this eruption, including a poor Pompeian dog straining at its leash, and a group of three hundred people stranded on the seashore at Herculaneum, waiting for evacuation by sea. The actual toll of the disaster must have numbered several thousand (some estimates go as high as 16,000) and many thousands more must have been injured or traumatized for the rest of their lives. By the end of the cataclysm, the volcano's profile had changed radically, from a single graceful, conical peak, like Etna and Mount Fuji, to a jagged-edged crater; the force of the eruption had blown the top right off the mountain.[10]

And then Vesuvius slept again. When it awoke in succeeding centuries, it continued its eerie habit of underscoring the turmoil of human events (right up to its last eruption, which occurred in 1944 at the height of World War II). The eruptions of 472 and 512 added to the chaos of a crumbling Roman Empire and invading barbarians, Visigoths, Ostrogoths, and Lombards. In 512, moreover, the volcano began to change its habits. Earlier eruptions, like the disaster of 79, expelled volcanic pebbles and produced pyroclastic flows, but now the mountain also began to spill real liquid: molten lava. When the volcano threw out pebbles in 1138 and again for eight days in 1139, Naples had just fallen to Norman warlords, who would soon transform the city into one of the most beautiful and populous settlements on earth—but at the time, the people of the region could see only the terror of invasion compounded by an exploding volcano. If there were any other eruptions in the Middle Ages, records have not survived. A small explosion occurred in 1500, and then, at a time when record keeping in the region had become both consistent and well preserved, Vesuvius seems to have fallen silent for decades. By the latter half of the sixteenth century, the younger Pliny's image of a column of smoke that rose like a huge umbrella pine had become a memory as dim as Vitruvius's talk about rivers of fire.[11] The serrated edge of the ancient crater had softened its lines after centuries of erosion, and the mountain now had two peaks: Somma, the remnants of the original slope, and the new cone—the "Great Cone" (Gran Cono) of Vesuvius—the one that had spewed forth the eruption of 79.

We can imagine what the mountain must have looked like in this dormant period from a poem, published in 1591 but probably written years earlier, by a native of the area, the wandering philosopher Giordano Bruno. Bruno remembered Vesuvius in his own day as a mountain of luxuriant greenery, the wine from the grapes that grew on its slopes so divinely exquisite that it was (and still is) called "Christ's Tears": *Lacryma Christi*. In the mid-sixteenth century, the volcano's jagged profile still showed the effects of the blast that had buried Pompeii, as we can see from Bruno's account of what Vesuvius looked like from a distance. His poem imagines a conversation between himself and the smaller mountain above his native Nola, Monte Cicala, which has just pointed out Vesuvius to him. The young Bruno (he must have been about thirteen) is unimpressed:

> Seeing that formless form, scrutinizing the figure
> Of that amorphous heap, I said: "You mean that
>   crookback?

You mean that sawtooth hunchback splitting the seamless
    sky?"[12]

When Bruno actually came closer to Vesuvius, however (as he
did for the first time as an adolescent in 1563), the "sawtooth
hunchback" turned into a "loving brother" of unimaginable
beauty:

Yet when at last I approached, and looked at Vesuvius
    closely,
Famous for Bacchus, his slopes superbly mantled in
    thickets,
Fertile, abundant in grapes in their burgeoning bowers,
    and fruits, too,
Of every kind, and shape, and color our nurturing mother
Nature sends forth, breathing in the bounteous air of our
    homeland—
He lacks for nothing, I thought; his treasures are more
    than a hundred.[13]

Although the volcano may have lain dormant throughout the
sixteenth century, the earth around the Bay of Naples had been
anything but sleepy. Year after year, the seaside city of Pozzuoli
sank gently into the bay, and then, suddenly, it began to rise again
(we call the phenomenon "bradyseism"—Greek for "slow shaking"). The bubbling mud of the crater called La Solfatara belched
out its foul-smelling vapors as it had ever since ancient times.
Most remarkably, an entire mountain ("Monte Nuovo," "New
Mountain") rose out of the ground just north of Naples between
September 29 and October 3, 1538, destroying a village in the process.[14] Yet Neapolitans in the later sixteenth century joked that
Vesuvius was more fearsome in their own day for its rainy-season
mudslides than for its subterranean fires.

FROM POMPEII

Those underground blazes, of course, continued to burn beneath the plug of solidified magma that had formed inside its crater, building up the underground pressure year after year, century after century. When the plug finally burst into the air again, and Vesuvius at last poured forth streams of fiery lava amid the pyroclastic flows, the volcano erupted onto a world that had become recognizably modern. With this dramatic explosion, the worst in a thousand years, the story of Pompeii's rediscovery really begins.

On the morning of December 16, 1631, Vesuvius began to rumble as it had not done in decades, and fires flickered down its flanks. As ever, the volcano seemed to be underlining the turmoil of human events: in 1631, the Swedish king Gustavus Adolphus and his crack artillery began a rampage through Germany, challenging the balance of power in Europe. As the morning progressed, the volcano's active cone began to spew dense clouds of smoke—the pulverized plug of hardened magma—and three fiery rivers of hot gas poured down the slopes of Vesuvius toward the bay.

The old crater of Somma, the one that had destroyed Pompeii and Herculaneum, stayed quiet as a new crater opened to the southeast. Pyroclastic flows (particulates suspended in gas) rather than flaming magma poured down the mountain's seaward slopes. The sea, as in the eruption of 79, grew as agitated as the mountain above it.

This eruption killed some three thousand people, most of them scattered along the Bay of Naples. But the ash also fell on Naples itself. By the seventeenth century, the city had become one of the most populous in the world: a quarter of a million people crowded into a dense warren of tall buildings lining narrow streets that had been laid out by Greek colonists more than two thousand years before—for a population one-tenth as great. Inside the walls of Naples, the risk of panic posed a danger nearly as grave as the eruption itself. The city, ruled (more normally misruled) by a Spanish viceroy who answered to Madrid, was as ready to erupt as Vesuvius. The viceroy maintained an antagonistic relationship with the local gentry: a small group of feudal barons whose vast wealth had been wrung for centuries from peasants and city dwellers who worked their lives away in desperate poverty.[15] In Naples, resentments between nationalities, between social classes, and between church and state, were never far from the surface.

As Vesuvius roared over the normal din of the crowded city, responsibility for managing the public safety fell to the brand-new Spanish viceroy, Manuel de Guzmán, Count of Monterrey, and to Archbishop Francesco Boncompagni. Boncompagni's first instinct was to hide, which he did for the entire evening of December 16. Guzmán, however, rushed to the cathedral to put the city's fate into the hands of a modest local saint, Januarius, whose cult had been fostered by the Spanish rulers ever since their arrival in Naples.

The true power of seventeenth-century saints resided in their ability to intercede with Christ, God, and the Virgin Mary in answer to prayer, but the church from its very beginnings had also ascribed miraculous qualities to the physical remains of holy people, not only whole bodies but also tiny fragments, and even secretions like the fat that dripped from Saint Lawrence as he roasted on the torturer's grill (preserved in three places in Rome) or drops of the Virgin Mary's milk (of which some was preserved in Rome's basilica of Santa Maria Maggiore, along with a lock of her hair). Italy, one of the cradles of Christianity, was a veritable treasury of such relics, and Naples was no exception. No one, however, collected relics more eagerly than the Spanish monarchs, who had ruled Naples since 1441.[16] Their attachment to physical remains extended from the company of saints to the members of the royal family; a surprising number of Spanish monarchs had taken long journeys accompanying the corpse of a relative: in 1504, Ferdinand of Aragón took the coffin containing his late wife, Isabella of Castile, from Granada to Medina del Campo. A generation

FROM POMPEII

later, their daughter Juana took what was left of her husband, Archduke Philip the Handsome, from Medina del Campo back to Granada, allegedly opening the coffin on at least one occasion to look at him (one of the actions that earned her the epithet "la Loca"—"the Mad"). King Philip II accompanied the body of his father, Charles V, from Yuste, near Spain's northern coast, to the Escorial, in the very center of the country.[17] Some Spanish monarchs were never buried at all: the Aragonese rulers of Naples, who reigned from 1441 to 1503, still lie to this day in lead-lined caskets high up on a shelf in the sacristy of the church of San Domenico Maggiore.[18]

It was one of these curiously preserved Aragonese kings, Ferrante I, who, in the late fifteenth century, transported the relics of Saint Januarius from the remote Benedictine abbey of Montevergine to a special chapel in Naples Cathedral. On December 17, 1631, Viceroy Guzmán de Monterrey and Archbishop Boncompagni took those relics up again, marching them out beneath a damask canopy in a glorious procession down the Via del Duomo and east to the Porta Nolana, straight toward the mountain's steaming slopes.

The decision to entrust the city's fate to Januarius, or "Gennaro," as he was known in the vernacular, stemmed from more than the simple fact that he was a local. His relics had a most peculiar quality: like the rocks of Mount Vesuvius, they could change from solid to liquid and back again. Though Januarius had never been a saint of major importance, he boasted a more colorful legend than most saints, with several ties to real places around Naples and its bay; by 1631, his relics had also acquired a long history of their own. The church marked his feast on September 19; on this day, in 305 A.D., at least according to a book of saints' lives called the *Roman Martyrology,* the minions of anti-Christian Emperor Diocletian had tried to torture Januarius, who served as a local bishop, by throwing him into a furnace. From this ordeal, however, the bishop emerged unscathed. Then, like so many early Christians, he was put into a Roman gladiatorial show as an intermezzo between animal fights and man-to-man combat. This venue was the amphitheater of Pozzuoli, a huge arena just north of Naples with impressive ruins that survive even today and are almost as imposing as those of the Colosseum in Rome. Here, the *Martyrology* says, Januarius was cast into the arena together with some hungry lions, but the lions refused to attack him.[19]

At last his life ended, as martyrs' lives almost always do, with a beheading—but not before a brave member of the bishop's congregation managed to catch some of the blood that spurted from the saint's severed neck. The Christian community also obtained Gennaro's mortal remains and guarded them in secret until Christianity became legal in 313. In 431 A.D., as waves of barbarian invaders swept through Italy (and Vesuvius prepared to spew lava for the first time rather than pyroclast), the body of Saint Januarius and two vials of his blood were moved for safekeeping to a maze of catacombs dug deep into the volcanic cliffs above Naples. Some records state that in the course of this first move, the saint's blood liquefied within its vials. Or perhaps it liquefied for the first time nearly a thousand years later, in 1389, when the relics were moved again, this time from the catacombs to the city of Benevento and then again to the Benedictine monastery of Montevergine. By the early fourteenth century, the physical remnants of Saint Januarius numbered only three: two crystal vials of his blood and an elaborate silver bust containing a piece of the martyr's skull. The reliquaries that still preserve these treasures were made in the early fourteenth century, when the relics themselves were already a thousand years old. At last, toward the end of the fifteenth century, when the relic-loving kings of Aragon had taken over the Kingdom of Naples, they moved Saint Januarius to his present honored place in Naples Cathedral.[20]

A painting by the Neapolitan artist Micco Spadaro (who probably witnessed the scene himself) shows what may have happened on December 16, 1631, when Viceroy Guzmán de Monterrey and Archbishop Boncompagni brought forth the skull of San Gennaro and the vials of his blood. As smoke fills the atmosphere and flames lap the margins of the volcano's crater, the two leaders, one sacred, one secular, march out of Naples with the sacred relics under a special white canopy, praying all the while that this act, by a holy process of analogy, will stanch the flow of fiery gases racing down the slopes of Mount Vesuvius. Because the worst of the damage was occurring in the countryside to the south of Naples, virtually in the same places that were destroyed in 79, Micco Spadaro takes pains to show that the procession has stopped just past the city walls at the Ponte della Maddalena.

Beneath the angry volcano, the archbishop's prayer, echoed by the huge, panicked procession of Neapolitans, made San Gennaro's blood liquefy within its crystal vials at the same moment that the pyroclastic surges from Vesuvius solidified on the slope of the mountain. With this miracle, San Gennaro, Saint Januarius, catapulted to confirmed status as the city's most beloved saintly protector.

The cult of San Gennaro spread with the speed of breaking news. The cathedral ordered the erection of a huge marble obelisk in his honor, designed and carved by the great sculptor Cosimo Fanzago.[21] The city of Pozzuoli, site of the saint's martyrdom, hired the famous team of Artemisia Gentileschi and Viviano Codazzi to paint the story of Gennaro's life, including a wonderful scene set in the amphitheater, where the kindly lions look, perhaps deliberately, like sweet-tempered Neapolitan mastiffs.

San Gennaro's reputation has never faltered since that December day in 1631. Today his chapel in the cathedral is an uncommonly privileged shrine, an independent piece of real estate governed by the mayor of Naples and the city council rather than the Curia in Rome. Its decoration is incomparably rich even by the lavish standards of Neapolitan Baroque. Altar, reliquaries, candlesticks, and lamps glitter with silver brought from the Spanish colonies of the New World, and the whole chapel creates a blaze of light within the dark, lofty recesses of the Gothic church.

The three relics of blood and skull, still in their fourteenth-century reliquaries, are ceremonially exposed to public view in his chapel three times a year: for a week at the end of May, a week in mid-September, and on December 16, the anniversary of San Gennaro's first great miracle.

In May and September, the bishop of Naples examines the vials of San Gennaro's blood, and on most occasions it liquefies. Its failure to do so is thought to foretell disaster, and in fact San Gennaro's blood was slow to liquefy in the revolutionary year of 1799 and withheld his miracle altogether twice in the twentieth century: in September 1939, just before the outbreak of World War II, and in September 1980, just before a devastating November earthquake.

In calling on San Gennaro in 1631, Viceroy Guzmán and Archbishop Boncompagni made several assumptions: first, that the eruption of Vesuvius was an act of God, and, second, that, in heaven, San Gennaro clearly exerted enough influence with the Almighty to convince the Lord to change his mind. Belief in a connection between the volcano's eruptions and events in Naples also meant believing that human behavior, especially human wickedness, could trigger natural disasters; to put it another way, natural disasters were God's warning that humanity's natural propensity for wickedness was getting out of control. It was hardly a new idea to connect the wrath of Vesuvius with the wrath of God; when the volcano erupted in 79, the Roman Jewish writer Josephus suggested that the disaster must be a divine punishment directed at the emperor Titus for having sacked Jerusalem nine years earlier.[22]

FROM POMPEII

In Naples in 1631, examples of human wickedness were uncommonly abundant: first, there were the Spanish viceroys, arrogant, greedy, and cruel, ingenious creators of new and ever heavier taxes. The rapacious barons of the local aristocracy were no better, nor were their haughty, overbearing servants. The clergy exhibited its own varieties of corruption and arrogance; the upper ranks were made up of Spaniards, barons, or aristocrats appointed in Rome (Archbishop Boncompagni, for example, was the nephew of a former pope, and the family originally hailed from Bologna). At the bottom of its elaborate social structure, Naples had its barefoot, quick-witted rabble, the *lazzaroni,* always scrambling for a better foothold on the kingdom's slippery social ladder. Neapolitans took it for granted that San Gennaro must be sensitive to politics—but every last one of them also knew that the kindhearted saint was on their side, whatever that side might happen to be. All told, the events of 1631 afforded Neapolitans ample proof that, beyond any doubt, the dread volcano responded to Christian appeals for mercy. Pagan Pompeii may have been buried under a rain of ash and pebbles, but now Naples and the whole region of Vesuvius could shelter under the protective mantle of San Gennaro, the saint who could soothe the mountain's anger with his miraculous liquefying blood.

3

Before Pompeii:
Kircher and Holste

Pompeii may have been buried in 79 A.D., but it has never been entirely forgotten. Much of the surviving population moved to the other side of the volcano, to the area around Nola, unaware that a Bronze Age eruption had once buried Nola, too, when the wind blew northeast rather than south, carrying a dense cloud of ash and volcanic lapilli.[1] Nola, however, was an inland city. Some of the refugees or their descendants inevitably moved back to the coast. Pompeii itself was still identified by name on a map of Italy drawn in 1264 and again on an antiquarian's map in the sixteenth century.[2] Local memory was powerful, too; in 1504 the Neapolitan poet Jacopo Sannazaro conjured up the last days of Pompeii in his romance, *Arcadia,* one of the best sellers of the sixteenth century. At one point in the long, convoluted story, a nymph escorts the hero, Sincero (Sannazaro's alter ego), through the underworld and tells him about its marvels:

"And then under great Vesuvius I would have you hear the fearsome groans of the giant Alcyoneus, although I think you will hear him when we draw near your Sebeto. There was a time when, to their misfortune, all the neighbors heard him, when with stormy flames and ashes he covered the nearby towns, just as the burnt and liquefied stones still bear clear witness to anyone who sees them, and beneath them who would believe that there are populations, and villas, and noble cities that lie buried? Truly there are, and they were covered by ruin and death, like the one that we see here before us, a city once celebrated beyond doubt in your countries, called Pompeii, watered by the waves of the chilly Sarno. It was swallowed by the earth in a sudden earthquake, when I believe the bedrock on which it was founded collapsed beneath its feet. Certainly it is a strange and horrible way to die; to see living people snatched from the ranks of the living in a second." . . . And with these words we were almost at the city she described, and its towers, houses, theatres, and temples could be picked out nearly intact.[3]

By the sixteenth century, however, the most important settlements in the region were Torre Annunziata to the north and Scafati to the southeast. The name "Pompeii" itself had disappeared from the map. Eventually, the name of a settlement called "Civita" would be seen as evidence of the onetime existence of a city (*civitas* in Latin) on the site once known as Pompeii.

Clues to the ancient city's location began to emerge again in 1592, when the famous architect-engineer Domenico Fontana moved from Rome to Naples. A wonder worker who moved the Vatican obelisk for Pope Sixtus V (and set up three more obelisks in Rome during the pontiff's five-year reign), Fontana was abruptly fired by his patron's successor, Clement VIII, who preferred burning heretics to raising obelisks. The viceroy of Naples was quick to offer Fontana a position as royal architect, and soon he was digging a channel to connect the River Sarno to a munitions factory at

Torre Annunziata under the supervision of the local landlord, Muzio Tuttavilla, Count of Sarno. When Fontana's workmen reached the fields around tiny Civita, they began striking standing architectural structures underneath the layers of volcanic soil. The royal architect's long experience in Rome meant that he could easily recognize the remains as ancient. From the ruins he also extracted a pair of inscriptions that said DECURIO POMPEI and passed them on to the count, but Fontana had been hired to dig a canal, not to conduct an archaeological excavation, and so he kept on channeling—so well that his waterway would continue in constant use until the early twentieth century. For his own part, the Count of Sarno, like the viceroy, was far more interested in his modern factory than in the ancient past. He kept the inscriptions because he thought they referred to the great General Pompey, a more glamorous subject than what had been, after all, a secondary Roman seaport even if that seaport happened to have been buried in a spectacular volcanic eruption and invoked by the likes of Pliny the Younger and the great "Sincerus" Sannazaro. Fontana's experience with Pope Sixtus V meant that he already knew a good deal about buried cities and the eagerness of popes and viceroys to transform them into modern metropolises; Pope Sixtus had ordered him to raze spectacular and illustrious ancient monuments such as the Septizodium of Septimius Severus, a third-century viewing terrace of superimposed colonnades along the Sacred Way between the Circus Maximus and the Colosseum, as well as the Lateran Palace, the residence of the popes since the very beginnings of official Christianity. In the late sixteenth century and especially in the expanding cities of Rome and Naples, feats of modern engineering almost always took precedence over exploring and preserving remnants of the ancient past.[4]

But antiquarian studies were developing, too, both in Naples and abroad, as we can see from the first real guidebook to Naples,

Giulio Cesare Capaccio's *Il forastiero (The Foreigner)* of 1634. Capaccio presents his information in the form of a ten-day, thousand-page dialogue between F, the Foreigner (Forastiero), and C, a helpful Citizen (Cittadino) of Naples who provides generous doses of local color to supplement what visitors might have learned about the region from books; F is quite well read, especially in the Greek and Latin classics. On the tenth day of their extended conversation, the two shift their focus from Naples itself to the smaller cities around the bay and inevitably to the inescapable mountain. "I would love to learn about this Vesuvius," Forastiero begins:

> having read in Philostratus that the Neapolitans brag about having the bones of the giant Alcyoneus, and the other Titans who were struck by lightning and imprisoned with him under that mountain. I have also read in Dio Cassius that up there was a huge fire long ago and that afterward a great drought followed, and terrible earthquakes, and that the plain caught fire, and huge groanings were heard, and agitation of the sea, and the sky resounded, and rocks came forth, and darkness fell, and beneath the ash fish and birds died, and the Romans were sure that the world had been turned upside down. There ought to be a mountain here that ranks among the marvels of the earth, although I have trouble with the name: is it Vesuvio, or Besbio?

The friendly Citizen replies as follows:

> This mountain is called Somma, Besbio, Vesevo, Vesuvio, and Vesuio, and there are poets to be found who speak of "Vesuvian Fires." What Dio Cassius reports is absolutely true history, and the fires have evaporated many times. At the time of the Emperor Titus not only did the things that Dio mentions happen, but two cities also perished under the

ashes, Herculaneum and Pompeii, whose remnants are called Torre del Greco and Torre Annunziata. . . . I will show you Herculaneum, where many ancient monuments are to be found: statues, inscriptions, subterranean places, and so many busts of Hercules that it certainly seems that the city must have been dedicated to that god; and it should be joined with Pompeii, the home town of Lucilius, Seneca's friend. And both cities were buried by the great fire of Vesuvius when Regulus, or Memmius, and Virginius were consuls.[5]

After these preliminaries, the Foreigner is eager to hear about the eruption of 1631, and the Citizen, as an eyewitness, is delighted to oblige him in exhaustive detail; at the end of his guidebook, Capaccio devotes another eighty-six pages of supplemental dialogue to "The Great Fire of Vesuvius."

To a Neapolitan, *forastiero* meant anyone born outside Naples, and the fact that Capaccio wrote his guidebook in the Italian vernacular suggests that many or most of its purchasers may have been visitors from the provinces, Rome, or port cities like Palermo, Genoa, and Venice. But *forastieri* also came from farther afield. In 1618 a German professor from the University of Leiden, Philipp Klüwer, visited the Bay of Naples as part of an ambitious plan to map the entire Italian peninsula. Together with his former student Lukas Holste, who had studied with Klüwer in Leiden and caught his teacher's enthusiasm, the man now celebrated as the founder of modern historical geography traveled the peninsula on foot, comparing what he saw with what earlier geographers had written. In Italy, as in university circles, the two were known by Latin versions of their names, Philippus Cluverius and Lucas Holstenius, and because they also published in Latin, this is how they are best known to present-day readers. Their search for Pompeii led Klüwer to conclude that the city must have stood on the site of Scafati, right along the bank of the River Sarno. Holste was not so sure.

It would take another nineteen years, however, before Lukas Holste had a second chance to investigate the site of Pompeii, years that carried him back to Hamburg, then to Paris, and finally to Rome, where he converted to Catholicism and took up a position in 1636 as librarian to Cardinal Francesco Barberini, the powerful nephew of the reigning pope, Urban VIII. Cardinal Barberini's library was one of the wonders of seventeenth-century Rome, packed with works of art and scientific instruments, including two armillary spheres showing a Copernican solar system, and a whole series of books that had been banned by the Inquisition; as a member of the Inquisition himself, Cardinal Francesco could read whatever he wanted.[6]

In 1637, however, Cardinal Francesco was willing to part temporarily with his librarian and sent him off to Naples along with another German intellectual he had summoned to Rome: the Jesuit Athanasius Kircher, who had been teaching mathematics at the order's Roman College since 1633, as well as studying Egyptology, magnetism, and a host of other subjects. In addition to their scholarly virtues, both Kircher and Holste turned out to have a talent for converting Protestants, especially German Protestants, to Catholicism, and in 1636 Holste, a convert himself, managed to persuade a wealthy German duke to follow suit. The duke in question was Friedrich, Landgrave of Hessen-Darmstadt (1616–1682), a third son with a penchant for spending money and an obsession with the swashbuckling Knights of Malta. The young man had lived in Rome since 1635, running up debts and dreaming of military glory; once converted, he was eligible at last for induction into the Knights Hospitalers of St. John of Jerusalem, Rhodes, and Malta, a transaction managed with the Grand Master by Cardinal Barberini and some of his fellow prelates. When the landgrave boarded a Genoese galley bound from Rome to

Malta, Holste came along as his tutor and Kircher as his father confessor, handpicked, presumably, by Cardinal Barberini. At every stop, including the ten-day stop in Naples, Holste wrote detailed reports to Cardinal Barberini, still carefully preserved among the Barberini manuscripts of the Vatican Library.[7]

In May 1637 the Genoese galley docked at Miseno, the seventeenth-century name for Cape Misenum, the ancient harbor of the imperial Roman fleet on the northern end of the Bay of Naples. It was from Misenum that Pliny the Elder had set out to rescue victims of Vesuvius in 79 A.D. and at Misenum that the younger Pliny saved his own life from the catastrophe by staying home and attending to his studies. In May of 1637 that long-ago disaster was all too easy to imagine in vivid detail, for it was only five and a half years after the cataclysm of 1631, and the volcano was still restless (as it would be until 1944). The events of 79 and 1631 both came after long years of dormancy, both exploded a stone plug and sent the fragments into the air before emitting deadly pyroclastic surges, and both produced ash and lapilli rather than lava (the 1631 eruption is now classified as "sub-Plinian," a less drastic version of the larger "Plinian" eruption of 79). Because we lack a visual record of the original "Plinian" event (we have the "before" picture from the House of the Centenary but not the "after") we do not know how the eruption of 79 changed the skyline of the Bay of Naples. The 1631 eruption, documented by eyewitness reports, opened a new hole in the mountain just before tearing its head off, leaving Vesuvius to cool with a jagged, two-pronged profile above the glittering slopes of black volcanic ash.

The Genoese galley that docked in the shadow of this jagged new Vesuvius was powered both by sail and by a crew of nearly two hundred oarsmen, making it one of the fastest ships in the world. Rumor had it that the stench of a galley preceded it long before it drew into port; the crews were mostly slaves and condemned criminals, whose comfort and hygiene were of little concern to anyone save themselves.

But this galley was carrying a precious cargo along with its hard-living oarsmen: the landgrave and his entourage, bound for Malta. And already, the landgrave's handlers realized that the transition from the idle comforts of Rome to the rigors of Maltese knighthood was not going to be an easy one. Among other advantages (speed, for example), docking in Miseno put some distance between the young landgrave and the temptations of Naples. By the time the galley finally anchored, its voyage barely begun, Holste also had serious doubts about Kircher's suitability as father confessor.[8] But as the two scholars pulled into port in this region rich in the wonders of nature and history, they could at least enjoy their own learned conversations. Energetic men in their thirties, they were eager to leave the evil-smelling galley as soon as it docked and see the legendary sights of the Phlegraean Fields and Naples, comparing their own notes with Holste's memories of his tramp through the area two decades earlier, now enshrined in the four volumes of Philipp Klüwer's *Italia antiqua*, finally published posthumously in 1624.[9]

For Father Kircher, the possible location of Pompeii was a much less interesting topic than the volcano that had buried it. He had arrived in Rome in October of 1633, a refugee from the butchery of the Thirty Years' War. Officially, he took up a chair in mathematics at the Jesuits' Roman College, but his unofficial duties were far more interesting to the upper ranks of the church. Alone among his contemporaries, Athanasius Kircher claimed to be able to read Egyptian hieroglyphs, and this was the real reason he was called to Rome at the behest of Cardinal Barberini, whose own scholarly interests ranged almost as widely as Kircher's own. Kircher quickly proved valuable for another, less conspicuous reason: he had grown up, like the landgrave, in the Hessian district between Catholic and Protestant Germany (later the borderland between West and East Germany). In Rome, that wartime experience made him one of the chief points of reference for German converts to Catholicism, an empathetic confidante, and a gentle guide to people often traumatized by the terrible things they had seen.

All of that skill was lost on the landgrave, as were most of Holste's lessons about history and literature. In this uncomfortable company of three, Holste and Kircher had little time to explore the Bay of Naples. Instead, they spent most of their disappointing stay driving from reception to reception, together with the papal envoy to Spain, Cardinal Spinola, and their pouting charge. But the stress and frustration of the trip also steeled their already steely wills; as a direct result of their ten-day visit to the Bay of Naples, Holste would become the first modern scholar to identify the site of Pompeii correctly, and Kircher would formulate a fanciful Baroque theory of terrestrial cycles, generated by deep motions within the earth, not quite modern plate tectonics, but a first move in that direction.

Holste was the first to win his way free of the landgrave; by September 7, 1637, he was back in Naples, scouting out books for the Barberini Library before returning to Rome and reporting to Cardinal Francesco on Kircher's behalf:

As I was leaving [Malta] the Father confessed that he did not much like this job, and that it bothered his conscience, because he thought he could not do what he regards as his proper duty, and he requested me to plead on my return to Rome with Your Eminence and his superiors to have him reassigned to his studies, or to some mission in Egypt or the Holy Land, so that he could see those lands and perfect his command of the Eastern languages, for that port [Malta] provides every kind of safe passage to those regions.[10]

　　　　　　　　　　　　　FROM POMPEII

A month later, Holste wrote to the cardinal from Benevento, describing a trip he had made through the area known as Contrada Arpaia, where the rains had uncovered a "beautiful and curious" inscription.[11] He had also taken another look at the inscriptions unearthed by Domenico Fontana forty years before and some inscriptions found in 1616, all of which led him to conclude that Scafati was not the real site of ancient Pompeii. Indeed, Pompeii had to have been sited at the place where Fontana had found ruins when cutting his canal, the little settlement called la Civita near Torre Annunziata, with its massive ruins—why else would a village with vineyards be called "The City"? In 1658 Holste set down his definitive conclusions in a long commentary on Klüwer's *Italia antiqua,* the product of years of thought, study, and literal scholarly footwork: "It is as certain as can be that Pompeii must have been where the biggest ruins can be seen, in the place that people call Civita, which Ambrose of Nola once thought must be Stabiae. But stones that have lately been excavated and transferred to Castellamare di Stabia show that it certainly had to be Pompeii. Furthermore, the very name Civita confirms this, as Cluverius has observed more than once elsewhere. Moreover, I have already shown that the distance between Nuceria and Pompeii had to be 12 miles beyond Scafati."[12]

As for Father Kircher, the Genoese galley that carried Landgrave Friedrich and his entourage off to Valletta in 1637 would pass by a whole series of volcanoes en route: first Vesuvius, then the islands of Stromboli and Vulcano, and finally Etna, the latter three perpetually active volcanoes, all spewing merrily as the galley passed. Kircher, an uncommonly curious man to begin with, conceived a new enthusiasm for volcanoes and rocks on this trip, and his enthusiasm only grew once they reached the limestone plateau of Malta. Here, more clearly than in the lush vegetation of Germany and Italy, he could see strata of rock laid bare along the barren sea cliffs and trace the process of erosion along shores and streambeds. The golden limestone of Malta was thick with fossils and hollowed-out caves, some of them still inhabited by locals.

In this curious, remote setting, the father confessor also had an unusual amount of time left over from his duties to observe the strange phenomena of nature and to ponder what he saw. He made a lifelong friend, Fabio Chigi, inquisitor and apostolic delegate to Malta. Nonetheless, as Lukas Holste had duly noted to Cardinal Barberini, the father confessor hated his job. Holste could not help adding, with a good academic gossip's barbed wit, that Kircher's shyness and diffidence rendered him almost useless in the society of the wealthy and powerful (this as Kircher cemented his friendship with one of the two most powerful men in Malta; the other was the Grand Master).[13] In 1638 Father Kircher was finally summoned back to Rome, the city that would become his home for the rest of his long life (he died there in 1680). First, however, he made the most of his return journey, which presented, as he knew, the chance of a lifetime to study volcanoes. He stopped en route to examine Etna, Stromboli, and Vesuvius at first hand. Etna and Stromboli obliged his curiosity with a burst of activity, as both mountains frequently do. But for the homebound Kircher, the earth put on a special show. He seems to have been the kind of person who attracted strange occurrences wherever he went: his autobiography claims that he was caught in a stampede, went over the falls in a millwheel (twice), was captured by Protestant soldiers, escaped a siege thanks to a prophetic vision, was stranded on a moving ice floe in a raging German river, and shipwrecked, all before he reached Rome at the age of thirty-one.[14] Now, at thirty-six, between Stromboli and Naples, Kircher experienced an earthquake at sea when his ship was rocked by a passing tsunami. Vesuvius was his last landfall before Rome, and this time, with no landgrave to mind or pressing schedule to keep, he made a special point of exploring it. Like the eruptions of 79 and 472, the explosion of 1631 had blown away a stone plug that had formed within the mountain's fumarole and eventually blocked it entirely, leaving the crater wide open, as Kircher could see. His account of the trip, published nearly thirty years later, suitably magnified his professions of horror (and the suggestions of his own bravery) for the delight of his readers:

> I arrived at Portici, a town located at the base of the mountain; from here, with a faithful peasant, familiar with the roads, for company, I climbed the mountain in the middle of the night by difficult, gravel-strewn and arduous paths. When I reached the crater—horrible to say—I saw that the whole thing was ablaze, with an unbearable stench of sulfur and pitch. Terrified at this unaccustomed sight, I began to believe that I might be looking straight into the house of hell—nothing was missing but the devils. You could hear the mountain's horrible moans and growlings, dark clouds of smoke mixed in with balls of fire erupting out of eleven different openings in the side and bottom of the crater, and I erupted, too: "O the depth of the wealth of God's wisdom and knowledge! How incomprehensible are thy ways!"[15]

As a devout Jesuit, Father Kircher would never have openly expressed doubts about a religious event like the miracle of San Gennaro any more than his friend in Malta, Inquisitor Fabio Chigi, would have dared to do. (Chigi, in fact, would keep a gallstone of Saint Francis de Sales to comfort him during his own surgery for kidney stones in 1642; today that same stone is preserved, wrapped in a label in Chigi's handwriting, inside a transparent glass obelisk commissioned by twentieth-century members of the Chigi family). Yet Kircher, in particular, was eager to rid Catholicism of its layers of superstition. He believed in prayer, but he also believed in reason, all the more so when disaster struck.

His climb up and into Vesuvius in 1638 forever changed Father Kircher's views about geology, and they were views that had nothing to do with saints, relics, or divine wrath. Pacing out the distances between the mountain, its summit, and the towns below provided him with a direct, physical sense of the volcano's size, the sheer immensity of the forces seething beneath its blackened cone, and by extension, the far greater immensity of the universe. Five years before this journey from Malta to Rome, in June of 1633, Galileo Galilei had been convicted of heresy by the Roman Inquisition and his *Dialogue on the Two Chief World Systems* consigned to the *Index of Prohibited Books*. Kircher knew that the dangers he faced in hiking up Vesuvius were more than equaled by the dangers he faced if his ideas about the universe ranged too freely, but his brain rushed ahead anyway, as it always did, in what he called a "mentis aestus" a "mental firestorm."[16]

For the next thirty years, Father Kircher carefully built his case that God had rooted nature's laws in the power of reason and applied these laws uniformly throughout the universe. When Vesuvius erupted, therefore, it did so in response to gigantic cycles within the earth itself rather than God's pique at individual sinners. Kircher's universe, like our own, moved simultaneously on many different orders of magnitude, from the minute actions of microbes to the great cycles of the cosmos, but unlike modern scientists he had to pay close attention to the way he expressed his ideas for fear of the Inquisition.[17]

In 1656 at mid-career, Athanasius Kircher knew that he stood near the volcano's rim of Catholic orthodoxy. His latest book, *The Ecstatic Heavenly Journey* (*Itinerarium Extaticum*, 1656), declared outright that the entire universe was made of the same basic matter, that it was infinite in its extent except in the mind of God, and that each one of its endless number of heavenly bodies was subject to the same kinds of constant change as the earth.[18] The sun and moon had seas and volcanoes; so did the stars. The solar and lunar volcanoes erupted for the same reasons that volcanoes erupted on Earth: this was how matter circulated throughout the cosmos. Still more controversially, because all of these bodies had fiery centers, there was no reason to presume that the fiery center of earth was a place called hell. The wrath of God had nothing to do with any of these phenomena: they were natural movements that occurred continually on a colossal scale, and regardless of their effect on individual human lives, they occurred because of God's benevolent providence.[19]

When the bubonic plague descended on Rome in 1656, Kircher blamed the disease on microbes and successfully convinced the pope to set up quarantines; fortunately that pope, Alexander VII, was none other than his old friend from Malta, Fabio Chigi.[20] The quarantine was successful enough to fortify Kircher's theory of a natural, not a moral cause for the epidemic; that success also helped to cement his reputation as a cool head in times of crisis. Thus, when Vesuvius began to spew smoke again in the summer of 1660, Athanasius Kircher was one of the first experts to whom people turned for an explanation. By that time, at the age of fifty-nine, he had published dozens of books, many of them lavishly illustrated, on subjects that included magnetism, Egyptology, music, optics, cosmology, and the plague. Everyone knew that he was also planning a magnum opus on geology; an indefatigable self-promoter, he had already advertised it for nearly twenty years in the pages of his other volumes.[21]

However, this new eruption called for more urgent action than a huge geological treatise because strange things were happening in the Bay of Naples and elsewhere in southern Italy. Kircher described the situation with his usual vehement rhetoric:

In the year 1660 on the third day of July around the first light of dawn, smoke on Mount Vesuvius, mixed with fire, gave the first intimation of storms and calamities to follow.

The smoke narrowed into the shape of an umbrella pine and gradually increased so much that, as observers have reported, it shot up to 300 miles into the air—the earth seemed to want to mix with the sky. This was followed immediately by a huge eruption of fiery globes, and then by a subterranean rumbling and crashes like those of horrible thunder, then by continuous flashes and lighting, and then huge amounts of blackish, ashy sand poured forth, which first seemed to present a moist surface, but quickly, as the sun dried it, it changed its color into bright white puffs, rather like silk, clear evidence of a mixed composition of nitre, salt, sulfur and pitch.[22]

These eruptions continued for the next several days, up until July 10, and the mountain never stopped its raging night or day, with such force and such an incredible discharge of smoke and sizeable stone that you could properly say that the mountain had vomited forth another mountain, and the ever-increasing flow spread so that Vesuvius seemed to be covered in snow. Nor was this the end of the portents: as the sun entered Leo [on July 21], crosses suddenly began to appear on people's linen clothing, to the wonder of everyone, imprinted by some hidden power, so that they seemed to have been painted [on the garments] not by the work of nature but by the brush of some hidden hand.[23]

The strange crosses also appeared on the altar cloths of churches, on sheets hung out to dry, and in chests where families stored their linens. In September of 1660, Giovanni Battista Zupo, a Jesuit mathematician based in Naples, sent Father Kircher drawings of the phenomena along with a detailed report.

Kircher concluded almost immediately that the crosses were nothing more than ash from Vesuvius precipitating back to earth on droplets of water vapor; when they landed on linen, they spread along the weave of the fabric. The crosses, therefore, carried no divine message about prayerful conversion or imminent doom, and he was quick to announce this fact.

Confirmation of his comforting words appeared right there in the laundry room of the Jesuit college, where the college cats liked to sleep among the piles of linen. Here the brother in charge of the laundry showed Kircher where one of the tomcats had sprayed a linen sheet; the drops of urine had spread in the same cross-shaped pattern as the "prodigious crosses" of Naples but in yellow rather than ashen gray. The very same thing, he asserted, had happened just the other day in the infirmary, when an old Jesuit of eighty had inadvertently wet his bed. In addition, spots of oil spilled from lamps, spills on tablecloths, all of these penetrated woven fabric in the same pattern of perpendiculars. Invariably, as any liquid soaked into woven filaments, it created crosses as it spread; the Jesuits' laundry hamper provided a gold mine of evidence.[24]

With his theory thus fortified by easily reproducible results, Kircher quickly drafted a reassuring pamphlet, *Diatribe de prodigiosis crucibus (Study of the Remarkable Crosses)* and sent his text to the Board of Reviewers, the Jesuit censors who reviewed all the order's manuscripts before permitting them to proceed to publication. And there, as so often in his career, he met with opposition. The reviewers handed down their decision on October 7; Kircher had drafted his study within a month of the first episodes, working speedily in hopes of calming the volatile situation in Naples. The censors in Rome, however, remained skeptical, despite the fact that it was their laundry room that had provided Kircher with his evidence: "We think that printing should be procrastinated and put off just a little bit because in these very days new apparitions have been reported, in the same crosslike form, not only on linen and silk but also on meat and fruit, and when the Sun has come back out of Leo and risen high again, then at last the September rains will repress the exhalations of Vesuvius, and then it will be clear whether the author has provided a full and faithful account of these phenomena and all the others."[25]

When *De prodigiosis crucibus* finally went to press in March of 1661 (five months later), Father Kircher had added a discussion about similar cross-like apparitions on fruit and meat. Although these organic substances were not woven, he noted, they nonetheless had their own fibrous structures, as could be confirmed by examining them under a *smicroscopium,* his term for the microscope.

As he encouraged people not to panic, however, Kircher had to draw a fine line between his own rational explanation of a phenomenon and his colleagues' narrower view of religious orthodoxy. If he insisted that the "prodigious crosses" were not so prodigious after all, he also had to assure his readers that God did indeed perform miracles; the Almighty had simply chosen not to do so on this particular occasion: "Now before we proceed to discuss the causes of this phenomenon, I must always protest that even if this phenomenon may be a pure effect of nature, nonetheless, nothing keeps GOD Supreme and Almighty, who controls all the effects of nature by his providence, from using these effects to communicate something to mortals."[26]

In other words, finding a rational explanation for the eruptions of Vesuvius and for the "prodigious crosses" had no bearing on the miraculous quality of unusual events like the liquefaction of San Gennaro's blood. Furthermore, as he noted, the very variety and irregularity of the crosses showed that they had to be the imperfect creations of irregular nature rather than the perfect creations of God.

Four years after publishing this calmly rational little pamphlet, Kircher finally produced the massive study that stood behind its bold claims. In 1665, nearly thirty years after his trip to Malta and his first passionate plunge into geology, Kircher's masterwork,

Mundus subterraneus, the *Subterranean World,* issued from the Protestant press of Johan Jansson in Amsterdam with a dedication to his old friend from Malta, Pope Alexander VII; Alexander's own copy of the work is still preserved in the Vatican Library.[27]

In this massive study, which sums up three decades of geological investigation, volcanoes feature as an essential cog in the great cycles of nature, and Vesuvius figures prominently among them (Figure 3.1). Like the vast majority of his learned contemporaries, Kircher believed that the world was composed of the four

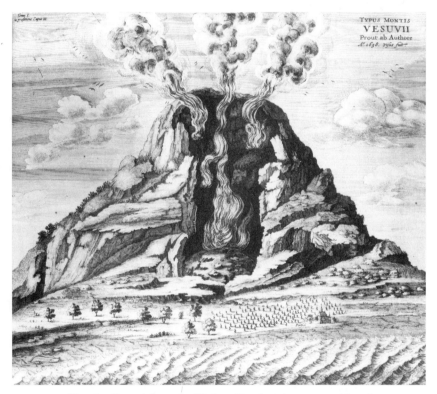

3.1.   Vesuvius. From Athanasius Kircher, *Mundus subterraneus,* 1665 and 1678. Photo: Snark / Art Resource, NY.

traditional elements, earth, air, fire, and water. Although the Jesuits' official curriculum, the *Ratio studiorum,* endorsed teaching the philosophy of Aristotle, Kircher openly rejected Aristotle's theory that the moon and the other heavenly bodies were made of a fifth element, quintessence. As far as he was concerned, the sun, stars, and planets had the same composition as the earth, with the advantage, he had noted in his earlier cosmological work, the *Itinerarium Extaticum,* that a person could therefore be baptized anywhere in the universe.[28]

Naturally the earth was made primarily of the element earth but that predominant element was mixed with the others in various proportions to create various forms of matter. Each of the other elements collected in huge underground reservoirs of fire, water, and air, as Kircher could assert from personal experience. In addition to his geological explorations in Sicily and Malta, Kircher had also been an eager spelunker; the porous limestone of the Italian peninsula, Sicily, and Malta had given him ample opportunities to explore what he liked to call "the Earth's viscera." He had seen underground reservoirs of air and water at first hand and surmised that the heat he could feel beneath Vesuvius and the Solfatara must be caused by underground reservoirs of fire that worked much like those of water and air. He had impressive Greek-derived terms for all of these reservoirs: *pyrophylacium* for fire, *hydrophylacium* for water, *aerophylacium* for air ("phylacium" means "reservoir"). These reservoirs could also collect more than one element at a time: water and air created hot springs, while water, air, and fire made bubbling hot springs, another common feature of central and southern Italy.

These primary elements never stayed in one place for long: they were constantly on the move, mixing and separating, bonding and breaking apart. Volcanoes spewed earth from their fumaroles, creating new mountains. Water reservoirs, tucked deep beneath the earth's mountain ranges, gushed forth rivers. Rain and river water gradually eroded the mountains, carrying the debris into the sea, where both silt and water were sucked back down into the earth by huge watery vortices. Kircher had seen the tidal swirls in the Straits of Messina and heard tales of a vortex off the Norwegian coast called the Maelstrom ("mill stream"); he had also seen how the waterfalls at Tivoli, outside Rome, plunge deep into limestone caves in the earth.

He concluded that the earth's surface must make huge circular movements over huge expanses of time, in which continents and seas rose and fell and rose again. The fate of lost Atlantis, buried under the waves, was the eventual fate of every tract of dry land, just as the eruption of volcanoes resulted from the eternal cycling of earth and fire.

Because his theory of terrestrial cycles is not unlike modern ideas about the movement of the earth's crust, some contemporary geologists, like Haraldur Sigurdsson, honor Kircher as the true father of plate tectonics and *Mundus subterraneus* as the first work to promote these ideas in detail. The Jesuit ran into difficulty, however, when he tried to imagine these massive geological movements all taking place in only six thousand years, given that the usual Catholic date for the creation of the world was 4004 B.C. With his reading knowledge of twenty-odd languages (his own tally of twenty-three included Egyptian hieroglyphs), Kircher knew that both the Greeks and the ancient Egyptians had imagined time as operating on a far longer scale than Catholic Christians would acknowledge. Plato had put the destruction of Atlantis at about 9500 B.C., several millennia before the ostensible date of the Creation, and the Egyptian lists of known and recorded kings extended as far back as 5000 B.C. It was hard to imagine mountains toppling or continents rising and falling at the rate a merely six-thousand-year-old world would dictate, and Kircher himself could not imagine a world so fast moving or so young.

He therefore searched for ways to reconcile orthodox doctrine with his observations and found a few serviceable loopholes. On the whole, however, his usual way of dealing with controversial topics was simply to state both the approved position and his own, side by side, as if there were no contradiction between them. That habit, needless to say, infuriated some of the Jesuit reviewers who examined his texts.

In the case of long-term geological phenomena, Kircher supposed that the universe had existed for eons as a "chaotic mass" *(massa chaotica)* before God called it to order with the Creation. This indefinite period gave the elements ample time to mix, coagulate, and come apart again without contradicting a single word of Scripture.[29]

More controversially, however, Kircher declared that volcanoes and volcanic activity were not restricted to Earth. The moon and the sun were subject to the same great cycles, for they, like our own planet, were also irregular elemental bodies that underwent constant, tumultuous change. The idea of imperfections in the heavenly bodies ran counter to Aristotle, but Jesuit astronomers had forged ahead with astronomical research from the very beginning of the order (chartered in 1540), especially at their college in Rome, where, for some reason, German astronomers had dominated the field long before Kircher. These astronomers included Christoph Clavius, deviser of the Gregorian calendar (1583), and Christoph Scheiner, an important investigator of sunspots. Kircher borrowed (or pillaged) both Scheiner's studies and his engraved plates for *Mundus subterraneus* and used them to assert that sunspots were traces of smoke from solar eruptions. As for the moon, Galileo's telescope had already shown (as of 1609) that it had mountains and seas like those on Earth, although Kircher argued that these elements on the lunar surface were lighter than their terrestrial equivalents.[30]

In its time, then, *Mundus subterraneus* represented an important account of volcanoes (although, as Sean Cocco has shown, the Neapolitans, with their firsthand access to every whim of the volcano, stood at the real forefront of geological research). Nonetheless, it was Kircher's illustration of the inner workings of Vesuvius, engraved by a professional in Amsterdam from his own charmingly clumsy, luridly colored autograph drawing (still preserved in Rome), that became the definitive cross-section of a volcanic cone for centuries to come.[31]

Importantly for posterity, then, *Mundus subterraneus* presented the eruption of volcanoes as a purely natural phenomenon; the cyclings of the earth's surface, like those of the sun, moon, and stars, took place in obedience to the laws of nature, which worked on a scale incalculably greater than that of human events. For Athanasius Kircher, moreover, as for Giordano Bruno before him, these huge natural events were only one part of a much more complicated story.

For nature also worked on a scale that was almost inconceivably tiny. Bruno had been a committed atomist who believed that chemical reactions took place in particles invisible to the naked eye; he formulated his ideas with help only from the eye of his imagination. Kircher, on the other hand, worked with both telescope and microscope, or, as he called them, the astronomical tube and the smicroscopium.

It was on this smallest, most elemental level, Kircher argued, that the primordial chaotic mass was charged with the spark of life, a force that he called *panspermia rerum:* the universal "seeding power" or "fertility of things."[32] That spark of life could be ignited by the sun's rays; it could also be found in the hearts of volcanoes. Like most dwellers on volcanic slopes, he had noticed (or heard from locals) that once the deadly heat of pyroclastic surges and lava flows have stopped, the soil around volcanoes is extraordinarily fertile. In the early twentieth century, the Swedish chemist (and Nobel laureate) Svante Arrhenius would borrow Kircher's concept of *panspermia* and use the term to suggest that life first originated in the cosmos and was transmitted to earth.[33]

As for Friedrich, the Landgrave of Hesse-Darmstadt, soon after his arrival in Malta he was appointed coadjutant to the commander of the German "Langue" (Nation) of the Knights of Malta. In 1640, financed by his brother, he assembled his own fleet and led them in a victorious operation against the Turks off the coast of Tunisia. Sadly, the spoils he acquired from that battle were not enough to maintain his little navy. In 1641 he resigned his commission and moved back to Rome, where Cardinal Barberini provided him with financial support as an important addition to the Catholic fold. A few months later the landgrave moved on to Vienna, and then to Madrid and Brussels before being named cardinal in 1650. For cardinals, military command was out of the question, but by then Friedrich had also become quite fat. Instead, he was ostensibly charged with representing German interests in the Curia, and he did so, famously, by throwing lavish parties.[34] It may be no wonder that his tutor and his father confessor had spent so much of their time in Malta discussing subjects like the site of Pompeii and the cycles of the earth's crust while their young charge strutted about in his armor, partied, and partied again.

Despite Holste's cogent arguments and the existence of inscriptions and physical ruins, the debate about the site of Pompeii would continue to rage for almost another century; after all, his Italian contemporaries noted, he was a German, and what did Germans know about Italy? They made the same criticism of Father Kircher even though both men spent most of their lives in Rome.

Ironically, however, it was another foreigner who would begin to solve the problem of Pompeii's location once and for all, Emmanuel-Maurice, Prince (later Duc) d'Elbeuf (1677–1763). The youngest son of a freewheeling French cavalry officer (who had been thrown into the Bastille in 1681 for bringing a leg of mutton down on the head of a fellow diner at Versailles), the younger d'Elbeuf was equally restless.[35] In a fit of pique, he had left the court of Louis XIV in 1706 to head a regiment for the Holy Roman Emperor in Vienna, the Sun King's sworn enemy, and Louis had duly hanged him in effigy. Having passed to the other side, the younger d'Elbeuf could easily move from Vienna to allied Naples, as he did in 1709. In Italy he became captain of the imperial cavalry and married a local duchess (apparently so annoying his commander that he nearly lost his job).[36] The next step for d'Elbeuf, like so many of his peers, was to build a country villa in the Neapolitan suburb of Portici, for which he engaged the brilliant local architect Ferdinando Sanfelice in 1713 (Figure 3.2). Hearing that a

3.2.   Ferdinando Sanfelice, Villa d'Elbeuf (later Villa Bruno), Granatello, Portici, 1713. Old postcard.

woman in nearby Resina had found colored marble after digging for a well, he contacted her as a potential supplier for the villa's interior decor. The well turned out to be a veritable mine of ancient marble, including three female statues that d'Elbeuf managed to spirit out of the country as a gift to his cousin. Soon anyone willing to dig sixty-five feet beneath the hard-packed soil of Resina was coming up with ancient artifacts. It was clear from ancient sources, as it had been to Giulio Cesare Capaccio a century earlier, that these objects must have belonged to Herculaneum rather than Pompeii, but now the discovery of subterranean structures provoked an entirely different response. Domenico Fontana may have forged ahead with his canal in the 1590s even when it sliced through the center of a Roman town, but the citizens of eighteenth-century Naples were eager to learn about their ancient past. The wells of Resina began to turn into something resembling a real archaeological excavation.

D'Elbeuf did not enjoy his villa for long. He was restored to the graces of the French Crown in 1719 and rushed back to Paris to press his advantage. He succeeded to the title of Duc d'Elbeuf in 1748, the year that an excavator's shovel struck another buried city: Pompeii. By then his beauteous villa had passed to the king of Naples.

In March of 2013, three hundred years after the construction of Villa d'Elbeuf, an extraordinary advertisement began appearing in Italian newspapers: a description of this same property, after a myriad of remodelings and one devastating world war (King Charles III snapped it up soon after d'Elbeuf left, and with the fall of the Kingdom of Naples it became in turn a hotel, an apartment house, and a restaurant). Now, the Villa d'Elbeuf, or what remained of it, was up for sale at auction to the highest bidder. The villa's name, Elbeuf, is consistently misspelled as "Elboeuf" in the auction documents and in newspaper accounts of the villa and its fate, but Elbeuf is a French town that has nothing to do with beef:

Lot 778269; Building complex sites in Portici (Naples), Via Peschiera 15.

Building complex Villa d'Elboeuf, derelict and in state of total abandonment, composed of a) a small house on the ground floor once used as a porter's lodge; b–c) a villa and "The Fisherman's House," with 40 units; d) open spaces used for gardens and courtyards, with underlying property once used as a restaurant, now used for storage, e) a complex of masonry walls, at present abandoned and vandalized, in part completely submerged by the sea and ascribed to the Domain of the State, Department of the Navy. 3960.6 square meters.[37]

This was the fourth such auction since 2009, when the villa was confiscated from its owners and put up for sale by the state; no buyers turned up for the first three auctions, and there were well-founded fears that the once-beautiful property would fall into the hands of the powerful Neapolitan criminal organization, the Camorra. The beach pavilions are described in these advertisements as "abandoned and vandalized" (another version of the advertisement, in the newspaper *La Repubblica,* said "ruinous"), and a series of articles by local journalists has revealed just how shockingly decrepit this formerly glorious property has become in recent decades.[38] The asking price for the main building in March 2013 was 3.5 million euros, the ruined pavilions a tenth of that amount. The whole property sold in April 2013 for 4 million euros to a consortium of local entrepreneurs.[39] The buyers of the Villa d'Elbeuf will need to contend with the modern highways and railway lines that did not exist in 1713 and which have divided the property and interfered with—destroyed, in fact—the esplanade that led down to the beach.

The national Ministry of Culture will supervise the restoration of the sad villa, whose grievous dereliction is a remarkably recent event. The Villa d'Elbeuf was still a magnificent and well-kept property when it was photographed for the mid-twentieth-century postcard that is Figure 3.2. It does not take an eruption of Vesuvius to produce a ruin. Indifference and neglect, given a little time, can be just as effective.

4

Mr. Freeman Goes
to Herculaneum

The well in Resina not only supplied Emmanuel-Maurice d'Elbeuf with antiquities but also led beneath the earth to a section of the ancient theater of Herculaneum. A climb down the shaft revealed a real version of Jacopo Sannazaro's dream of Pompeii, where "towers, houses, theaters, and temples could be picked out nearly intact."[1] The English painter George Knapton (who became the official limner for the Society of Dilettanti) provided a chatty account of what it was like to visit the place in 1740, when he managed to track down some of the original well diggers and marble purveyors for the "Duke di Belbosi":

At our coming to the Well, which is in a small Square, surrounded with miserable Houses, filled with miserable ugly old Women, they soon gathered about us, wondering what brought us thither; but when the Men who were with us, broke away the paltry Machine with which they used to draw up small Buckets of Water, I thought we should have been stoned by them. Till perceiving one more furious than the rest, whom we found to be *Padrona* of the Well, by applying a small Bit of Money to her, we made a shift to quiet the Tumult. Our having all the Tackle for descending to seek, gave Time for all the Town to gather round us, which was very troublesome: For, when any one offered to go down, he was prevented either by a Wife, or a Mother; so that we were forced to seek a motherless Batchelor[2] to go first. It being very difficult for the First to get in, the Well being very broad at that Part, so that they were obliged to swing him in, and the People above making such a Noise, that the Man in the Well could not be heard, obliged our Company to draw their Swords, and threaten any who spoke with Death. This caused a Silence, after which our Guide was soon landed safe, who pulled us in by the Legs, as we came down. The Entrance is 82 Feet from the Top of the Well: It is large, and branches out into many Ways, which they have cut. We were forced to mark with Chalk, when we came to any Turning, to prevent losing ourselves. It gives one a perfect Idea of a City destroyed in that Manner.[3]

An earlier English visitor, the evidently portly William Hammond, wrote in 1732 that he "never cared to venture down, being heavy, and the ropes bad."[4]

Resina, as the poor neighbor of posh Portici, was only too happy to become that wealthier community's chief supplier of antiquities. Portici had become an increasingly popular site for villas in the early eighteenth century, replacing the old favorite haunts that had been turned into suburbs of the ever-expanding city of Naples: places like the broad sweep of the Riviera di Chiaia, just north of the old city walls, now the preferred place for city folk to promenade in the afternoon, or the peninsula just north of Chiaia, known as Posillipo, from Greek *Pausilypon,* "Care's End."[5] The slopes of Vesuvius, looming above Portici, no longer seemed quite as forbidding as they had three generations earlier, in 1631; though the volcano continued to smolder, the damage was comparatively mild. Besides, San Gennaro was standing watch over Naples, his blood reliably and reassuringly liquefying year after year as a pledge of his constant vigilance.

There was also great satisfaction to be had in doing precisely what the ancient Romans had done along the Bay of Naples, creating a retreat for themselves from the crowds, noises, and smells of the capital city. In the early decades of the Roman Empire, every citizen with aspirations knew that the most important people were as likely to be found in Campania as in Rome, luxuriating in the domed splendor of the thermal baths at Baiae, consulting the Cumaean Sibyl, or performing the ritual of the *ambitio* (making the rounds) from villa to villa. These are the activities we hear about most from ancient authors, but this busy buzz of leisure activity was sustained, needless to say, on hard work, both slave and free, like staffing the imperial fleet anchored at Cape Misenum, not to mention the vast fortunes to be made (and occasionally lost) in the emporia of Puteoli, Naples, and Pompeii.[6] The list of prominent Romans who died in or en route to Campania shows how completely the area had been incorporated into the rhythms of life in the capital: Augustus died in Nola, Vergil in Naples, and Pliny the Elder, of course, on the beach at Stabiae. The explosion of Vesuvius in 79 therefore buried not only a series of settlements but also what had become a whole way of life for Rome itself. Romans of the later imperial age made sure to build their villas and baths on safer ground.

The first enthusiastic local revival of villas and "villeggiatura" in Campania occurred during the Renaissance, that self-conscious "rebirth" of classical culture in the fifteenth and sixteenth centuries. But these new villas were not simply attempts to recreate the settings and substance of Roman "dignified leisure" *(otium cum dignitate)*. Throughout the medieval period, Campania had maintained close contacts with the Islamic world by importing and adopting architectural motifs and amenities perfectly adapted to the Mediterranean climate, refinements like tiled courtyards, fountains, baths, orchards, and gardens. No Renaissance villa on the Bay of Naples would have seemed complete without an Islamic-style paradise garden, bursting with citrus fruits, peaches, apricots, and cherries (all fruits virtually unknown to the ancient palate) and, after 1492, with exotic plants from the New World. The most enchanting of all these retreats must have been the fifteenth-century royal villa just outside the Nolan Gate of Naples: Poggioreale, the "Royal Hill," created in 1483 for Ferrante I of Aragón.[7] Although the king employed a Florentine architect to execute its design, Poggioreale was nothing like a fifteenth-century Tuscan villa: it reflected its own very different and idyllic local conditions. Experienced as a whole, in fact, it must have been a place like almost none other on Earth. The grounds stretched from the rim of an old extinct volcano (the "Royal Hill," which gave the villa its name) right down to the beach. Because the complex stood along the chief northward route out of Naples, it was ringed by high walls to protect it from bandits, pirates, and invading armies, but inside its bristling exterior Poggioreale combined the best of the ancient and medieval worlds in a glorious blend of gracious architecture, fountains, gardens, and wandering animals.

Sadly, the villa's fortification walls failed to protect it from the troops of King Charles VIII of France, who nearly destroyed this earthly paradise a scant decade after its construction.[8] The site of Poggioreale must have been desolate indeed if its grounds could be turned over for the grim pair of public works it has hosted since the nineteenth century; part of the onetime royal gardens became the city cemetery, the special destination for victims of the new epidemic disease, cholera, and a modern prison rose next to the cemetery to relieve pressure on the wretched Spanish-built dungeons of the Tribunali.[9] In today's Naples, the word "Poggio-reale" conjures up vivid images, none of them pleasant. Once upon a time, however, the name evoked a wonderfully eclectic combination of ways to achieve the good life.

The creators of Poggioreale and the string of similar fifteenth- and sixteenth-century villas that began to appear along the coast had no intention of returning to antiquity. The ancient world inspired them, but they would no sooner have lived in the past, giving up the benefits of modern trade, food, and technology, than they would have renounced their Christian faith. Typically, the poet Jacopo Sannazaro, the same Sannazaro who wrote so eloquently of buried Pompeii, restored Vergil's tomb and built his own villa, Pausilypon—"Care's End"—close by. He spent his time at Pausilypon as Vergil would have, writing Latin poetry, which Sannazaro (or "Actius Sincerus," as he signed these Latin works) did in an excellent emulation of Vergilian style,[10] but he turned all of his efforts, both architectural and literary, to Christian subjects. His shorter Latin poems, the "Piscatory Eclogues," were the fisherman's equivalent of the pastoral verse that Vergil devoted to sheep, goats, trees, shepherds, and Augustus, but for Sannazaro the fisherman was just as much a Christ symbol as he was a fixture of the Neapolitan seascape. Like Vergil, "Sincerus" Sannazaro crowned his career by writing an epic, but *De partu virginis*, "On the Virgin's Delivery," tells the Christmas story in heroic Latin hexameters.

Sannazaro's older friend Giovanni Gioviano Pontano may have been the kingdom's most eager promoter of classical culture; he, too had his villa, his elegant writings in Latin and the vernacular, and his architectural projects, but when he and his friends met in their new version of Plato's Academy, they often assembled in the chapel he had built in the center of Naples along strikingly classical lines; their academy never lost sight of an ultimate Christian purpose. He might exhibit an Olympian arrogance—apparently he addressed his fellow academicians by saying, "How goes it, mortals?"—but all of his prodigious cultural efforts were firmly directed toward the Christian salvation of his immortal soul.[11]

Michelangelo's friend Vittoria Colonna, a Roman aristocrat from an old feudal family married to a Neapolitan of comparable lineage, the Marquis D'Avalos, pursued this same combination of classical and Christian interests at a still higher rung of the social ladder (that of the "barons," the oldest and most powerful of feudal landowners), using her castle on the island of Ischia much as Pontano and Sannazzaro used their villas: to withdraw from the world with like-minded friends.[12]

Neapolitan villa life was interrupted in the mid-sixteenth century by marauding Turks (who captured Chiaia for a few weeks in 1563) and the Spanish state's insatiable hunger for money, but by the end of the seventeenth century, piracy no longer posed a significant threat to Naples or the cities around its bay, and thus the dashing horseman d'Elbeuf was just one of the many aristocrats, both native and foreign, who resolved, once again, to build villas along the coast. These villa dwellers looked not only to antiquity for their inspiration but also to more recent local history, from the chivalrous world of medieval and Renaissance Naples to the region's unique local traditions, which linked villa life specifically with learned discussions of natural and political philosophy. For despite (or perhaps because of) its long history of foreign occupation, Naples had always been a center of political and what we would call scientific discussion (the Neapolitans themselves would have called their activity natural philosophy). In the thirteenth century, the majestic and magisterial Thomas Aquinas, himself a Neapolitan noble, had taught at the Dominican College of San Domenico Maggiore, a convent so large that it was able to host the royal university as well as its own college and often acted as a law unto itself. Two centuries later, Giovanni Gioviano Pontano, from his villa on the hills above Naples, made astronomical discussions an important part of the agenda in the late fifteenth and early sixteenth centuries. In the mid-sixteenth century, it was the turn of Bernardino Telesio in his palazzo on Via Medina; here the philosopher had proposed his physics of heat and cold to Giordano Bruno, then a friar at troublemaking San Domenico Maggiore, leading the younger man to develop his own theory of an infinite universe. Another friar from San Domenico, Bruno's younger contemporary Tommaso Campanella, would help foment a rebellion against the Spaniards, for which he would suffer torture and twenty-seven years of imprisonment in various Neapolitan dungeons, all the while writing undaunted about astronomy and politics. Neapolitan gentlemen also continued to meet in literary academies, both private and state sponsored, like the illustrious Accademia degli Oziosi, the "Academy of Men of Leisure," founded in the presence of Viceroy De Lemos in 1611 as a way of keeping an eye on the city's most restless and well-connected intellectuals. These "men of leisure" modeled themselves directly on the "dignified leisure," *otium cum dignitate,* of ancient Roman villa dwellers, but at the same time they kept a sharp eye on the latest modern developments in art, science, literature—and that new subject of fervent interest, antiquarian study.[13]

Eighteenth-century Naples continued this long tradition of learned gatherings, reviving the idea of *villeggiatura* in the beautiful stretch of coast just south of Naples and expanding these meetings to include, at least on occasion, outsiders: visitors, Grand Tourists, and officials from northern Europe, as well as permanent foreign residents like Emmanuel-Maurice d'Elbeuf. The French cavalryman may have been the first person to discover a large deposit of antiquities while digging the foundations for his villa at Portici, but no construction site could compare in size to the zone that was marked out in Portici for the new villa of young King Charles Bourbon in 1734.

Charles represented a new, auspicious episode in the life of Naples. At the end of the seventeenth century, the inbreeding of Spain's royal family had finally reached a point of no return in poor King Charles II, the deformed, mentally retarded son of two cousins, Philip IV and Anne of Austria, who were also uncle and niece (in fact, they looked so much alike that the court painter Diego Velázquez recycled a planned portrait of Philip as a portrait of his wife).[14] Charles II, though duly married, was unable to beget children, and in 1734, after a series of pitched battles by means of which France, Spain, and Austria settled the question of the "Spanish succession," Naples at last became a royal capital in its own right. It owed its ascendancy in great measure to the Italian-born queen of Spain, Elisabetta Farnese, who sent her eighteen-year-old son, Charles III Bourbon, over from Madrid to rule the Kingdom of Naples. This Charles, unlike his genetically doomed predecessor, was both intelligent and enlightened. He moved to Naples with the intention of making it a capital of truly European significance. The beauty of the bay and the balmy climate made it easy to love his adopted city, and the city loved Charles in return.

Part of Charles's campaign to propel Naples to prominence involved reconnecting the city with its ancient past. His mother had inherited a vast collection of antiquities from her forebears, including the colossal statues from the Baths of Caracalla in Rome, a family property, as well as a dazzling assemblage of decorative arts: metalwork, rock crystal, cameos, and gems, some ancient, some purchased from the treasury of Lorenzo de' Medici by a Farnese cardinal (the future Pope Paul III), some created on commission.[15] The Old Master paintings that came along with the antiquities were equally exquisite, with works by Raphael, Titian, the Carracci brothers, and many others. King Charles moved this collection from Rome to Naples in 1734 and distributed its components among the various palaces he had started to build in the region, all of them on the titanic scale the Farnese had favored ever since they acquired the Baths of Caracalla.

As king, and encouraged by his enthusiastic German queen, Maria Carolina, Charles insisted that the archaeological excavations that were beginning to excite so much interest in the Bay of Naples should became a royal prerogative. King Charles acquired both the Villa d'Elbeuf and the famous well in Resina as properties of the Crown. All further official investigations in the area were supervised by his staff and carried out by his own teams of convict laborers. The convicts, many of them captured pirates, were men who had been sentenced to row in the galleys or embalm corpses in the crypt under Santa Maria della Sanità. Life spent in a chain gang chipping away pyroclastic rock was slightly better than life spent rowing a galley or preparing corpses under ground; nonetheless, it was grim work that was carried out in dark tunnels, where the men were assailed by the constant damp and constantly threatened by underground seepage of poisonous gas. Karl Jakob Weber, the Swiss engineer who oversaw their work, died of the respiratory disease he contracted in these tunnels; so, no doubt, did many of the workers—the ones lucky enough to be spared death by asphyxiation on the spot.

The king's archaeological activity, such as it was, aimed almost exclusively at enhancing the royal collections. Buried buildings, once emptied of their booty and stripped of their decorations, were reburied. Wall paintings that were judged insufficiently beautiful were destroyed so that no one but the Charles, his family, and his close associates would ever have access to them. Visitors were admitted to the excavation sites only after applying directly to the monarch. Initially, then, the experience of the ancient cities of Herculaneum and Pompeii, for Charles himself and for visitors, could not help focusing on the immediate present—on how it felt to plunge into the ground and see what marvels lay buried underneath. Visitors wrote about excavations, individual artifacts, and the royal collection, often complaining about how little could be seen by anyone but the monarch and his court.

Because the first excursions to Herculaneum took place beneath a thick layer of rock-hard pyroclastic debris, they were virtually journeys to the underworld, torch-lit processions down wells and through tunnels to see the remains of paintings that often struck their viewers as monstrous rather than beautiful. One English visitor to Herculaneum reported to the Royal Society in London with an almost palpable shudder:[16]

> The designs of the greatest part of these paintings are so strange and uncouth, that it is difficult, and almost impossible, to guess what was aimed at. A vast deal of it looks like such Chinese borders and ornaments, as we see painted upon skreens. There are great numbers of little figures, dancing upon ropes; some few small bad landscapes; and some very odd pieces, either emblematical, or perhaps only the painter's whim. Of which last the writer gives two specimens: one, of a grasshopper driving a parrot; the other, of a vast great head, in the midst of what seems to have been intended for a green field encompassed with an hedge.

Yet when the artists of the Renaissance crawled down into the ruins and tombs of ancient Rome in the late fifteenth and early sixteenth centuries, they thought that the paintings they saw on the walls were the most beautiful works imaginable, and eighteenth-century antiquarians entered the tunnels of Herculaneum fully prepared to have the same experience.[17] What had happened in the meantime to make their reactions so different and so surprisingly negative?

Surprise was one factor. Most early visitors to Herculaneum were convinced, in one way or another, that the ancients painted like Raphael, the early sixteenth-century Italian artist who had, in the eyes of his own contemporaries, achieved full equality with the legendary painters of antiquity: Zeuxis, who portrayed grapes so realistically that the birds pecked at them, or Apelles, the favorite artist of Alexander the Great. Pliny the Elder mentioned both men in his chapter on soils, which included a long discussion of pigments and painters.

Raphael's later artistic style was, in fact, famously inspired by his own direct contact with ancient Roman art, and his contemporaries often insisted that his work looked just like ancient painting. It looked ancient to eyes trained even decades later, when direct contact with antiquity was still important to artistic success, but so was a display of familiarity with the great masters of the sixteenth century: not only Raphael but also Titian, Michelangelo, Giorgione, and Correggio. To eighteenth-century eyes, in effect, the Renaissance version of antiquity had become the real thing.

Ironically, the ancient paintings that Raphael saw were very much like those that greeted eighteenth-century visitors to Herculaneum. Raphael and his contemporaries crawled down into the ruins of Nero's Golden House, built after the disastrous fire of 64 A.D. and decorated in an extravagant new style, which they called "grottesco" because they found it in the underground grottoes near the Colosseum. The painters who worked in the Bay of Naples after the earthquake of 63 adopted the same carefree style as their Roman counterparts; thus, the very kinds of figures that captivated Raphael and his companions were the ones that shocked the later explorers of Herculaneum. Where the sixteenth century saw perfection, the eighteenth century saw monstrosity. "Grotesque" had taken on the negative connotations it has for us, whereas for the sixteenth century it meant extravagant, fanciful, but also beautiful.

When Raphael worked with ancient Roman painting, moreover, he could enter into its spirit while still remaining fervently

Christian. In 1514, he decorated a suite within the Vatican for Cardinal Bernardo Dovizi da Bibbiena, a close friend of Pope Leo X. The cardinal enjoyed reviving an ancient Roman habit that had become a rarity since the Middle Ages: bathing. Just a few years earlier, Pope Julius II had installed hot and cold running water in the Vatican, and Bibbiena decided to have a bathroom (*stufetta,* a combination of bath and sauna) of his own, with frescoes by Raphael on the wall (Figure 4.1). These frescoes still survive; Raphael's associate Marcantonio Raimondi also reproduced the decorations as engravings.

From these wall paintings in their striking cinnabar red (which was called "Pompeian red" in the eighteenth century) it is clear that Raphael had explored Nero's Golden House because he duplicated one of its designs on the upper portion of a wall of the *stufetta.* However, he also saw a series of paintings that must have been an exact duplicate of the atrium decorations in Pompeii's House of the Vettii: a series of cupids driving chariots drawn by different kinds of animals (another example of this subject appears in the Museo Nazionale in Naples, taken from yet another Pompeian wall). Marcantonio Raimondi's engravings gave these winged babies charming names: "Slow Love," for example, is the infant charioteer who struggles with a pair of gigantic snails.

We do not know where Raphael saw such cupid charioteers, but they must have been visible somewhere in Rome; he never went to Naples, much less to buried Pompeii (and the House of the Vettii was not excavated until 1894 and 1895). But what he saw was almost identical to what appeared on walls in the Bay of Naples, and this tells us that the painters of ancient Rome traveled between Rome and Campania and that the people who commissioned paintings for their walls could ask for favorite designs.[18]

Love may seem like an odd subject for a cardinal's bathroom, as it is not for the fun-loving Vettius brothers of Pompeii, but Bibbiena would have been ready to reassure us, with the Bible in

4.1.   Raphael, *stufetta* of Cardinal Bibbiena, Vatican Palace, 1514. Photo: Scala / Art Resource, NY.

one hand and Plato's *Symposium* in the other, that love was God's greatest blessing and that its earthly physical forms were simply signposts on the way to understanding its ineffable, transcendent reality. (Besides, in his own day priestly celibacy really meant no more than agreeing not to marry.) In the loggia next door, he had Raphael paint grotesques in the ancient style but with Christian figures mixed in.

The influence of ancient painting on the Italian Renaissance was fundamental, but the trail of inspiration hardly stopped there. Nor did it involve only academic painting. Even artists who rejected their own contemporary traditions of decorum let ancient art work its charm on them; they simply drew their inspiration from the ancient forms in new and different ways. The renegade painter Caravaggio, for example, modeled some of his most moving compositions on ancient Roman sculpture, and we will see how deeply Pompeii affected Renoir.

When the wall paintings of Herculaneum and later Pompeii became visible in the eighteenth century, they struck people as strange in part because their own vision of ancient art had been so powerfully conditioned by long tradition, one shaped by Raphael and his followers, including the great seventeenth-century Baroque masters, from Caravaggio and Annibale Carracci to Rubens. Ancient painting was supposed to look like Raphael's Vatican Logge or the Loggia of Cupid and Psyche he had painted for the merchant Agostino Chigi. The fact that it did not quite do so was a shock, and that shock underlines how carefully and subtly artists like Raphael and Michelangelo transformed the exuberance of ancient art by bringing it under iron control. There is a discipline to the designs of Raphael's Vatican Logge and Michelangelo's Sistine Chapel ceiling that is simply absent from ancient Roman art. The Renaissance aimed for order, whereas the painters of Herculaneum and Pompeii (and Rome itself) aimed for wild variety. Every piece of a design by Raphael or Michelangelo fits into a masterfully organized compositional structure, just as their Catholic worldview was governed in every detail by an omnipotent, providential God. The ancient Romans saw the world much more loosely, from their rambunctious gods to their choices in decor.

Roman houses were places where the imagination could run wild in every direction: landscapes, myths, gods, heroes, wildlife, architecture, jewels, monsters, and sometimes, amid all this fanciful activity, the portraits of real people. If we feel that our own culture has been overwhelmed by an onslaught of visual stimuli, ancient Rome was not so different.[19] The qualities that Vitruvius admired were *copia* (abundance) and *poikilia* (variety). There is order, too, but it is looser than that imposed by the Renaissance version of the classical spirit.

Ancient Roman homeowners, no matter how modest, liked to decorate their walls and courtyards with little painted gardens or mythological scenes. In the great houses of the rich, who owed their wealth to trade and military conquests that linked Italy with Europe, Africa, and Asia, the décor included originals or copies of famous works of painting and sculpture, some looted, some purchased, some simply evoked—like the huge mosaic in Pompeii's House of the Faun, which shows Alexander the Great defeating the Persian emperor Darius at the Battle of Issus. Dating from about 100 B.C., it is probably a copy in stone of a painted original produced three hundred years earlier, when Alexander was still alive and conquering the world, in all likelihood by none other than Apelles, the most famous ancient painter of them all.[20]

Original ancient paintings may be rare, but reproductions in other media are not. The ancient Roman world was filled, almost as much as our own, with tourists and other travelers and therefore with souvenirs. Visitors could not bring back postcards of famous works of art, but they could bring back an image in some other form: a vase, a plate, a mosaic, a necklace, a cameo—even a statue, like the universally popular Hellenistic scene of a tipsy

Bacchus uncovering the beautiful sleeping Ariadne or the mosaic of Alexander conquering a Persian army at Issus.

Ancient Romans had picture galleries to rival those of Greece; the wealthiest houses all tried to include fine old paintings (especially Greek works) as well as portraits of ancestors. Ancient writers like Vitruvius tells us that Roman householders sometimes set ancient paintings directly into the walls of their house, but more often they commissioned a copy of an Old Master painting they liked in a medium they liked. And they did not set those paintings into blank white walls; they set them into walls with a riot of other decoration.

As Pliny the Elder reminds his readers, the traditions of Roman painting developed from classical Greece by incorporating its further developments in the Hellenistic era, especially in cosmopolitan Alexandria. Many of the artists who worked in Roman Italy continued to come directly from the Greek-speaking world, making sure to sign their works in Greek as a mark of their sophisticated training. Inevitably, though, once they arrived in Italy, their work responded to the region's golden light, its abundance of plants and animals, and the particular forms of a local architecture that had absorbed elements from the Etruscans and ancient Egypt as well as classical and Hellenistic Greece. Pompeian painting is almost never, if ever, a pure copy of painting from someplace else; it always reflects the special, ravishing beauty of the Bay of Naples delighting in juxtapositions like copies of Old Masters set into walls decorated with the most complicated, up-to-date filigree architecture imaginable.

Well into the twentieth century, archaeologists were convinced that the art of Pompeii and Herculaneum must be provincial work compared with that of Rome itself, but by now the houses of Rome, including that of Augustus himself, are fairly well understood. It now seems more likely that painting along the Bay of Naples reached a level just as high as that anywhere else in the

Roman Empire, including the capital. And this should really come as no surprise. Travel along Rome's roads and seaways was relatively safe and could be remarkably swift; if wealthy home-owners could travel easily between Rome and Campania, so could the artists who decorated their houses on commission. The result was often a busy hodgepodge of objects, media, styles, eras, colors, and tastes (most Pompeian peristyles look positively cluttered), but Roman art struck most of its ancient viewers (Vitruvius ex-cepted) as charming rather than chaotic. It made quite a different impression, however, when Enlightenment taste, in the form of eighteenth-century explorers, plunged into the subterranean world of Herculaneum.

However, the eighteenth-century shock value of the art from Pompeii and Herculaneum also came from its subject matter. Everyone who explored the ruins knew that the ancient Romans' view of sex was very different from that of the Christian Church. The Bible provided ample evidence of that, from the doom rain-ing down on sinners in the book of *Revelation* to Saint Paul's fulminations against fornication, which literally meant loitering around arcades (Latin *fornices*) waiting for prostitutes. Paul also launched strict injunctions against first-century Roman common-places such as divorce and marital infidelity.

What Saint Paul denounced as "fornication," most ancient Romans lingered over in detail. In story, song, and verse they explored every aspect of human coupling (and tripling and more), from unfulfilled longing to enduring marriages to quick inter-ludes between men and women, men and boys, not to mention a memorable poem by Propertius, in which his lady friend, Cyn-thia, catches him with two other women at once and raises poetic hell.[21] Ancient vases, cameos, and wall paintings showed couples, almost always young and beautiful, joined together in extrava-gantly athletic embraces. By the first quarter of the sixteenth cen-tury, thanks to the Renaissance revival of interest in every aspect of ancient culture, there was really very little that scholars, courtesans, and connoisseurs did not already know about sexuality in ancient Rome. But here, too, Christian convention imposed order where ancient Rome reveled in variety and abundance. The preservation of so many personal items from Herculaneum and Pompeii showed exactly how varied and abundant an erotic experience was on offer for the average ancient Roman: a vast range of titillating new objects, preserved in their original settings, provided vibrant proof of the extent to which sex, in boundless exuberance, seemed to have pervaded Pompeian life.

The real picture, of course, was more complicated than that of a long, unbridled orgy. Sex in the Roman world was still a sacred and terrifying thing, the domain of the goddess Venus, normally shown working in tandem with her young son, Cupid, desire personified as a capricious child. Like the drinking of wine, the act of love was a holy act even when casual indulgence seemed to profane it.

Venus was also, like many ancient goddesses, a protectress of cities, including both Rome and Pompeii (Herculaneum, of course, had that burly hero Hercules). From 80 B.C. on, the city of Pompeii was officially know as the Colonia Cornelia Veneria Pompeianorum, the "Cornelian Venusian (or Venereal!) Colony of the Pompeians," its "Venusian" identity clinched by the dedication of a new temple to Venus on the headland above the main entrance to the city, the Porta Marina. The lavish Corinthian-style temple was meant to dominate the view of Pompeii from the sea as well as the land, and for about ninety years it did just that. Then the earthquake of 63 toppled its showy marble colonnade, the price of projecting so far above its surroundings. Rebuilding went slowly, and then, in 79, Vesuvius buried the city once and for all. Now two lone capitals and a square block of concrete core are all that is left of the chief shrine to Pompeii's divine guardian. Modern visitors to the site will hardly notice any of it, because the ruined temple stands right by the main exit from the site, the Porta Marina. Today, the fallen columns arranged around this stub of a building mostly serve as shady benches, idyllic vantages for a last lovely view of the ancient city, at a moment when most people's thoughts have long since turned from archaeology to food, drink, and rest. This is where a disconsolate Ingrid Bergman sits in a still from *Viaggio in Italia,* the film she made in Pompeii and Naples with her husband, Roberto Rossellini (see Chapter 18 and Figure 18.5).

Venus was not simply the goddess of sex; she was also the mother of fertility in all of its forms, including the abundance of commodities that drove commerce. The philosopher-poet Lucretius celebrates this commercial aspect of the goddess in the opening lines of his poem *On Nature (De rerum natura):*

> Dear Venus, who underneath the gliding
> heavenly signals busies the seas with ships and makes
> earth fruitful (for only through you are living things
>   conceived
> and because of you they rise up to bask in the light of the
>   sun):
> from you the harsh winds flee and the skies' black storm
>   clouds scatter
> at your approach; for you the intricate earth sprouts
>   flowers,
> wide ocean roads subside into gentle smiling, and furthest
> reaches of heaven grow serene in response to your
>   prompting.[22]

Most Pompeian businessmen seem to have entrusted their good fortune to less high-mindedly philosophical versions of the Golden Goddess's divine protection, appealing not directly to Venus herself but to her ubiquitous henchman, the phallic god Priapus.

Priapus had no philosophy; a god of action, pure, simple, and mindless, he lived in gardens and the countryside and between the legs of animals and men, springing into action whenever he chose, and only when he chose. There was one temple of Venus, but the shrines to Priapus in Pompeii outnumbered even the shrines to the Lares and Penates, the household gods. So persistent was his cult that he still shows up in the early Christian catacombs of San Gennaro, standing guard over a Christian tomb, not to mention the ubiquitous spray-painted graffiti that now mar Italian walls everywhere, American in their medium but relentlessly traditional in their subject matter.

The wealthy Vettius brothers, Pompeian freedmen who may have owned a perfume business, put a painted image of the phallic god Priapus in the vestibule of their house, weighing an abundance of produce against his own engorged, evidently fertile member (Figure 4.2). He is telling evil spirits to give up on haunting this house because they cannot possibly compete with his glorious virility.

Other Pompeians tied phallic amulets to their wrists, lit their rooms with phallic lamps, drank from cups decorated with sexual scenes, or cheered their gardens with phallic wind chimes. Bricks embossed with phallic symbols have been set into the walls of Pompeii to guide customers to the *lupanare*—the "wolf house," Roman slang for "brothel" (needless to say, Romans, those civic descendants of Venus, were well aware of the double entendres suggested by the legend that the city's twin founders, Romulus and Remus, had been suckled by a female wolf).

Pompeii's *lupanare* is a grim, low-budget affair, its tiny cubicles furnished with built-in masonry couches (which must have been covered by cushions), a prominent cashier's desk, and a little one-seat latrine. A series of tiny frescoes above the cubicles presents graphic ideas of what the "she-wolves" and their clients might have gotten up to behind the curtain that would have provided

4.2.   Priapus, House of the Vettii, Pompeii. Photo: The Bridgeman Art Library.

their only privacy (one scene involves two women). The smells, noises, and press of flesh must have been suffocating when this den of wolves was in its heyday; cramped and dismal, it was never a high-budget establishment. The workers were probably slaves: human property, devoid of rights, exploited relentlessly to enrich the establishment's owner.

Herculaneum also had its share of lascivious paintings. Private houses all over the Roman world featured erotica on their walls, even places like the elegant Farnesina House in Rome, which may well have belonged to Julia, the daughter of Augustus, when she was married his close associate, the general Marcus Vipsanius Agrippa. The Farnesina House may have been the place where Raphael and his associates came into contact with ancient Roman erotic art in the early sixteenth century; they certainly came across it somewhere.

Raphael himself always maintained a scrupulous decorum in his work, but his associates entered enthusiastically into the ancient world of sex, especially his most gifted protégé, the Roman painter Giulio Pippi (Giulio Romano), and the engraver Marcantonio Raimondi. Shortly after Raphael's death in 1520, Giulio made a series of drawings based on ancient Roman erotic scenes, which Marcantonio duly engraved, emphasizing the quality that most struck Christian visitors about eros in the ancient world: the wide variety of positions that lovers seem to have assumed in its pursuit. Not surprisingly, the series took on the name *I modi,* "The Ways [to do it]," and its distribution in 1524 caused both a sensation and a scandal. Soon their friend, the Venetian poet Pietro Aretino, had supplied each of the engravings with a sonnet in the vernacular, all minutely descriptive, if not particularly poetic.

For all its refinements of design and execution, *I modi* presented a challenge to Christian Rome and its ruler, the pope, and finally the pontifical authorities cracked down, charging Marcantonio with copyright violation in 1524. Prudently, his collaborators left town: Giulio moved on to Mantova and Aretino to Venice, where each happily continued to produce lascivious words and pictures for their new northern Italian patrons. Only fragments survive of the original *Modi* of 1524, but knockoffs of the engravings quickly appeared throughout Europe, pornography vindicated by a classical veneer. At least some of the erotic visions from Pompeii were not entirely new to their eighteenth-century viewers, but it was surprising to see such intimate scenes painted in public places rather than carefully hidden away in books.

Furthermore, compared with the decorations on the walls of the *lupanare* at Pompeii, *I modi* are the essence of elegance; Giulio Romano's lovers perform their supple feats on stately, carved canopy beds, though one plump mattress has slipped halfway off its bedstead, and one woman has embraced her standing partner in a flying leap.

The sight of Pompeii's painted sporting couples would have surprised eighteenth-century visitors more with their crudity and with the women's proportions (small breasts, massive posteriors) than with their activities, for which *I modi* had prepared them well. On the other hand, the Pompeians' carved stone cameos and intaglio gems were exquisite. Here again, however, these objects were familiar; from his mother, King Charles had inherited the incomparable Farnese collection of gems and intaglios, some of which had erotic subjects.

Even the erotic subjects of the bronze lamps and wind chimes from Herculaneum and Pompeii had been imitated in the Renaissance. It was the sheer numbers of these objects and their extravagant enthusiasm that took everyone aback: flying phalluses, many of them hung with jingling bells, and the bronze sistra, ritual rattles for the cult of Isis, topped with reclining cats, symbols of loving motherhood and sexual abandon.

Finally, there was a certain suggestive power to the setting in which these early visitors saw the art of the ancient Romans: by making a journey into the bowels of the earth to see prurient pictures in a kind of earthly hell. An English "Mr. Freeman" describes this underground progress vividly in letters of 1750 and 1751 to Lady Mary Capel, Countess of Essex, who in turn relayed his correspondence to the Royal Society in London. This is "Mr. Freeman" on his experience of Herculaneum in 1751:

I was first conducted down a narrow passage, which they have dug wide enough barely for two persons to pass by each other; and descended, by a gradual slope, to the depth of about 65 feet perpendicular. Here I saw a great part of the ancient theatre, being a building in the form of an horseshoe. That part of it, where is supposed to be the orchestra and stage, was not so cleared out, as to be distinctly seen: the other [part], where the spectators sat, is very visible, and consists of 18 rows of broad stone seats, one above another, in a semicircular form, and are sufficiently wide to place the feet of those, who sit behind each other; so that they may be said to be both seats and footstools. Altho' this theatre is not emptied of the matter or earth, that filled it, yet they have dug quite round the exterior part, by which one may judge of its spaciousness. . . . The pavement of this theatre must have been very beautiful, by the different-colour'd marble, that has been taken out of it, and some that remains. In short, by the broken pieces of cornices, mouldings, and carved work, and the many fragments of pillars, etc., which have been found within and without the theatre, it appears to have been a most magnificent edifice.[23]

This Mr. Freeman also explored the rest of the city, noting that "Here they seem to have dug infinitely more than about the theatre; for one may ramble, as in a labyrinth, for, at least, half a mile." On the very same day that he penned this letter to London, May 2, 1750, the head of the king's archaeological team, Karl Jakob Weber, began excavating a new area, which would turn out to be the richest location in all of Herculaneum, the Villa of the Papyri, with its bounteous hoard of statues, small finds, and a whole library of papyrus books.[24]

Perhaps a merchant based in Naples but clearly a man with intellectual interests (his letter appeared in the *Philosophical Transactions of the Royal Society,* after all), Mr. Freeman was most unimpressed by the excavators' methods and their habit of transferring everything of quality to the royal collections, to which, as a gentleman but not an aristocrat, he seems to have had no access: "It is great pity, that they did not, at the first discovery, open the ground at the top, and clear it away as they worked, in order to have seen those fine things in open day-light. But I have been told, it was impossible, seeing the vast depth of earth and stone they must have been obliged to have made way thro'. That reason does not all satisfy me; they having slaves enough, of the rascally and villainous sort, to complete such a work."[25]

Herculaneum was not the only disconcerting element in this experience. In the mid-eighteenth century, the buried city was only a sideshow to a much larger circus: the phantasmagoria of Naples itself, a city that was not only densely populated, filthy, and strange but also riddled with tunnels of its own, carved into the soft volcanic bedrock since time immemorial. The entire city sat above an intricate network of underground cisterns that connected one building to another, tended by a clan of workers it was best to treat with elaborate respect—or face the odoriferous consequences. Herculaneum was normally not the first subterranean journey that visitors to Campania would have undertaken, especially in the early days of excavation. Their stay almost invariably included not only caverns like the Grotta del cane and the Sibyl's cave in Cumae but also the underground haunts of Naples itself, from the crypt of the church of San Pietro ad Aram to the city's intricate network of catacombs.

For in Naples, as in Rome, the bodies of saints and sinners alike were stored away in catacombs, the vast graveyards that were hewed into the volcanic stone on which both cities sit. Although the catacombs served as important meeting places for Christians, they were never hideouts; the graves were all registered with city authorities. Pagans and Jews also buried their dead in these underground galleries, often side by side. It was to a catacomb, therefore, that the Christians of Naples brought the body of San Gennaro in 472, cajoling or stealing him away from his resting place in Pozzuoli.

San Gennaro's new Neapolitan tomb was doubtless more impressive than his seaside grave had been. The solidified lava known in Italian as *tufa* is soft and relatively easy to cut, especially the golden stone of Naples; it hardens only on contact with air. Rome's tufa is denser than that of Naples, and consequently Rome's catacombs are cramped, dark places, but the underground spaces of Naples soar to fantastic heights, virtual underground cathedrals. The catacomb of San Gennaro is carved into a steep hill above the city, and there, tucked in among the tombs of the first bishops of Naples and other members of the early Christian community, it became a destination for pilgrims. Living worshippers came to pray and also tried to arrange eventual burial for themselves and their families as close to the saint as possible. At some point early in the catacomb's existence, one pious visitor or prospective occupant, still partly pagan at heart, carved a protective phallus into the tufa to give his (clearly not her) grave some extra protection from evil spirits. Even after the saint's relics had been moved to Benevento in 831, the underground chapel was still venerated as a holy place and continued to grow, a multistory rabbit warren of tombs and what amounts to an underground cathe-

FROM POMPEII

dral, carved directly out of the soft rock with pillars, arcades, and a spectacular balcony looking out into a cavernous vestibule.

We do not know when San Gennaro's relics were reduced simply to his skull and the two vials of his blood, but the preservation of his skull reflects an ancient Greco-Roman conviction that the soul resided in the brain so long as a person lived. This belief persisted for centuries; Leonardo da Vinci's drawings of the human skull are part of his own attempt to pinpoint the anatomical location of the soul within our heads. Nor has it ever entirely died out, for in Naples, as in some parts of Greece, skulls have played an important part in local religious life.[26]

Just down the hill from the catacombs of San Gennaro, another catacomb, this one dedicated to San Gaudioso, shows how dramatic the Neapolitan attachment to skulls could be. In the seventeenth century, the Dominicans dedicated a church to Santa Maria della Sanità, Our Lady of Health, to serve a growing settlement outside the city walls. The congregation decided to revive the ancient practice of burial in catacombs but added a new twist, reputedly inspired by Spanish funeral customs: the dead were lowered through one of three trapdoors into a newly carved crypt, where they were arranged to crouch in the fetal position on tufa thrones, each of which contained a basin rather than a seat.

Within the moist, even climate of the underground chamber, the bodies' fluids gradually drained into the basins until they became desiccated. At that point the grave workers removed the skulls, which were partially sunk into the plastered walls of the catacomb at head level so that they grin eerily out at visitors. The headless bodies, meanwhile, were laid out on horizontal shelves carved into the rock. On the plaster beneath the immured skulls, artists have painted the deceased as dancing skeletons: men carrying the tools of their trade, women clad in modest red skirts to cover their pelvic bones. The people who performed the distasteful task of preparing the bodies in this dark, putrid crypt were condemned criminals who undertook this work rather than rowing as galley slaves, the same class of people who would be pressed into service as excavators at Herculaneum and Pompeii. This extraordinary custom seems to have lasted for about a hundred years at Santa Maria della Sanità, that is, up to the advent of the Bourbon monarchy and the first royal investigations of the buried cities.[27]

After two decades of exploration and ten years of official royal attention, the ruins of Herculaneum seemed to be running out of portable treasures; at that point the military engineer in charge of the royal excavations, Rocco Alcubierre, decided to take soundings in other areas around Vesuvius. Encouraged by the fact that, for a century, scholars like Lukas Holste had proclaimed that Civita must be the site of Pompeii, Alcubierre started a series of exploratory tunnels around the village. At first he dug tunnels because this is what he had always done, but soon the workers, Alcubierre himself, and above all his second in command, a Swiss engineer named Karl Jacob Weber, realized that conditions in Pompeii were different from those in Herculaneum, with a different kind of soil and nothing but scattered farmhouses on the land. Piled volcanic lapilli were easy to remove, and in the countryside, no obstacles prevented simple open-air digging. Excavating in Pompeii turned out to be infinitely easier than it had been in Herculaneum. It was also far safer, at least after Alcubierre gave up the idea of tunneling; his Pompeian tunnels, dug into piles of volcanic pebbles rather than hardened pyroclast, collapsed with alarming ease. Once Alcubierre had realized that he could dig out in the open, he also began to perceive that the friable, fertile soil released no poisonous fumes, and working in the open meant that the excavation trenches could drain and dry after a rain rather than turn into stagnant pools like the underground caverns of Herculaneum. A healthier workforce and easier conditions also meant that digging at Pompeii was a much more economical undertaking than digging at Herculaneum, and Alcubierre, as a military man, knew all about managing budgets.[28] Most important, the soundings at Pompeii produced results that went far beyond a new supply of objects and paintings for the royal collection. Weber, frustrated by the haphazard efforts at Herculaneum, had insisted from the outset that exploration of the new site follow the actual layout of the city, guided by the course of the ancient streets, and that every street, monument, and building be carefully recorded on measured plans. An urban street grid began to emerge along with the tombs, villas, houses, walls, and theater complex.

Thus, although they were driven by the same combination of antiquarian enthusiasm and treasure hunting, the excavations of Pompeii soon provided a completely different experience from those of Herculaneum. The sun beamed down from an open sky in the midst of a fertile countryside, and rather than crawling down mephitic tunnels, visitors had a gorgeous outing in the country. Under these conditions, it was easier to evoke wholesome thoughts of a living city as much as a city of the dead, especially in the early days, before excavators had learned how to produce plaster casts of the buried bodies. It is no wonder that the more southerly city quickly outstripped Herculaneum in popularity—it was accessible to nearly everyone, easy to negotiate, and pleasant to visit. The city had been much more important in antiquity than Herculaneum; it was not by chance that a well-informed Neapolitan like Jacopo Sannazaro had woven his Arcadian reverie around Pompeii. It was the real antiquarian's dream along the Bay of Naples.

5

The Rediscovery of Pompeii

In 1748 Abbot Giuseppe Martorelli opened the first excavation trench at what he thought was ancient Stabiae, bringing up coins, statues, small objects, wall paintings, and a skeleton, nothing exciting enough to steal attention away from Herculaneum; as a result, king and scholars kept their sights fixed on Herculaneum for another several years. When findings at Herculaneum began to peter out, soundings were again taken at Civita in 1754, but it was not until 1763 that the discovery of an inscription with the phrase RES PUBLICA POMPEIANORUM definitively proved Lukas Holste's conjecture: the hill of Civita covered ancient Pompeii.[1]

Excavators working just outside the ancient city wall uncovered what would prove to be a suburban villa situated a few steps above a road paved with big rounded blocks of volcanic basalt, the same basalt that paved the streets of Naples. The road itself clearly led to Herculaneum, and, like the consular roads that lead to Rome, it was lined with tombs: the monuments of Pompeians who still clamor for passersby to read their epitaphs, thereby ensuring that their names will never die (ancient Romans normally read aloud, which must have made their libraries interesting places). Some of the deceased even provided benches for weary travelers to rest a bit before moving on and perhaps spare a grateful thought for the benefactor who had so thoughtfully foreseen their weariness. A tomb almost directly in front of the villa commemorated a Pompeian freedman named Marcus Arrius Diomedes. Wishful thinking quickly turned Arrius Diomedes into the villa's owner. Mariano Vasi's 1844 guidebook still told a story that by that time went back nearly a hundred years:

> The house of Arrius Diomedes situated in the suburb Pagus Augusto Felix in the direction of Vesuvius was the first discovered. Its interior is a long square surrounded with a portico supported by stuccoed pilasters; in the middle was a small garden with six columns, a basin of white marble and a well; some of the rooms are painted on a red ground with figures and grotesques. A skeleton supposed to be that of Diomedes was found here holding in one hand a key, in the other coins and gold ornaments; behind this another [skeleton] holding bronze and silver vases. Under the garden portico is a cellar which contained many of the vases used by the ancients for preserving wine. Two stair cases lead to the second story placed in the midst of a covered court with 14 brick stuccoed columns and a mosaic pavement.
>
> The tomb of the Arria family to the left of the house bears the inscription that it was raised by M. Arrius Diomedes, the freedman of Caja.[2]

Proceeding down the road in the direction of the city walls, the digging uncovered a crush of tombs that crowded in on one another, all clamoring for attention, and another suburban villa, called the Villa of Cicero. This structure, once emptied of its wall paintings, was buried again and remains buried to this day.

Additional structures came to light in other areas nearby: in 1764 a temple with Egyptian-themed decorations that allowed excavators to identify it almost immediately as a temple of Isis (an exciting prospect) in a city block that also included a portico, a large theater, and a smaller concert hall, all explored between 1764 and 1769.[3]

As an above-ground site, Pompeii had the potential to attract visitors who would never think of lowering themselves into a well and scrambling in the dark: less adventurous, more corpulent visitors, perhaps, but not necessarily any less interested in antiquity than the lithe young men who sent back reports from the tunnels of Herculaneum. Ongoing excavations added to Pompeii's allure of the site holding out the prospect of an exciting find right then and there: an artifact, a painting, a skeleton, a new building. By 1765 Neapolitan tour guides, *ciceroni,* had all added Pompeii to their repertory of routes. For the most important tourists, "discoveries" could be arranged as part of the package.

The buried city made a convenient day trip by carriage from Naples on a road fit for a king. There was always time for an additional stop in Portici or at least a slow drive through to see the villas of the royal, rich, and famous. The king's permission was required to make the trip, as was the payment of a fee. A 1775 French guidebook to Italy, the *Guide d'Italie pour faire agréablement le voyage de Rome, Naples, et autres lieux (Guide to Italy to Make the Journey Pleasantly to Rome, Naples, and Other Places),* provides a list of prices: royal apartments at Portici, 4 *carlini* (a gold coin named after King Charles); Herculaneum, 3 *carlini;* antiquities collection, 2 *carlini;* a guide for the trip up Vesuvius, 2 *carlini;* lunch and red wine of Vesuvius, 1 *carlino;* the carriage, 11 *carlini.*[4]

The most earnest visitors devoted three days to the towns around Vesuvius, but the site of Pompeii itself, tiny, agricultural Civita, had little to offer either excavators or tourists; instead, under royal sponsorship a separate workers' settlement began to grow up along the road to Salerno. The Crown was also responsible for upgrading the Rapillo tavern, an old wayside inn that accommodated carriage drivers and their horses as the visitors and *ciceroni* made their tours. As director of excavations in the 1780s, Francesco La Vega addressed a specific request to the king for such a facility, noting that many foreign visitors had complained about the lack of "comfortable lodgings, which necessitated a short, hurried visit in order to return to Naples by the end of the day. . . . The best place to build such an inn would be where there is already one called the Rapillo . . . which is found on the Royal Road, just outside the perimeter of the ancient city at a nearly equal distance from the Herculaneum Gate and the Amphitheater."[5]

La Vega also suggested that the plan of the new inn mimic the construction of an ancient Pompeian house "to serve as a teaching tool and provide the most reliable means for understanding the remains that have been found in the city." He designed this new building himself, modeling it on his own experience of Roman domestic architecture: the Villa of Diomedes. Until 1814, visitors entered the site of Pompeii straight through the peristyle of the Villa of Diomedes, and so La Vega designed the Rapillo with a spacious portico at its entrance, perfect for outdoor dining most of the year. The fact that this was the equivalent of entering a house through its back door bothered no one at all. The porticoes, ancient and modern, were delightful places to dine, and besides, Vitruvius said that suburban villas put the peristyle before the atrium.

There were good reasons, as La Vega well knew, to locate both the new inn and the workers' village at a distance from Civita itself. Conditions in that settlement had changed drastically for the worse in 1659, when the local feudal lord, Alfonso Piccolomini, tried to divert the River Sarno to power a series of water mills at Scafati to the east. Domenico Fontana's canal had been cut to serve one of the first industrial establishments in the area, the munitions factory in Torre del Greco, but over the course of the seventeenth and especially the eighteenth century, factories became increasingly popular investments for Neapolitan aristocrats. Not all of them were successful. Piccolomini's project, for example, backfired, disastrously flooding the fields around Civita before the water could be drained away. Then the mosquitoes moved in, and the region between the ancient city and the Sarno quickly became a malarial swamp. Few, if any, tourists came from Naples to Civita expecting to spend the night.

6

Wolfgang Amadeus Mozart

When Leopold Mozart took his talented son to Naples in May 1770, it was for an open-ended business trip. They had already spent the winter in northern Italy before moving on to Bologna, Florence, and Rome. Leopold was realistic about their chances for success in Naples, one of the world's largest cities at the time and perhaps the greatest musical city in Europe. "I can't tell you how long we'll be staying here," he wrote his wife on May 19, five days after their arrival from Rome. "I've no choice in the matter. It could be 5 weeks or 5 months. I think it'll be 5 weeks, but it all depends on the circumstances."[1]

"The circumstances," for working musicians like the Mozarts, meant finding sponsors for their music. In their search for patronage, Leopold and his prodigiously talented children had learned to move among the loftiest ranks of society, but they knew that they would never belong to those ranks themselves. They were phenomenally well connected, but they were not, by contemporary standards, wellborn. At seven, Wolfgang may have proposed marriage to Princess Marie Antoinette (a family story claimed that she had picked him up when he tripped and fell after his concert in the Hofburg Palace, and he gallantly proposed on the spot), but Leopold Mozart, at least, knew about the rigid social distinctions that ruled courtly life and courtly careers.[2] As a child, Wolfgang had played for the empress of Austria, but it remained to be seen whether he would play as a young adult for the king of Naples.

At fifteen, the young prodigy could still, if barely, capitalize on his youth; many musicians made their debuts at about the same age (like the castrato Farinelli, whom we will meet shortly). And so, with an eye to the future, Leopold had already begun pointing his son toward adult responsibilities, including the commission of his first *opera seria*. The Mozarts, then, were not really Grand Tourists in Italy. In a certain sense, they were a privileged variety of traveling performer, giving concerts to pay their expenses as they went and devoting most of their time abroad to carrying on the business of music: commissions, performances, keeping track of new developments. But they were also energetic and curious visitors, well informed about their temporary home long before they arrived and eager to see all the sights that the Bay of Naples had to offer. They were also well inserted into society, here as elsewhere; as Leopold wrote his wife from Milan in March: "Tomorrow, to mark our departure, we're dining with His Excellency [Leopold's employer, the archbishop of Salzburg, Count Firmian], who is providing us with letters of recommendation for Parma, Florence, Rome and Naples."[3] There were twenty letters of recommendation for Rome alone.[4]

Leopold Mozart can be a remarkably informative correspondent, as when he tells his wife about the logistics of their trip to Naples:

We left Rome at 10 in the morning on 8 May in the company of three other sedias—2-seater carriages—and had a light lunch at 1 o'clock in the Augustinian monastery at

Marino, and on the evening of the 11th we were again well looked after at another Augustinian monastery at Sessa. We then called in on the Augustinian friars in Capua at midday on the 12th in the belief that we'd be in Naples that same evening. [Instead they spent the night in Capua]. . . . On the Monday we slept until 10 and after lunch drove to Naples, where we arrived in good time that same evening. We spent 2 nights in a house belonging to the Augustinian monastery of San Giovanni a Carbonaro, but we're now in rooms for which we're having to pay 10 silver ducats—4 ducats in our own currency—a month.[5]

Throughout their Italian journey, the Mozarts were able to travel in the company of Augustinian friars and stay cheaply at Augustinian convents, thanks to Leopold's position as deputy Kapellmeister to the archbishop of Salzburg, a city with its own important Augustinian church. Italian inns were another matter, as the elder Mozart told his wife: "But I won't bore you with a long description of our appalling journey here. Imagine only a largely uncultivated country and the most appalling inns, filth everywhere, nothing to eat except—if we were lucky—the occasional meal of eggs and broccoli: and sometimes they even made a fuss about giving us eggs on fast days."[6]

In Naples, the Augustinian convent of San Giovanni a Carbonara (Leopold mistakenly spells it with an *o*) provided an illustrious point of reference for the newcomers, a beautiful old Gothic building set on a hill on the eastern side of the city, looking out toward the slopes of a gently smoking Vesuvius, for the volcano was in one of its active periods.[7]

One enduring legacy of ancient Rome is clear from Leopold's letter of May 19: the roads, which enabled a post chaise to travel the two hundred kilometers from Rome to Naples in two days despite the region's mountainous terrain. The old Roman roadbeds were remarkably well maintained by a collaborative effort between the governments of the papal states and the kingdom of Naples, both, for once, working together rather than in opposition to one another. The eighteenth century, at least until Napoleon's invasion in 1798, was a time of rare political stability for the Italian peninsula, making travel relatively easy and secure—an important factor in promoting the Neapolitan tourist trade. The risk of attack by bandits was less daunting than it had been since the breakup of the Roman Empire (and would be again in the war-torn nineteenth century). Still, the Mozarts clearly traveled in a little convoy for safety, and they took the mountainous route that led over the hills from Marino to Sessa Aurunca rather than risk the shorter Appian Way, whose straight trajectory, lined with umbrella pines, shot through the middle of the malarial swamps known as the Pomptine Marshes. The same excellent roads would facilitate their travels around the Bay of Naples.

Travel within Italy may have been easier in the later eighteenth century than at any time since the fall of the Roman Empire; nonetheless, it was not easy. No visitor in those days would think of planning a tour of Pompeii without making a protracted stay in Naples, one of the world's most populous and important cities, with its own wealth of attractions. In any case, access to the kingdom's archaeological sites required connections—they were all royal property—and making use of those connections required paying courtesy calls in Naples and the royal villa at Portici, where the king kept one of his collections of antiquities. Only a few buildings had been unearthed in Pompeii itself, as we will see, and the usual round for visitors to the site took in "the two buried cities" of Pompeii and Herculaneum in a single day. Thus Wolfgang Amadeus Mozart's experience of Pompeii was only one part of his larger experience of Naples; if his memories of Pompeii have exerted any effect on his music, then they are more likely to be memories of his whole Neapolitan experience rather than one part of a single, action-packed day trip.

Leopold Mozart estimated that three hundred professional musicians must have been living in Naples when he arrived with his brilliant son. The people in the little border town of Sessa Aurunca had clearly received them warmly (and still cherish the memory of an evening concert that Leopold so took for granted that he failed to mention it in his letter), but the sophisticated capital of the Kingdom of Naples was another matter entirely. In Rome, too, Wolfgang had caused a sensation with a caper that hints, like his boyish proposal to Marie Antoinette, at a spirit that pushed relentlessly against the limits of social convention. At first, Leopold shared his son's delight at the coup by telling his wife about the incident:

> You'll often have heard of the famous Miserere in Rome, which is held in such high regard that the chapel musicians are forbidden on pain of excommunication to remove even a single part from the chapel, still less to copy it out or to give it to anyone else. But *we already have it*. Wolfg. has already written it down, and we'd have sent it to Salzb[urg] with this letter except that it would require our presence to perform it; the manner of its performance must play a greater role than the work itself, and so we'll bring it home with us, and as it's one of Rome's secrets, we don't want it to fall into the wrong hands, *ut non incurremus mediate vel immediate in Censuram Ecclesiæ* [so that we don't incur a censure from the church sooner or later].[8]

Two days later he wrote again with what sounds like a touch of nervousness amid the bravado: "When we read the article about the *Miserere* [presumably in a Salzburg newspaper], we couldn't help laughing out loud. There's not the slightest cause for worry.

People are making far more of it elsewhere. The whole of Rome knows about it; and even the pope knows that Wolfg. wrote down the *Miserere.* There's absolutely nothing to be afraid of: quite the opposite, it's done him great credit, as you'll shortly be hearing."[9]

This *Miserere,* Gregorio Allegri's elaborate seventeenth-century setting of Psalm 51, is a repetitive piece—as is the psalm itself. Its fame lies in the stratospheric lift of its soprano line, which was carried in those days by castrati, giving the whole piece an eerily otherworldly sound. According to official church doctrine, castration, like any other deliberate mutilation of the body, was a sin so grave that it could be properly punished only by excommunication. Yet this same church was Europe's chief employer of castrati as singers, and the center for their production was Italy, Naples above all. Eighteenth-century visitors, like the English diplomat Charles Burney, reported that Neapolitan barbers hung out signs saying "Boys castrated here."[10] As a result, the city was also a center for the training of boys who had undergone the traumatic and dangerous operation. (It was performed with a set of formidable shears.)

Of the three hundred professional musicians that Leopold estimated to be working in Naples, the castrati enjoyed the greatest prestige. The most famous castrato of them all had started out in this very same city: Carlo Broschi (1705–1782), nicknamed Farinelli, whom the Mozarts had made a special point of visiting on his estate outside Bologna in March.[11] Unusually for singers, Broschi belonged to the kingdom's minor aristocracy and had moved to the capital in 1712, when his elder brother, Riccardo, enrolled in one of the city's conservatories. Carlo, too, showed extraordinary musical talent as a boy and began training with the maestro Nicola Porpora, the greatest voice teacher in Naples. Castrated at twelve to preserve the soprano range of his voice, the young Broschi made his debut only after several more years of rigorous training, at which point, like most castrati, he took a professional name.

Castration did more than preserve a singer's upper range by keeping his vocal cords boyishly short. His long bones would never receive an adult male's hormonal message to fuse, so the arms, legs, and ribs of castrati continued to grow and grow. By the time their careers had developed, most of them were big men, tall, long-limbed, and large-footed, but oddly shaped, with wide hips and substantial bellies. Above all, they developed huge chests and phenomenal lung capacity. Castrati are sometimes described as sopranos with the lung power of a full-grown man, but in fact they were something much more remarkable: singing giants who could sustain uncannily high notes with uncanny power for an uncannily long time.[12] They towered over most of their intact peers, blasting so loudly from their outsized lungs that many of them, Farinelli included, staged—and won—competitions with trumpeters.

In Mozart's time, as women singers were becoming increasingly acceptable socially and increasingly popular, castrati began to lose some of their pull outside Italy. In Naples, however, they still dominated church and theater, and Mozart wrote his motet "Exsultate, Jubilate" for this surreal, supple voice in 1773; the venue, needless to say, was Italian—Milan.[13] Yet perhaps, as we will see, this joyous motet is not his only response to hearing the castrato voice on his Italian journey.

Today, Naples has only one conservatory, housed in the deconsecrated Gothic convent of San Pietro of Majella, but this state-run institution incorporates what were originally four separate church-sponsored conservatories scattered about the city.[14] In addition, Naples harbored hundreds of musicians who worked for secular patrons, from local aristocrats to impresarios.

The Mozarts soon discovered that the music lovers of Naples seemed to be perfectly satisfied with what the city already had to offer. As Leopold Mozart finally complained to his wife, the best appointments he and Wolfgang could get in this promising but elusive musical panorama were an evening with the English envoy,

Sir William Hamilton, and an afternoon—not an evening—with the queen, who was German by birth. In other words, the only locals who showed much interest in these two foreign musicians were foreigners themselves. The *regnicoli* (kingdom dwellers) of the Kingdom of Naples kept to their own circles. The plural is necessary here: the royal family had been imposed on Naples from outside, and its circles were not those of the native Neapolitans, who had learned over millennia of invasions, colonizations, occupations, and pirate raids to keep to themselves as they watched the world go by: Greeks, Etruscans, Samnites, Oscans, Romans, Goths, Arabs, Normans, Swabians, French, Spaniards, the odd shipload of Ottoman Turks, and the domineering presence of British ships in port, masters of the Mediterranean ever since the defeat of the Spanish Armada, almost two hundred years before.

One visit in particular would have whetted the Mozarts' appetite for seeing both Vesuvius and Pompeii: their soirée with Sir William Hamilton and his refined, musically talented first wife, Caroline, one of their very first appointments in Naples (Figure 6.1). Hamilton's position, established in 1764 (he would hold it until 1800) reflected the ever-increasing importance of the British presence in Naples.[15] An aristocrat of scant means, he realized that could live far better in Italy on his limited income than he could in London. Even so, he could not afford a villa in the prestigious neighborhood of the royal villa at Portici, along what had come to be known as the Golden Mile. Instead, he and Caroline rented a small palazzo within Naples itself, scenically perched on the ancient volcanic rim of Pizzofalcone and overlooking the promenade of the Riviera di Chiaia, a long, gently arching cove lined with sixteenth- and seventeenth-century villas, where Neapolitans and visitors turned out every afternoon for their ritual *passeggiata*—in a carriage if they could afford it, on foot if they could not. (The Mozarts made the *passeggiata* in a carriage.)

6.1.   Pietro Fabris (fl. 1768–1778), Concert party at the Neapolitan residence of Kenneth Mackenzie (1744–1781), 1st Earl of Seaforth, May 1770 (oil on canvas). Scottish National Gallery, Edinburgh / The Bridgeman Art Library.

Hamilton, who was forty when the Mozarts met him, may have lacked money, but he had culture, imagination, charm, and initiative. He developed passionate interests in volcanoes and in the buried cities along the bay. He also devised an ingenious way of making money: peddling the ceramic vases removed from ancient tombs to English customers, encouraging them to look carefully at the painted figures and their inscriptions, so different from the wall paintings of Pompeii and Herculaneum.[16] He and his contemporaries decided that these spare, severe works must be Etruscan rather than Greek or Roman, and one buyer, potter Josiah Wedgwood, named his factory "Etruria" in their honor. (We now know that they are largely Greek, made for both Greek and Etruscan clients in Italy.)

In most eighteenth-century visitors' accounts of the buried cities along the Bay of Naples and the images of their archaeological excavations, the greatest focus of attention is the refinement that closer acquaintance with ancient style brings to contemporary life. Characteristically, then, both Etruria, Josiah Wedgwood's pottery works in England, and the porcelain factory the monarchs of Naples set up in their summer palace of Capodimonte mined the excavations and the royal collections for motifs, designs, and compositional ideas, which were applied to the industrial creation of modern furnishings such as table services, clocks, vases, and decorative pieces. Hamilton's own house provided a wealth of material.

But Leopold Mozart, who had studied science in his youth, may have taken even greater delight in Hamilton's passion for volcanoes. The Englishman had been able to study the eruptions of March and April 1766 and October 1767 at close hand. In the case of the latter eruption, he saw the events from a closer vantage point than he had planned. Since spring, Vesuvius had been exploding periodically on a minor scale, building up a small cone inside the cone of 1631. On the basis of his experience the previous year, Hamilton was confident that once lava began to erupt, the mountain would be safe to explore. On October 19, 1767, "a thick black smoak" began to appear at 7:00 a.m.; as Hamilton later reported to the Royal Society, "by degrees, the smoak took the exact shape of a huge pine tree, such as Pliny the Younger described in his letter to Tacitus." By 8:00 a.m. lava had begun to erupt from the little peak. In his villa on the slopes above Riviera di Chiaia, Hamilton reassured his family that there was nothing to worry about (much as Pliny had reassured his family in 79). He himself rushed up the mountainside with "one peasant only," probably, as Alwyn Scarth suggests, his usual companion,

Bartolomeo ("Tolo") Pumo.[17] But Vesuvius had more surprises in store:

> On a sudden, about noon, I heard a violent noise within the mountain, and . . . about a quarter of a mile off the place where I stood, the mountain split, and, with much noise, from this new mouth, a fountain of liquid fire shot up many feet high, and then, like a torrent, rolled on directly towards us. The earth shook, at the same time that a volley of pumice stones fell thick upon us; in an instant, clouds of black smoak and ashes caused almost total darkness; the explosions from the top of the mountain were much louder than any thunder I ever heard, and the smell of sulphur was very offensive.

Obviously, Hamilton lived to tell the hair-raising tale of his experience, which did nothing to dim his fascination with Vesuvius. In 1776 he would publish his volcanic research in a book that is as historically important in its own way as his studies of Greek pottery, the *Campi phlegraei*.[18]

It seems unlikely that Hamilton and his musical guests, the Mozarts, discussed his other great intellectual passion: the phallic cults of southern Italy.[19] The subject would have appealed greatly to the adolescent Wolfgang, who spent most of his Italian trip thinking about a girl in Salzburg and whose letters home testify to his lifelong delight in puns and scatological jokes. However, Mrs. Hamilton was in attendance, and Sir William would never have talked about such subjects in mixed company. Besides, music was the supreme topic of this particular visit.

For her part, Caroline Hamilton, then thirty-two, was awe-struck by the chance to play with the daunting Wolfgang, but Leopold praised her musicianship in his letter home of May 19: "Yesterday evening we called on the English ambassador Hamilton (our acquaintance from London), whose wife plays the keyboard with exceptional feeling and is a most pleasant person. She trembled at the prospect of having to play for Wolfg[ang]. She has a valuable instrument made in England by Tschudi, with 2 manuals and pedal stops that can be uncoupled by means of the foot. Also present were Mr. Beckfort and Monsieur Weis, our acquaintances from England."[20]

"Mr. Beckfort" (as Leopold's German pronunciation had it) was William Beckford of Somerley, part of an English dynasty that made its fortune on Jamaican sugar plantations (and legions of slaves). Beckford of Somerley's *Descriptive Account of the Island of Jamaica,* published in 1790, would reflect his Italian stay of 1770 by comparing the Jamaican landscape with the region between Rome and Naples, while lamenting the lack of "those picturesque and elegant ruins which so enoble [*sic*] the landscape of Italy."[21] This Mr. Beckford's cousin, William Thomas Beckford, would study briefly with Wolfgang Amadeus Mozart and make his own Grand Tour in 1781, at the age of twenty-one; we will meet him shortly in the ruins of Pompeii.

By the end of May, when an evening at the Hamiltons' and an afternoon with the queen had failed to lead to greener pastures, it was clear to Leopold Mozart that their stay in Naples would indeed last only five weeks. It was time at last to become a tourist, now that father and son had explored and apparently exhausted the city's immediate musical possibilities. On June 9 Leopold wrote his wife (the odd spellings are his): "Next week we'll be visiting Vessuvius, the 2 buried cities, where entire rooms from classical antiquity are currently being excavated, then Casserta, etc., in a word, all the sights of which I already own copperplate engravings."[22]

Leopold Mozart, in other words, had come well prepared for their expedition. His copperplate engravings might have come (or been pirated) from the huge volumes published under royal sponsorship as "The Antiquities of Herculaneum on Display" (*Le antichità di Ercolano esposte*) beginning in 1759.[23]

After a month in the city and with contacts like the Hamiltons, he must have had good advice about guides, or *ciceroni,* as the Grand Tourists called them (perhaps because their Italian speeches and gestures on-site reminded Anglo-Saxon clients of Cicero's oratory). As a workingman himself, Leopold Mozart may have been kinder to their guide than many an aristocratic client, and the presence of the young Wolfgang seems to have charmed everyone.

Their first outing took place on June 13, at a manic pace that explains how Mozart could have composed so many works in so short a life. Leopold send back a detailed account to his wife, with his usual complement of creative spellings for Italian words:

> On the 13th—St. Anthony's Day—you'd have found us at sea. We took a carriage and drove out to Pozzolo [Pozzuoli] at 5 in the morning, arriving there before 7 and taking a boat to Baia, where we saw the baths of Nero, the underground grotto of the Sybilla cumana, the Lago d'Averno, Tempio di Venere, Tempio di Diana, il Sepolchro d'agripina, the Elysian Fields or Campi Elisi, the Dead Sea, where the ferryman was Charon, la Piscina Mirabile, and the Cente Camerelle etc. on the return journey many old baths, temples, and underground rooms, etc., . . . il Monte Nuovo, il Monte Gauro, il Molo di Pozzoli, the Coliseum, the Solfatara, the Astroni, the Grotta del Cane, the Lago di Agnano, etc., but above all the Grotto di Pozzuoli and Virgil's grave. The Grotto di Pozzuoli is like our New Gate [in Salzburg], except that it took us 8 minutes to drive through it as it is 344 *cannas* long [a *canna,* "reed," was somewhat longer than a meter].[24]

A postscript tells us a bit more about the day's outing: "In order to see all the curiosities, you always have to take a torch along because many of them are underground. Wolfg. and I were completely alone with our servant, we had 6 sailors and the cicerone, none of whom could conceal their astonishment at seeing Wolfg. as the 2 old grey-bearded seamen declared that they had never seen such a young boy come to these places to see these antiquities."[25]

This agenda is about twice as long as that of a modern tour of the Campi Flegrei with a modern bus on the viaduct known as the Tangenziale (whatever advantage of speed the bus might have over an eighteenth-century carriage is lost in the tangles of modern Neapolitan traffic). What the Mozarts knew as the Sibyl's cave was a different grotto from the cave that now bears the name, and one of the attractions, the Grotta del cane, no longer appears in guidebooks because subsequent earthquakes have stopped its flow of poison gas.

Just to the north of Naples, this cave in the area of Agnano was called the "Dog's Grotto" because its carbon dioxide fumes could stun or kill a dog, and for many Grand Tourists, this experiment apparently marked one of the salient points of their journey to Naples.[26] In 1867, almost a century after Mozart, Mark Twain was among their number. His account of those travels, *The Innocents Abroad* (1869), tells about his visit to the grotto with relish:

> Everybody has written about the Grotto del Cane and its poisonous vapours, from Pliny down to Smith, and every tourist has held a dog over its floor by the legs to test the capabilities of the place. The dog dies in a minute and a half—a chicken instantly. As a general thing, strangers who crawl in there to sleep do not get up until they are called. And then they don't, either. The stranger that ventures to sleep there takes a permanent contract. I longed to see this grotto. I resolved to take a dog and hold him myself; suffocate him a little, and time him; suffocate him some more, and then finish him. We reached the grotto about three in

the afternoon, and proceeded at once to make the experiments. But now, an important difficulty presented itself. We had no dog.[27]

This is where the story stops in Twain's final version, but his original dispatch back to a San Francisco newspaper, the *Alta California,* reports that he and his traveling companion, Mr. Brown, bought a dog from a local peasant and dragged the poor creature toward the grotto, only to have it expire at a whiff of Mr. Brown's breath. The fact that Twain deleted the joke about Mr. Brown's halitosis from his final account may show where this report turned into a Far Western tall tale.

By the early twentieth century, attitudes toward the experience were changing, as we can see from Arthur Norway's *Naples Past and Present* of 1901:[28]

But I forget!—the compelling interest of this day's journey is not literary. A short walk from Fuorigrotta brings me to a point where the road turns slightly upward to the right, leading me to the brow of a hill, over which I look into a wooded hollow—none other than the Lago d'Agnano, once a crater, then a volcanic lake. Oddly enough, it is not mentioned as a lake by any ancient writer. Pliny describes the Grotta del Cane, which we are about to visit, but says not a word of any lake. This fact, with some others, suggests that the water appeared in this old crater only in the Middle Ages; though it really does not matter much, for it is gone now. The bottom has been reft from the fishes and converted into fertile soil. The sloping heights which wall the basin have a waste and somewhat blasted aspect; but I was not granted time to muse on these appearances before a smiling but determined brigand, belonging to the class of guides, sauntered up with a small cur running at his heels and made me aware that I had reached the entrance of the Dog Grotto.

I might have known it; for in fact, through many centuries up to that recent year when it pleased the Italians to drain the lake, the life of the small dogs dwelling in this neighborhood has been composed of progresses from grotto to lake and back again, first held up by the heels to be stifled by the poisonous gas, then soused head over ears in the lake with instructions to recover quickly because another carriage was coming over the hill. Thus lake and grotto were twin branches on one establishment, now dissolved. . . .

The little dog—he was hardly more than a puppy—looked at me and wagged his tail hopefully. I understood him perfectly. He had detected my nationality, and I resolved to be no less humane than a countrywoman of my own who visited this grotto no great while ago, and who, when asked by the brigand whether he should put the dog in, answered hastily, "Certainly not." "Ah!" said the guide, "you are Englees! If you had been American you would have said, 'Why, certainly.'" I made the same condition. The fellow shrugged his shoulders. He did not care, he knew another way of extorting as many francs from me; and accordingly we all went gaily down the hill, preceded by the happy cur, running on with tail erect, till we reached a gate in the wall though which we passed to the Grotta del Cane.

A low entrance, barely more than a man's height, a long tubular passage of uniform dimensions sloping backwards into the bowels of the hill—such is all one sees on approaching the Dog Grotto. A misty exhalation rises from the floor and maintains its level while the ground slopes downwards. Thus, if a man entered, the whitish vapour would cling at first about his feet. A few steps further would bring it to his knees, then waist high, and in a little more it would rise about his mouth and nostrils and become a shroud indeed; for the gas is carbonic acid, and destroys all human life. King Charles the Eighth of France . . . came here . . . bringing with him a donkey, on which he tried the effects of the gas. I do not know why he selected that animal, but the poor brute died. So did two slaves, whom Don Pietro di Toledo, one of the early Spanish viceroys, used to decide the question whether any of the virtue had gone out of the gas. That question is settled more humanely now. The guide takes a torch, kindles it to a bright flame, and plunges it into the vapour. It goes out instantly; and when then act has been repeated some half-dozen times the gas, impregnated with smoke, assumes the appearance of a silver sea, flowing in rippling waves against the black walls of the cavern.

With all its curiosity the Dog Grotto is a deadly little hole, in which the world takes much less interest nowadays than it does in many other objects in the neighbourhood of the Siren city, going indeed by preference to see those which are beautiful, whereas not many generations ago it rushed off hastily to see first those which are odd.

Today tourists no longer gas dogs at the Grotta del cane; instead, they admire the black mosaic guard dog in the vestibule of the House of the Tragic Poet in Pompeii, with its inscription, CAVE CANEM (beware of the dog), and pity his counterpart, who died at his chain during one of the pyroclastic surges that finished off every living thing in the city—plant, animal, and human. Both dogs belong to a recognizable Italian breed, the needle-nosed *segugio,* an excellent hunter. The poor Pompeian dog may well have been left on its leash in order to discourage looters— further evidence, amid a host of clues, that most of the residents must have run away early in the eruption cycle of Vesuvius. The Anglo-Greek poet Constantine Trypanis has left a haunting tribute to the dog's agony (though we now know that its twisted pose is the result of muscle contraction in the heat generated by the pyroclastic surge. This the dog never felt; death came quietly a few moments before):

POMPEIAN DOG (1964)
Like that Pompeian dog chained to a stone
I howl as living cinders pour, half-blind
Howl as I search the cracking street to find
An answer to this freak of storms sky-thrown.
I howl, but cannot turn to blame
The hand that tied me to these gouts of death,
A sheet of cinders chars my staggered breath
Chained to a world of unforgiving flame.[29]

The situation of animals in this still-impoverished region of Italy remains difficult and often tragic, though the dogs of the Campi Flegrei no longer need to fear the fumes of the Grotta del cane. Neither do the residents.

After recounting the wonders of their day in the Campi Flegrei (all that Wolfgang's addition says is "we saw Fesufius," revealing his father's German accent when pronouncing the name of the mountain), Leopold Mozart goes on to tell his wife about their plans for exploring the southern stretch of the Bay of Naples: "On Monday and Tuesday etc. we're going to take a closer look at Vesuvius, Pompea and Herculaneum—the towns that are currently being excavated—and admire the curiosities that have already been discovered, and also take a look at Caserta etc. and Capo di Monte etc., all of which cost money."[30]

In 1770 a visitor to Pompeii would have been able to see only a tiny fraction of what is visible today. The House of Diomedes had already been cleared, and the excavators were centering their efforts on the temple of Isis (Figure 6.2). Thanks to a frieze showing

6.2.   Jean-Louis Desprez, Temple of Isis, Pompeii, 1799. Engraving. Besançon, Musée des Beaux-Arts. Photo: Gianni Dagli Orti / The Art Archive at Art Resource, NY.

a procession in honor of the goddess and a series of other painted ornaments and decorative stuccoes, there was little doubt about the identity of the building. Unfortunately, the Mozart males did not provide Maria Anna and Nannerl with any details about their Pompeian visit. Instead, we might turn to the account published eleven years later, in 1781, by Wolfgang's sometime pupil, William Thomas Beckford, an aesthete (and English snob) of the first order. Much more of the site had been cleared in the ensuing decade, but the mood of both tours must have been much the same: a combination of frenetic activity in the present—both *ciceroni* and tourists obeyed a relentless schedule—and a brooding consciousness of disasters past. Beckford writes: "We made our excursion to Pompeii, passing through Portici, and over the last lava of Mount Vesuvius. I experienced a strange mixture of sensations, on surveying at once the mischiefs of the late eruption, in the ruin of villages, farms, and vineyards; and all around them the most luxuriant and delightful scenery of nature. It was impossible to resist the impressions of melancholy from viewing the former, or not to admit that gaiety of spirits which was inspired by the sight of the latter."[31] Beckford was extravagantly moved by the Temple of Isis, but then he was extravagantly moved almost everywhere and never shy about describing his transports of emotion:

> We were now conducted to the temple, or rather chapel, of Isis. The chief remains are a covered cloister; the great altar on which was probably exhibited the statue of the goddess; a little edifice to protect the sacred well; the pediment of the chapel, with a symbolical vase in relief; ornaments in stucco, on the front of the main building. . . . We next observe three altars of different sizes. On one of them is said to have been found the bones of a victim unconsumed, the last sacrifice having probably been stopped by the dreadful calamity which had occasioned it.[32]

The story of the preserved sacrifice is probably a *cicerone*'s fiction. But Beckford was perfectly capable of supplying a fictional scene himself. His Pompeian reverie is worth quoting at length because it had such an effect, through publication, on later visitors' imaginings:

> As I lingered alone in these environs sacred to Isis, some time after my companions had quitted them, I fell into one of those reveries which my imagination is so fond of indulging; and transporting myself seventeen hundred years back, fancied I was sailing with the elder Pliny, on the first day's eruption . . . The course of our galley seldom carried us out of sight of Pompeii, and as often as I could divert my attention from the tremendous spectacle of the eruption, its enormous pillar of smoke standing conically in the air, and tempests of liquid fire continually bursting out from the midst of it, then raining down the sides of the mountain, and flooding this beautiful coast with innumerable streams of red-hot lava, methought I turned my eyes upon this fair city, whose houses, villas, and gardens, with their long ranges of columned courts and porticos, were made visible through the universal cloud of ashes, by lightning from the mountain; and saw its distracted inhabitants, men, women, and children, running to and fro in despair. But in one spot, I mean the court and precincts of the temple, glared a continual light. It was the blaze of the altars; towards which I discerned a long-robed train of priests moving in solemn procession, to supplicate by prayer and sacrifice, at this destructive moment, the intervention of Isis, who had taught the first fathers of mankind the culture of the earth, and other arts of civil life. Methought I could distinguish in their hands all those paintings and images, sacred to this divinity, brought out on this portentous occasion, from the subterranean

apartments and mystic cells of the temple. There was every form of creeping thing and abominable beast, every Egyptian pollution which the true prophet had seen in vision, among the secret idolatries of the temple at Jerusalem. The priests arrived at the altars; I saw them gathered round, and purifying the three at once with the sacred meal; then, all moving slowly about them, each with his right hand towards the fire: it was the office of some to seize the firebrands of the altars, with which they sprinkled holy water on the numberless bystanders. Then began the prayers, the hymns, and lustrations of the sacrifice. The priests had laid the victims with their throats downward upon the altars; were ransacking the baskets of flour and salt for the knives of slaughter, and proceeding in haste to the accomplishment of their pious ceremonies; - when one of our company, who thought me lost, returned with impatience, and calling me off to some new object, put an end to my strange reverie.[33]

The Mozarts, too, were called sharply back from antiquarian reverie to hard reality. It was time to leave Naples. Leopold had even begun to tally his souvenirs:

In some ways, it's a pity that we can't stay any longer here as there are various interesting things to be seen here during the summer; and the choice of fruit, herbs and flowers changes from one week to the next. The situation of the town, the fertility of the area, the liveliness of the people, the unusual sights etc. and a hundred other beautiful things make me regret having to leave Naples; but the filth, the hordes of beggars, the appalling and, indeed, godless townsfolk, the poor education of the children and the incredibly licentious goings-on even in church allow us to leave even the good things with a clear conscience. I shall not only bring back with me all the rare sights in the form of many beautiful copper engravings but have also received from Herr Meuricoffre a fine collection of Vesuvius lava—not the kind of lava that anyone can easily get hold of, but choice pieces with a description of the minerals that they contain and that are rare and hard to come by. If God allows us to return home in good health, you'll see some beautiful things.[34]

As for Wolfgang, it is often said (for example, by the catalogue of the British Museum's Pompeii exhibition of summer 2013) that this visit to Pompeii, and especially to the Temple of Isis, inspired parts of his *Magic Flute,* like Sarastro's majestic aria "O Isis und Osiris." It is a lovely thought but difficult to prove. How exactly are we to recognize the reflection of an archaeological site in a musical composition?

More to the point, how do we separate the single experience of this Pompeian temple from that of the other Egyptian artifacts the Mozarts saw in Rome? For many European travelers in the Mozarts' day, Rome provided a kind a homegrown Egypt, with its obelisks, statues, and a real marble-clad pyramid from the time of Augustus: a funeral monument to the wealthy Roman official Gaius Cestius.[35] If Mozart drew his inspiration from what he saw in Italy, he was more likely to have remembered a series of sights and sounds than a tour through a single building.

Furthermore, the composer was only partly responsible for the *Magic Flute.* He wrote the music, but the libretto, like the opera itself, came from the head of his friend Emanuel Schikaneder, a German singer, actor, and impresario who never set foot in Italy but was always willing to dream of faraway lands; thus Mozart's first production for Schikaneder's Kärntnertortheater in Vienna had been a revival of his "Turkish" opera, *The Abduction from the Seraglio* (1785).

Like its plot line, the *Magic Flute*'s Egyptian overtones also owe an evident debt to Freemasonry; both Mozart and Schikaneder belonged to the Viennese lodge, "Zur neugekrönten Hoffnung" (New-Crowned Hope), and their German-language *Singspiel* was directed at an audience of their Masonic brothers (including Leopold Mozart). Thus the most vivid "Egyptian" experiences in Wolfgang Amadeus Mozart's life were probably the Egyptian fantasies conjured up by Masonic ritual and Schikaneder's fertile brain in the 1780s rather than one stop in a whirlwind Grand Tour of Italy more than a decade earlier.

Neither Leopold nor Wolfgang Mozart had been inducted into their Masonic lodge at the time of their trip to Naples in 1770, but this is not the only reason that they never met the city's most prominent Freemason at the time, Don Raimondo di Sangro, Prince of Sansevero.[36] Don Raimondo belonged to the old baronial aristocracy of the city, the exclusive group of feudal lords who looked upon the king and queen as modern interlopers (and had so looked upon all of their predecessors for centuries). Within the closed circles of that aristocracy, Don Raimondo stood at the very center. His palazzo in the Piazza San Domenico Maggiore had been the home of a musical forebear, Don Carlo Gesualdo, Prince of Venosa, the late sixteenth-century writer of strange, discordant (and ravishingly beautiful) music, who had killed his wife and her lover in the palazzo and exposed their bodies in the doorway.[37]

Don Raimondo was only slightly less eccentric than his notorious forebear. He had shown such intelligence as a child that he was sent to Rome to study at the Jesuits' Roman College, a generation too late to know Athanasius Kircher but well acquainted with Kircher's successor, Filippo Buonanni, and Kircher's marvelous museum. Don Raimondo's own interests eventually ranged as widely as those of Kircher himself. He conducted chemical experiments, invented powerful cannons, and collected curiosities;

FROM POMPEII

he wrote an essay on *quipu,* the knotted belts that served the Incas as documents. When King Charles III began to excavate Herculaneum and Pompeii, it was clear that the learned Prince of Sansevero would enter into the picture. Perhaps no visitor to the Temple of Isis has ever been more inspired by this trace of Egyptian wisdom on Italian soil than Don Raimondo, who had been initiated as a Freemason by none other than Don Manuel Pinto de Fonseca, Grand Master of the Knights of Malta. Neither man was particularly bothered by official church hostility to Freemasonry; they were too distinguished for the laws of the world to apply to them. Don Raimondo, indeed, established the first Scottish Rite Masonic lodge in Naples.

A remarkable synthesis of Don Raimondo's interests in art and science can be seen today in the crypt of his family chapel, just behind the family palazzo, on Piazza San Domenico in Naples, where a tall display case houses the "anatomical machines," two full-scale models of the human circulatory system: a man and a pregnant woman, her fetus displayed at her feet. The intricacy of these webs and branches of blood vessels is so fantastic that for centuries the rumor has persisted that the "anatomical machines" were not models at all but servants of Don Raimondo, injected while still living with some chemical fluid he had devised in his laboratory. For years after the widespread use of DNA testing, Don Raimondo's descendants stubbornly refused access to the "machines" in their glass case, adding to the crypt's air of mystery and the Masonic prince's sinister reputation. At last, in 2007, the family relented and let two young women scholars into the sanctum. The anatomical machines, they discovered to general relief, really are models, made of wax, wire, and silk thread. Somehow the fact that they are artificial makes them seem all the more incredible (and makes a visit to the chapel, the Cappella Sansevero, slightly less chilling).[38]

Mozart almost surely never saw Don Raimondo's macabre scientific models, but he may have seen the Cappella Sansevero itself, a project that took the prince from 1749 to 1771 to complete. In one of the most astonishing Baroque assemblages in this dramatically Baroque city, the tombs of Don Raimondo's Sansevero forebears are adorned with white marble statues depicting abstractions like "modesty" and "temperance" and are centered on Giuseppe Sammartino's life-sized depiction of the dead Christ (1753), swathed, with almost archaeological precision, in a winding sheet that deliberately evokes the famous relic known as the Shroud of Turin, a large piece of linen identified by the faithful as the winding sheet of Jesus, miraculously impressed with his image.

The fabric clings so tightly around Sammartino's sculpted Christ that it reveals every single finger and toe, along with muscles, veins, and the five stigmata that pierce the figure's hands, feet, and sides; the winding sheet penetrates slightly into Christ's nostrils as if he has just breathed in. To contemporaries, Sanmartino's workmanship seemed more than human, and here, too, rumors maintained that Don Raimondo had somehow managed to petrify a real person by the use of some alchemical formula.

The *Veiled Christ* is only one of the Cappella Sansevero's ghostly apparitions in marble (and suggests why Pompeii, in turn, would become a city populated by plaster ghosts). To the left of the *Veiled Christ* as we face the chapel's altar, Antonio Corradini's *Modesty* decorates the tomb of Don Raimondo's mother, demurely covered from head to toe, with only a hand and a foot emerging from the fabric. Yet every contour of *Modesty*'s body shows through the clinging drapery, presenting an unusually voluptuous version of motherhood. But then Cecilia Gaetani Dell'Aquila D'Aragona had died as a young woman, before Don Raimondo was a year old. Premature death is symbolized as well by a broken marble stele that records Donna Cecilia's name, her long list of noble titles, and the tragic blamelessness of her life. On the opposite side of the chapel, Fernando Queirolo's *Undeception (Disinganno)* (1750s) depicts an older man freeing himself from a net, a tour de force of sculpted transparency. Not surprisingly for a Freemason's chapel set in the center of the old Egyptian quarter of ancient Naples, an area called the "Nile region," *regio nilensis,* Egyptian imagery abounds in the Cappella Sansevero, inspired less by the ruins of the Isis Temple in Pompeii than it is by Don Raimondo's Freemasonry and by the Egyptological studies of Father Athanasius Kircher (see Chapter 3), whose fat, two-thousand-page folio opus, *The Egyptian Oedipus* (so massive it took three years, from 1652 to 1655, to publish it all), conditioned nearly everyone's view of ancient Egypt until the Napoleonic expeditions at the very close of the eighteenth century.

Don Raimondo, with all of his scientific curiosity, kept up with news of the excavations in Herculaneum and then Pompeii. He was especially captivated by the rolls of Egyptian papyrus emerging from the tunnels of Herculaneum, tightly rolled bundles with writing in Greek and Latin that could be read through the charred gray of their surface.[39] By sheer chance, Karl Jakob Weber's workers had stumbled onto the remains of an ancient library, but its secrets were frustratingly inaccessible; the fragile papyrus broke into pieces at every attempt to unroll it.

In hopes of solving the problem, Don Raimondo took to his laboratory, where he cooked up a loosening potion made of mercury and other chemicals and urged the king to sink a papyrus into the mixture until it was soft enough to unroll. Unfortunately, the result must have been just like throwing a roll of toilet paper into water; the papyrus promptly disintegrated into pulp, and the whole mess had to be thrown away. Ultimately, the most successful technique for opening up the ancient books also seemed to be the simplest: to unscroll the papyrus slowly, flattening each opened section by sitting on it.[40] Eventually a Neapolitan priest, Father Antonio Piaggio, devised a special machine to unfurl the scrolls extremely slowly, and this eighteenth-century device is still used today.[41] There is great hope that digital techniques will help with reading the charred texts, but so far the unfurling of the scrolls remains a largely physical task.

On several occasions during their visit to Naples, the Mozarts must have seen Don Raimondo di Sangro, if only from a distance. Perhaps they saw him at a concert, for the prince loved music as much as art and scientific research. They must have seen him when, along with everyone else in Naples, they made their afternoon promenade along the Riviera di Chiaia. The Mozarts went by carriage—they could afford at least that luxury—and they must have noticed that the most elegant "carriage" of all was not rolling down the boulevard with everyone else; instead, out in the bay, it seemed to be coasting over the water, its horses cresting the waves as if they belonged to Neptune himself. The vehicle belonged to Don Raimondo, and it was amphibious. This seaborne coach and four was one of his last extravagant inventions; he died in 1771, the year after the Mozarts' visit.

For Wolfgang Amadeus Mozart, the most vivid memories of Naples may well have been purely musical. He wrote the part of the Queen of the Night in *The Magic Flute* for his sister-in-law, Josepha Weber, but the Queen's vocal pyrotechnics are more like those of a castrato than a prima donna. Like the "Exsultate, Jubilate," she may come from the realm of his Neapolitan memories. There may also be other genuine echoes of his Italian tour in his Masonic *Singspiel,* but because they resided largely within Mozart's skull, they are neither simple nor simple to uncover.

With later set designers for *The Magic Flute,* on the other hand, the connection with Pompeii's Temple of Isis is clear and deliberate. The team of Gayl and Nessthaler convincingly reproduced the building in their late nineteenth-century set. The Prussian architect Karl Friedrich Schinkel (1781–1841) made his first study trip to Italy in 1805; by 1816 he had produced his own marvelous series of neoclassical sets for a production of Mozart's *Singspiel* in

FROM POMPEII

Berlin. And in an era when travel to Egypt remained difficult, the Temple of Isis joined the monuments of Rome as part of the standard repertory of "Egyptian" designs.[42]

Between William Beckford's "reverie" and the evocations of Isis from the *Magic Flute,* it is hard to shake off the impact of Pompeii on our own imaginations and infinitely tempting to project these images, not without reason, onto Wolfgang Amadeus Mozart.

7

Further Excavations

In 1771, the year after the Mozarts' visit to Pompeii, excavations extended into the basement level (cryptoporticus) of the Villa of Diomedes, where Francesco La Vega and his team found the skeletons of eighteen people huddled together in the corner of one of the underground chambers, including a child and a baby. In some cases the bodies of the victims had left impressions in the volcanic mass before decomposing. By the time the excavators came across them, everything but bone had long since turned to dust, but the shapes of flesh and clothing had left behind their traces in the hardened volcanic deposit. The all-male team was particularly taken by the imprint of a young woman's arms and breast. As La Vega wrote on December 12, 1772:

> Having begun last week to remove the earth in a corridor . . . we have found 18 skeletons of adult persons, along with those of a youth and a little child. It is easy to see that they. . . . were surprised in this part of the house . . . by a rain of ashes, and that afterwards the rain of lapilli fell. . . .

This flood of fluid material so embraced and surrounded the bodies on every side that they, for their fragility, had to succumb. This material has preserved the imprint and the hollow. . . . To provide some proof of what is asserted to have occurred I have decided to cut away up to 16 pieces of these imprints of corpses, where among others can be distinguished the breast of a woman covered in a dress . . . and I have sent all these things to the Museum.[1]

This relic of a real person became one of the best-known sights in the royal collection, recorded by Madame de Staël, the famous French feminist, on her visit in 1803.[2] The English poet Felicia Hemans remembered the children's skeletons among the group and turned the phantom breast into a maternal symbol in her poem "The Image of Lava" (1829); like the vast majority of her contemporaries, she either did not know or did not care about the distinction between lava and lapilli:

> A strange, dark fate o'ertook you,
> Fair babe and loving heart!
> One moment of a thousand pangs
> Yet better than to part!
>
> Haply of that fond bosom
> On ashes here impress'd,
> Thou wert the only treasure, child!
> Whereon a hope might rest.[3]

For male viewers, on the other hand, the disembodied breast tended to evoke erotic, romantic dreams. In 1852 the French novelist Théophile Gautier would dedicate a novelette (and a good deal of romantic fantasy) to its unknown owner. He called the work *Arria Marcella,* certain that the breast must have belonged to the daughter of the house; by a similar process of wishful thinking, the villa's owner was still routinely identified in Gautier's time as Marcus Arrius Diomedes simply because that name is mentioned on the tomb just outside, which takes advantage of a prominent position along the road to Herculaneum (we will meet both Gautier and Arria Marcella again). Somewhere in the long process that transformed the Royal Collection of the Kingdom of Naples into the National Museum of the Republic of Italy, this enigmatic fragment quietly disappeared from sight. In 1950 Amedeo Maiuri, the legendary twentieth-century superintendent of Pompeii and director of the Naples Museum, made a concerted search for it but came up empty-handed. The fragile bit of earth may have disintegrated; but it had also lost some of its appeal after 1863, when Superintendent Giuseppe Fiorelli started making whole-body casts of other victims.[4]

Madame de Staël's novel *Corinne, or Italy* (1807), sets a crucial scene of its tragic love story in Pompeii, evidently drawing its descriptions from the author's visit in 1803. The strongest impression the site seems to have made on this strong-willed, supremely intelligent visitor was an acute sense of human mortality:

> When you stand at the centre of the crossroads, on every side you can see almost in its entirety the still surviving part of the town; it is as if you were waiting for someone, as if the master is about to arrive, and the very semblance of life in this place makes you even more sad at feeling its eternal silence. It is with pieces of petrified lava that most of these houses have been built, and they have been buried beneath other pieces of lava. So there are ruins upon ruins and tombs upon tombs. This history of the world where periods are counted from ruin to ruin, this human life whose trail is followed by the gleam of the volcanic eruptions that have consumed it, fills the heart with profound melancholy. What

a long time men have existed! What a long time they have lived, suffered, and perished! Where can their feelings and thoughts be found again? Is the air you breathe amongst these ruins still marked with their traces or are they forever deposited in heaven where immortality reigns? A few burnt manuscripts found at Herculaneum and Pompeii, which people at Portici are trying to unroll, are all that is left to enable us to learn about the unfortunate victims consumed by earth's thunderbolt, the volcano. But as you pass by those ashes which art manages to bring back to life, you are afraid to breathe, in case a breath carries away the dust perhaps still imprinted with noble ideas.[5]

Madame de Staël came to Naples at a moment when local events rivaled Vesuvius for activity and Vesuvius was in a particularly active state. In *Corinne* she furnishes her own eyewitness account of an eruption:

The torrent is a funereal color; when it burns the vines or the trees, however, you can see a clear bright flame coming from it. It flows slowly like black sand by day and red by night. When it comes near you can hear a little noise of sparks, all the more frightening because it is slight, and cunning seems to combine with strength. Thus the royal tiger arrives secretly with measured tread. . . . Its glare is so fiery that for the first time the earth is reflected in the sky, giving it the appearance of continual lightning; in turn the sky is repeated in the sea and nature is set ablaze by this triple image of fire.[6]

The years between 1799 and 1815 were years of great political changes for Naples, and because archaeology was a government-subsidized operation, the fortunes of Pompeii shifted with every change in authority. In January 1799, with Napoleon's troops already stationed in Naples, a rebellion led by progressive aristocrats expelled King Ferdinand and established a republic for a few months; this in turn was overthrown by conservative forces, and the king was reinstated. In 1806 Napoleon drove away King Ferdinand again and imposed his own brother, Joseph Bonaparte, as king until 1808, when the crown passed to their dashing brother-in-law, Joaquin Murat. Murat's consort, Napoleon's younger sister, Caroline Bonaparte, put her own funds into a huge push to excavate Pompeii, engaging six hundred workmen for the task.[7]

In June 1815 King Ferdinand returned, now as King of the Two Sicilies, and sent Murat before a firing squad in September of the same year. The restored monarch cut the number of excavators at work in Pompeii from three hundred to thirteen. Some of the land that had been requisitioned from local owners for future exploration was ceded instead to a landowner named Giuseppe dell'Aquila, who built an elegant farmhouse on the property (it still stands today).

Between 1818 and 1826 King Ferdinand decided to make Pompeii's excavations entirely accessible by carriage so that he and his guests could see all of the principal sights without ever descending from their vehicles. This meant removing some of the ancient basalt stepping-stones at intersections; the gauge of the royal axles was far broader than that of ancient carts. Workers continued to clear the forum of Pompeii and the adjoining Temple of Apollo, as well as the forum baths. Visitors could now progress along the ancient road from the Villa of Diomedes, down the Street of the Tombs, through the Herculaneum Gate, and all the way to the center of the city. From there a path over farmland led them to the two other excavated zones: the area around the theaters, including the Triangular Forum and the Temple of Isis, and the amphitheater, together with a peculiar structure one block to the north, which had been excavated and carefully documented by Karl Jacob Weber before his death in 1764.[8] This building was known as the *praedia* (property) of Julia Felix from an inscription on its outer wall. Weber was not quite sure what the structure was; part of it seemed to be a house, and another part a public bath. Both of these impressions were correct: Julia Felix was a homeowner who made extra income by renting out her peristyle to bathers. The walls of Pompeii were largely cleared in the early nineteenth century, which may also be the moment when umbrella pines were planted alongside the access roads to the site as a means of stabilizing the roadbed. Under the canopy of these majestic trees, Pompeii still seems to belong to the romantic past rather than the frenetic present (Figure 7.1).

As of 1828, visitors to the buried city might come armed with a two-hundred-page guidebook, *Plan de Pompeii*, written in French although it was published in Naples (an Italian translation followed in 1836). Its author, Andrea De Jorio (1769–1851), was a canon of the cathedral in Naples who served the Neapolitan Crown as inspector of public schools in 1810. By 1811, however, he had moved on to

7.1.   Sacred Way, Pompeii. From Fausto and Felice Niccolini, *Fouilles de Pompéi: Monuments choisis*. Naples: Antonio Niccolini: s.n. [1879]. Photo: Gianni Dagli Orti / The Art Archive at Art Resource, NY.

become curator of the "Etruscan" vases in the royal collection, a position that inspired him to write guidebooks to all of the archaeological sites around Naples as well as to the royal collections of antiquities and papyri.[9] However, De Jorio's best-known work is a delightful study of Neapolitan hand gestures, *La mimica degli antichi investigata nel gestire napoletano (The Mimicry of the Ancients Investigated in Neapolitan Gestures)*. Published in 1832, it is the first serious ethnographic study of its kind.[10] De Jorio arranged his book alphabetically to create what he called an "ABC of gestures," analyzing them in action by examining sixteen plates he called *bambocciate,* scenes of daily life in early nineteenth-century Naples.[11]

De Jorio's ultimate purpose in assembling that ABC was, however, to illuminate the gestures he observed in ancient art; for him, the physical motions of Neapolitans were as natural as speech itself, and he assumed that things had been no different in antiquity (with good reason: the rhetorical writer Quintilian supplies a whole list of gestures and their meaning for aspiring orators, most of which are perfectly current in modern Italy, and the *Life of Augustus* by Suetonius mentions a spectator raising his middle finger to the emperor in the middle of a theatrical performance). With the gusto of a true connoisseur, De Jorio applied his insights to the most spectacular recent find from the excavations of Pompeii in his own day: the Alexander mosaic from the House of the Faun, uncovered in 1831. His rhetoric in describing the famous pavement is as flamboyant as the gestures he describes with such relish:

> Pompeii, to which, after Herculaneum, there seems to be reserved the glory of rending ever more completely this dense veil behind which the ancient world has been hidden from us, Pompeii, beyond a doubt, has given us the gift of an imposing monument. This, more than any others that have appeared up to now, triumphantly reveals to what a degree of perfection the fine arts had arrived in those centuries, and

what force of expression was given by those artists to their lively gestures. We mean to speak about the Great Mosaic. Already learned pens have explained it in erudite terms, and perhaps they shall never tire of praising its qualities, as well as contributing new archaeological information. Amid this river of deep and cosmopolitan erudition let it be permitted us, too, to present the following observation, regarding the great and fascinating use of gesture among the ancients, as well as its correspondence among the Neapolitans.[12]

As with the "Bambocciate" that illustrate hand gestures in his own time (Figure 7.2), De Jorio offers a learned analysis of gesticulated language in antiquity:

7.2.   Hand gestures in the Alexander mosaic, Museo Nazionale, Naples. Photo by author.

To us it seems that one can recognize the following gestured conversation. The soldier who raises his hand held in such a way as not to straighten any fingers but the index and the middle, because he is closer to the great event, sees it and quickly turns back to tell his fellow soldiers, who, ignorant of the fact, were galloping full speed ahead into the thick of the battle; he turns, we repeat, and uses gesture (which in such circumstances is worth far more than speech) and with a simple instantaneous sign tells them: *our champion is dead*, or *it is all over for us; we are lost*.[13]

Sales of De Jorio's books did not suffer because of his local reputation in Naples as a *iettatore,* a natural bringer of calamity; his actual presence was required to bring on that bad luck (apparently one reason for De Jorio's reputation as a *iettatore* was his great ugliness).[14] For visitors to Pompeii, in his printed incarnation as a writer of guidebooks, the good canon was a valuable resource who provided a learned discussion of the monuments, together with plans of public buildings and private houses. His study of gesture is now considered a milestone of social anthropology. It seems more than likely that when an ambitious young Russian painter named Karl Bryullov traveled to Pompeii in 1838, he must have carried a copy of De Jorio, most probably the brand-new French edition of the guidebook. Ambitious, headstrong, and enterprising, Bryullov was also studious, an academic painter in the purest sense of the word, in an era when academic painting was in its heyday.

8

Karl Bryullov

Among the most sought-after visitors to nineteenth-century Italy (as they have become again in the past few years), the Russians were both cultivated and rich, avid collectors of Western art and eager to participate in the European artistic tradition. The most successful of all the Russian artists who came to study in Italy was surely Karl Pavlovich Bryullov (1799–1852)—"Carlo Briullo"—whose secret to success was the painting he created after a trip to Pompeii in 1828. This work was so important to nineteenth-century Europe that since 2001 it has merited a plaque in Russian and Italian on the side of the Roman palazzo on the Via di San Claudio, where Bryullov painted and displayed his huge, ambitious canvas just off the Via del Corso in the heart of Grand Tourists' Rome.[1]

Bryullov's large, artistic family descended from French Huguenots named Brulleau, who had escaped to St. Petersburg in the eighteenth century. In their new home, they engaged in a wide variety of arts and crafts: Karl's great-grandfather had worked in the imperial porcelain factory, his grandfather had been a sculptor, his father was a woodcarver and an engraver, and his elder brother, Alexander, became a well-known painter and architect. Karl and Alexander's father, Pavel, also held a professorship at the St. Petersburg Academy of Art, where Karl was admitted in 1815. Pavel Bryullov must have been a stern taskmaster—he once boxed his second son's ears hard enough to make Karl partially deaf for the rest of his life (the same abuse that happened to Ludwig van Beethoven, his slightly older contemporary).[2] In 1821 the academy awarded Karl a gold medal for one of his paintings, as well as a three-year fellowship to continue his studies in the same institution where his father held a position. But when the academy's president refused his request to study with a particular professor and denied him his right to a travel grant, Karl and his brother Alexander decided to study in Rome, financed by the state-run Society for the Encouragement of the Arts. The two brothers set out for Italy in August 1822, stopping in Dresden, Munich, and Venice before they arrived in Rome in 1823. Karl started immediately on a rigorous program of copying ancient statues and Old Master paintings, dutifully reporting back to the academy and his sponsors on his progress.

In 1824, however, he broke from the academy's classical traditions by exhibiting a brightly lit genre painting of a bare-breasted peasant girl drinking from a fountain. This work, evocatively titled *Italian Morning,* appealed to Italians and Russians alike; best of all, it pleased the tsar, who ordered a companion piece, *Evening.* When both paintings went off to the imperial collection in St. Petersburg, their author could finally think seriously about making a living as an independent artist.

In 1828 Bryullov made a trip to Pompeii, sketching madly as he moved about the ruins, and it was there that he must have conceived the idea of creating a monumental history painting of the city's destruction. *The Last Day of Pompeii* (Figure 8.1) fulfilled the society's requirements that each of its pensioners create

8.1. Karl Bryullov, *The Last Day of Pompeii*, 1830–1834. Russian State Museum, St. Petersburg. Photo: Scala / Art Resource, NY.

at least one large historical painting while studying abroad.³ By 1829, however, Bryullov had tired of the society ad its incessant advice on how to paint; he had garnered more broad-minded sponsors in the Russian art collector Anatoly Demidoff, who commissioned *The Last Day of Pompeii*, and his probable mistress, the beautiful countess Yulia Samoilova.⁴ The huge canvas (465.5×651 cm, or about 15×21 ft) took him three years to compose and execute, but when he put it on display in the Roman studio on the Via di San Claudio in 1833, the whole world came to see it and to exclaim in wonder.

Only the French were tepid in their enthusiasm; they compared the Russian's work unfavorably with the equally ambitious painting that Eugène Delacroix had unveiled in Paris in 1830, *Liberty Leading the People,* where the warlike mood was no less dramatic than Bryullov's vividly depicted panic beneath the fulminations of an erupting Vesuvius. Furthermore, Delacroix used brushwork that was as thrillingly loose and voluptuous as that of Rubens, whereas Bryullov's surfaces were crisply linear in the old-fashioned tradition of Jean-Dominique Ingres and Jacques-Louis David.

Whether or not it fell short of the technical genius of Ingres or Delacroix, Bryullov's *Last Day of Pompeii* was huge, colorful, dramatic, learned, and above all, timely. The most powerful eruption of Vesuvius in the nineteenth century occurred in October of 1822, when the Bryullov brothers were making their way south to Rome, a full-bore Plinian eruption with a huge cloud of ash that was still going strong when the great German naturalist Alexander von Humboldt visited on November 23, guiding the king of Prussia. With almost two centuries of experience of regular eruptions from the temperamental volcano, the local populations were well prepared for its latest outburst; the cities of Ottaviano, Boscotrecase, and Resina stood ready to evacuate, and sometimes it was possible to divert slow-moving lava flows by digging ditches and erecting walls to minimize damage to life and property. For

Humboldt and his sovereign, however, the trip still seemed like an excursion to the margins of hell.[5]

Despite the vagaries of Vesuvius, excavations in Pompeii continued at a rapid rate during the first quarter of the nineteenth century. Workers cleared the forum between 1817 and 1826 and then moved outward into the surrounding neighborhoods. Beginning in the 1820s, a series of spectacular houses began coming to light, including the huge House of the Faun, with its marvelous mosaics (excavated 1829–1830), and the lavishly painted House of Meleager (1829–1830). Bryullov had thrilling new material, both scientific and artistic, to include in his composition, and he made inventive use of his opportunities.

The Last Day of Pompeii is a bold, public claim to mastery of what its painter and his contemporaries regarded as the highest form of art: history painting. Epic in scale, the canvas revels in close details that provide proof of the artist's industrious research and up-to-date archaeological knowledge. Bryullov adapts Pliny's account of the ancient eruption to his own scrutiny of the volcano and the sketches he had made of Pompeii itself; at the same time, his composition makes learned visual quotations from the work of other artists, from the ancients to the Old Masters, sculpture as well as painting, insisting on Bryullov's right to a distinguished position in this exalted artistic company.

The Last Day of Pompeii takes place at a recognizable spot along the Street of the Tombs, the road to Herculaneum, uncovered in the eighteenth century and one of the best-known areas of the city. The big basalt paving stones are clearly visible, littered with bodies, treasure (a mirror, an oil lamp, a candelabrum), and a broken cartwheel. In the foreground, a young boy and a soldier are carrying off an old man wrapped in green, who is looking toward the bolts of lightning splitting the ashen sky; the boy is a quotation from Raphael's *Transfiguration,* but the old man is probably meant to be Pliny the Elder, expiring in Pompeii rather than on the beach at

Stabiae. To the right of this group, a young man is saying good-bye to his elderly mother, who has collapsed on the pavement and is urging him to go on without her. A youth with a floral crown carries the limp body of a maiden crowned with roses, their joyous festivities turned to sudden tragedy. The left-hand side of the painting is dominated by a fleeing family sheltering under the husband's cloak; just behind them a statuesque woman balances a water jug on her head (a figure purloined from Raphael's Vatican fresco, *Fire in the Borgo,* which in turn illustrates Plato's dialogue *Hippias Major*). A beam of eerie volcanic light falls on the attractive face of a young painter, who has saved his colors and brushes, jumbled together in a box he carries on his head: this dedicated artist is Bryullov himself. At the cloaked couple's feet, a baby clings to its dead mother, a vignette borrowed from Nicolas Poussin's *Plague of Ashdod;* just behind, a priest is rushing away with some of his paraphernalia, every implement a scrupulous replica of a piece from the Royal Museum. In the lower left corner, a mother is embracing her terrified daughters in a pose that artfully echoes two famous ancient sculptural groups: the Three Graces, and the tormented father and sons of the Laocoön in the Vatican Museum; the trio probably also portrays Bryullov's beloved Countess Yulia Samoilova with her two adopted daughters, Giovannina and Amazilia.

In the background, Vesuvius has become an inferno of sparks and flashes. The inspiration for Bryullov's menacing clouds and many of his figures comes from Peter Paul Rubens's great *Allegory of War* in the Louvre, where the clouds of disaster are man-made rather than natural, a deadly pall rather than a crackling blaze. (This is the painting that also inspired Delacroix's *Liberty Leading the People*.) But the colors of an erupting volcano belonged to a register all their own, a series of white-hot whites and sizzling reds, developed from firsthand experience by generations of Neapolitan gouache (opaque watercolor) painters who had been selling souvenir scenes of the eruption to tourists ever since the late eighteenth century. With evident glee, like the gouache painters, Bryullov has heightened and saturated his own oil colors to match the red-hot glow of Vesuvius, whose phosphorescent lava spills he may well have witnessed in person. The artist punctuates the milling throng of panicked Pompeians with accents of powder blue and sea green drapery rippling in the pyroclastic breeze.

Unlike Rubens, however, whose loose brushwork can be almost abstract, Bryullov keeps tight control over his paint; as noted before, he has given his figures the pearly flesh, high-gloss finish, and nearly photographic realism perfected by the supreme French painters of the Napoleonic era, Jacques-Louis David and Jean-Dominique Ingres. The result is a dramatic canvas, but in the nineteenth-century sense of that description; the figures, even in their fear and agony, pose with studied grace.

Viewers must have been moved by the painting's decorum as well as its pathos. To modern eyes the whole scene probably seems much too artificial, given the fact that many of the figures are pantomiming great works of art as they run for their lives. In Bryullov's day, however, artifice captured the very essence of art: the word, after all, means "art making." Lurid and learned at the same time, *The Last Day of Pompeii* became one of the most famous and most beloved works of the nineteenth century. Soon St. Petersburg was begging for the artist to make a hero's return, and in 1835 "The Great Karl" Bryullov came back to Russia and his own distinguished position at the Imperial Academy of the Arts, lionized at last as the best of what Russia had to offer to the civilized world. *The Last Day of Pompeii* became one of the outstanding sights of St. Petersburg, where it still hangs proudly in the State Russian Museum. But Bryullov's health began to fail in the freezing Russian winters, and in 1850 he returned to his beloved Italy.. He died in Rome in 1852, still at the height of his reputation.

The Great Karl's great canvas was only one of many artistic responses to the fertile combination of a particularly dramatic eruption and a series of new archaeological finds at Pompeii. Writers reacted just as eagerly. In these same years, an American cleric, Sumner Lincoln Fairfield, and an English dandy, Edward Bulwer, penned their own tributes to, respectively, *The Last Night of Pompeii* (1832) and *The Last Days of Pompeii* (1834), the latter book directly inspired by viewing Bryullov's phantasmagoria in the studio on the Via di San Claudio; in effect, *The Last Day of Pompeii* had become part of the Grand Tour in its own right. All three of these last visions of Pompeii are careful to feature close descriptions, verbal or pictorial, of buildings, artifacts, people, and the fiery rage of the volcano. When Vesuvius began to erupt again in 1834, a comparable explosion had already erupted in the world of culture.

Early visitors to Pompeii generally agreed that the city had perished by fire and brimstone for the same reason as the biblical cities of Sodom and Gomorrah: the Romans were cruel, licentious pagans. Flame, as the Inquisition well knew, could not be surpassed as a punishment for cruelty and dissolute morals, and that same trust in refining fire, in its Protestant version, guided the sentiments of Fairfield, Bulwer, and their legions of readers in thrilling over the destruction of Pompeii in poetry and prose.

If Bryullov assumed that the ancients should strike artful poses even in mortal distress, Fairfield and Bulwer assumed, like most writers of the nineteenth and early twentieth century—and quite unlike Shakespeare—that the ancients should speak a language more formal and decorous then their own colloquial tongue. The passage of time, on the whole, has not been kind to these deliberate attempts at classical eloquence. Any reader who begins the long march through Fairfield's poignantly earnest verse will find it high minded and well meaning, a colossal expenditure of industry (the same might be said of Bryullov's gigantic painting)—but often it is hard to fathom just what his Pompeians are actually talking about.

Bulwer's prose also marches to a strictly artificial rhythm. The opening line of his 1830 novel, *Paul Clifford,* "It was a dark and stormy night," has become the proverbial example of overwrought Romantic oratory in English, while Bulwer's name (in the form it assumed in 1844, Bulwer-Lytton) lives on in an annual Bulwer-Lytton award for bad fiction.[6] In his own day, however, "Mr. Bulwer" was almost universally admired; his *Rienzi* of 1835 was turned into a theater piece with an overture by Beethoven and set to opera by no less than Richard Wagner. *The Last Days of Pompeii* proved yet another immediate, universal favorite, the early nineteenth-century counterpart to Dan Brown's globally popular fictions in the twenty-first century. Pompeii is always a compelling subject for readers: *Pompeii,* the 2003 novel by Robert Harris, has also enjoyed great success. But not even a subject as riveting as *The Last Night of Pompeii* could make a bestseller of Sumner Lincoln Fairfield's long, earnest poem in 1832.

The similarity of title between Fairfield's verse and Bulwer's novel infuriated the American, whose most eloquent writing may well be the accusation of plagiarism he leveled at his rival in 1834, from the pages of the periodical he published in Philadelphia, the *North American Magazine:*

Mr. Bulwer has read much and skillfully appropriated, without acknowledgement, all that has suited his designs. He has artfully clothed the lofty thoughts of others in his own brilliant garb, and enjoyed the renown of a powerful writer and profound thinker, when he was little more than an adroit and manoeuvering plagiary. This we long since perceived, and therefore denied his claims to a high order of genius, though we readily accorded to him the possession of much curious knowledge and a felicitous use of language. We never imagined the labors of an unrewarded and little regarded American could be deemed by the proud, *soi-disant* highborn, and affluent Mr. Bulwer as worthy of his unquestioning appropriation. We fancied that so deep a scholar would continue to dig for treasures in ancient and recondite literature, and pass triumphantly over the obscure productions of a poor cisatlantic. But we erred.[7]

Fairfield, it goes without saying, was a thin-skinned soul, distressed, his wife would later recount, if ever a short poem of his received a bad review, let alone his massive, ambitious Pompeian opus, the crowning achievement of his career. Bulwer's popularity and financial gain stung him, for the prose novel had clearly been a better commercial choice than spinning out long tracts of verse. Most galling of all was the fact that Fairfield had actually sent the British writer a copy of *The Last Night of Pompeii,* but the gift had never been acknowledged, only pillaged, at least as the unfortunate poet saw it.

Fairfield had further objections to *The Last Days of Pompeii.* These were moral, and they had to do both with the book and with its author's personal life. In 1833 Bulwer's wife, Rosina, had left him, citing his many infidelities. The separation would become fully legal in 1836. To the prim American, therefore, the English author was evidently as loose in his writing as in his conduct, aiming merely to entertain rather than to instruct and edify his readers. In fact, Bulwer wrote, like Doctor Johnson, for the money. His aristocratic family had disinherited him when he married Rosina, outraged that she was Irish. Fairfield, on the other hand, was outraged for his own reasons. Bulwer had no choice but to write, and laugh all the way to the bank. Fairfield classed him among the most shameless of libertines:

> While we have never failed to acknowledge and applaud the brilliant imagination and the eloquent and fascinating style of Mr. E. L. Bulwer, we have never feared to assert that he

was a sophist in ethics and a libertine in love, and that *effect* was apparently the only law which influenced his mind or guided his pen . . . his characters not only exist in, but actually create an atmosphere of impurity which infects the very hearts of his admirers. He invests the seducer with irresistible attractions, and paints the highwayman and the murderer as examples for imitation. The old Portuguese Jew Spinoza and his disciples Hobbes, Toland, Shaftesbury and Bolingbroke have contributed their licentious stratagems and impure dialogues to augment the claims and heighten the charms of his coxcombs, libertines, and menslayers.

Fairfield's *Last Night of Pompeii,* needless to say, is morally impeccable. It focuses on a pair of Christian lovers who manage, because of their faith, to escape the fury of the volcano that devours their pagan neighbors. Its reams of verse linger over the Romans' obstinate devotion to their traditional gods and their old habits of self-indulgence:[8]

> Yet men repented not of foregone crime.
> Denied them not their wonted festivals,
> Their pomp of garniture and banquet mirth.
> Tornado, pestilence, earthquake and war.
> Awe not the criminal inured to guilt;
> So the barbed poison arrow flies his heart,
> His pageants and night orgies brighter glow—
> Though death sighs float along the wine cups
>   brimmed
> With nectar mocking of all calamities.

Fairfield's two protagonists have already survived an earlier cataclysm: the conquest of Jerusalem in 70 A.D., during which Pansa, a Roman soldier in Titus's army, had rescued the Jewish maiden

Mariamne. The poem begins when the two, now married and converted to Christianity, are hiding in a cave outside the city to escape persecution for their faith (Fairfield, unlike Bulwer, had clearly never been to Pompeii, where caves are hard to find on the alluvial skirts of the great volcano). As flying lapilli begin to bury the pagans under a fiery hail, Pansa and Mariamne take to sea, just in time to see the galleys of the Roman navy, under the command of Pliny the Elder, row out from Cape Misenum on their mission of rescue. But the Christian refugees are already safe, as Pansa points out in "The Farewell of the Christians," one of the many rhymed songs that break up the rhythmic roll of Fairfield's blank pentameter verse:[9]

> Alone, in darkness, on the deep,
> Spirit of Love! redeemed by thee,
> While fear its watch o'er ruin keeps,
> Thy grace our sign and shield, we flee.
> The billows burst around our barque,
> The death streams roll and burn behind—
> Thy mercy guides our little ark.
> Thy breath can swell or hush the wind.
> Thy footsteps ruffled not the wave
> When drowning voices shrieked for aid;
> The cavern'd billow yawn'd—a grave—
> "Be still!" it heard Thee and obeyed!
> From idol rites and tyrant power,
> Now o'er the midnight sea we fly—
> Be with us through our peril's hour!
> Saviour! with Thee we cannot die!

To modern taste, the opening of Bulwer's novel is no less comically portentous than Fairfield's poem, but at least *The Last Days of Pompeii* demonstrates the advantages of prose over verse for writing about the distant past; it is perfectly clear what Bulwer's characters are discussing: "'HO, Diomed, well met! Do you sup with Glaucus to-night?'" said a young man of small stature, who wore his tunic in those loose and effeminate folds which proved him to be a gentleman and a coxcomb. "'Alas, no! dear Clodius; he has not invited me,'" replied Diomed, a man of portly frame and of middle age. "'By Pollux, a scurvy trick! for they say his suppers are the best in Pompeii.'"

In this coxcomb Pompeii, as in *Paul Clifford*'s London, it promises to be a dark and stormy night. Diomed, of course, is the owner of the Villa of Diomedes, through the peristyle of which Bulwer himself would have entered the site of Pompeii. He concentrates, however, on another character, the Greek Glaucus, he of the sumptuous dinners, and his blind slave, Nydia, who loves her master with unrequited devotion. Tragically, however, Nydia will fare less happily than Fairfield's Pansa and Mariamne: her blindness will allow her to guide Glaucus and his lover, Ione, through the pall of volcanic ash that clouds Pompeii's streets, but at the last moment the press of the fleeing crowd will separate her from the couple she has so selflessly rescued (Bulwer may have modeled her fate on that of Vergil's Creusa, the wife of his hero, Aeneas, who disappears in the flames of burning Troy so that the epic can move on to Carthage and Italy). The death of Nydia thus took its place as one of the most poignant sorrows of nineteenth-century literature.

Despite Fairfield's objections to *The Last Days of Pompeii*, it, too, imparts its own nineteenth-century moral lesson. Bulwer reserves a plain-spoken message to the ancient Christian character Olinthus, who directly compares Pompeii's fate with that of Sodom and Gomorrah: "'Medon!'" said Olinthus, pityingly, "'arise, and fly! God is forth upon the wings of the elements! The New Gomorrah is doomed!—Fly, ere the fires consume thee!'"[10] As pumice continues to fall, a congregation of Christians shouts the same warning to the citizens at large: "'Woe! woe!'" cried, in a shrill and piercing voice, the elder at their head. "'Behold! the Lord descendeth to judgment! He maketh fire come down from heaven in the sight of men! Woe! woe! ye strong and mighty! Woe to ye of the fasces and the purple! Woe to the idolater and the worshipper of the beast! Woe to ye who pour forth the blood of saints, and gloat over the death-pangs of the sons of God! Woe to the harlot of the sea!—woe! woe!'"[11]

At the novel's end, Glaucus, delivered from destruction by poor Nydia's self-sacrifice, addresses a letter to his friend Sallust (a real Roman, the historian Gaius Sallustius Crispus), in which he announces that he and Ione have converted to the new religion:

> You speak of the growing sect of the Christians in Rome. Sallust, to you I may confide my secret; I have pondered much over that faith—I have adopted it. . . . I listened—believed—adored! My own, my more than ever beloved Ione, has also embraced the creed!—a creed, Sallust, which, shedding light over this world, gathers its concentrated glory, like a sunset, over the next! We know that we are united in the soul, as in the flesh, for ever and for ever! Ages may roll on, our very dust be dissolved, the earth shrivelled like a scroll; but round and round the circle of eternity rolls the wheel of life—imperishable—unceasing! And as the earth from the sun, so immortality drinks happiness from virtue, which is the smile upon the face of God! Visit me, then, Sallust; bring with you the learned scrolls of Epicurus, Pythagoras, Diogenes; arm yourself for defeat; and let us, amidst the groves of Academus, dispute, under a surer guide than any granted to our fathers, on the mighty problem of the true ends of life and the nature of the soul.[12]

Religion is not the only object of moral scrutiny in *The Last Days of Pompeii*. Like the eighteenth-century visitors to Herculaneum, Bulwer continues to takes a dim view of Pompeian art:

The reader will now have a tolerable notion of the Pompeian houses . . . in all you find the walls richly painted, and in all the evidence of a people fond of the refining elegancies of life. The purity of the taste of the Pompeians in decoration is however questionable; they were fond of the gaudiest colors, of fantastic designs; they often painted the lower half of their columns a bright red, leaving the rest uncolored; and where the garden was small, its wall was frequently tinted to deceive the eye as to its extent, imitating trees, birds, temples, &c. in perspective—a meretricious delusion which the graceful pedantry of Pliny himself adopted, with a complacent pride in its ingenuity.

Nonetheless, this was the account of Pompeii that English-speaking visitors were most likely to have in mind for nearly a century and a half when they toured the ruins or remembered them when they returned home. It was certainly my father's chief point of reference when we visited Pompeii in 1962.

For many twenty-first-century visitors, novelist Robert Harris has performed the same role as Bulwer, but rather than pondering Sodom and Gomorrah, his readers will be scouring the site for its waterworks. First published in 2003, *Pompeii* obeys many of the same narrative laws as Fairfield's *Last Night* and Bulwer-Lytton's *Last Days of Pompeii,* an important reason for this recent book's popular success. The good guy wins, the bad guy loses, and the damsel in distress is saved; the same timeless laws of narrative govern the myths portrayed on Pompeian walls: Theseus saves Ariadne from the hideous Minotaur, Perseus saves Andromeda from the sea monster, baby Hercules throttles the snakes that have come to strangle him in his cradle. Harris, true to this eternally satisfying formula, makes sure that his sadistic villain dies horribly, incinerated in a pyroclastic flow, the hero escapes the catastrophe together with the woman he loves, and the depressing

reality of Pompeii's tragedy is softened by a series of compassionate details: the elderly slave woman who has seen her son cruelly
devoured by eels (warned by friends, I actually have not read this
passage in Chapter 2) is rescued by the hero, Attilius, after he
finds her beaten and abandoned to die. Families escape from the
danger zone with belongings and pets in tow, and an ash-covered
man carries his cat to safety. (Harris is thinking, like his readers,
of the plaster cast of the poor dog incinerated at his leash by a
pyroclastic flow, either abandoned by his escaping master or,
more likely, helping his equally unfortunate master stand guard
against looters. Interestingly, parts of only two feline skeletons
have ever been found on site).[13] As in *The Last Night of Pompeii*,
Pliny's fleet rescues boatloads of refugees. But what redeems the
hydraulic engineer Attilius is not his Christian faith; it is his
straightforward, practical reliance on the principles of science and
the writings of Vitruvius (along with a generous dose of human
decency, the same decency that saves Harris's other refugees).

Harris also captures readers by exploring a part of Rome that
fiction so far has barely touched. Rather than lingering on the
painted houses and luxuriant gardens of Pompeii, he sets most of
his action in the heart of the Roman water system, from its aque-
ducts to the reservoirs that served the Bay of Naples. His own
hero's hero, therefore, is that crusty old architect Vitruvius, and
what eventually saves Attilius and his beloved Corelia is clever
application of the advice that Vitruvius provides at the very end
of his *Ten Books:* "in defense, it is not so much machines that
should be put at the ready, but strategies" (Vitruvius 10.16.8). Harris faces the cruelty of ancient Rome with the same perplexity as
his nineteenth-century predecessors; experience of slavery has
sharpened the viciousness of his villain, Ampliatus, but does not
explain it; greed, graft, and corruption abound in Pompeii just as
they do in every city. Attilius has no more use for the Roman
gods than Pansa, Mariamne, Glaucus, or Ione, but he puts his

trust in the laws of nature rather than divine Providence to effect his ingenious escape from the eruption of Vesuvius. The heroine, Corelia, is not only a plucky damsel in distress but gratifyingly exact about taking her revenge on her vile father, Ampliatus, opening his prized aviary and letting the birds fly away (one is caught by the family cat, who surely escapes destruction along with her mistress). Free from the classical ambitions of nineteenth-century books on Pompeii, Harris settles down to the practical business of a page-turning techno-thriller and does so with an evident gusto that has created a genuine bond with his many readers. Aside from its one luridly gruesome passage in Chapter 2, *Pompeii* is not a violent book despite the violence of the age and the events it treats. Best of all, by praising the wonders of Roman hydraulics, it has brought readers into a whole new realm; the thrill of this thriller is all the more thrilling because it is so unexpected.

9

Railway Tourism

Inaugurated in 1839, Italy's first railroad stretched from the eastern end of Naples to the little port of Granatello, below Portici, the site of Villa d'Elbeuf. The steam-powered locomotive drew a royal car and three classes of passenger cars, some of them open-air "charabancs," which allowed passengers the best possible view as they sped along the coast. By 1844 the line had been extended to Nocera Inferiore and included a stop at Pompeii. After this point, the level Campanian plain gave way to the precipitous volcanic mountains of the Sorrento Peninsula, which made construction a great deal more difficult. Then, in 1848 a wave of republican rebellions swept through Naples along with many other European capitals. The Bourbon monarchy struck back, but with only temporary success. By 1860 the Kingdom of the Two Sicilies no longer existed; it had dissolved into the unified Kingdom of Italy under a new monarch, Victor Emmanuel II, onetime king of Piedmont and Sardinia. The railroad line finally reached Salerno, its final destination, in 1866.[1]

Train travel brought Pompeii within reach of tourists who might not be able to afford a carriage and cicerone for the day, like the three French students Octavien, Fabio, and Max, who are the protagonists of Théophile Gautier's novelette of 1852, *Arria Marcella:*

The route of the railroad that goes to Pompeii runs almost entirely along the seaside; long foamy waves break on a blackish sand that looks like filtered carbon. In fact, the coast is formed from flows of lava and volcanic ash and contrasts, because of its dark hue, with the blue of the sky and the blue of the sea; in the midst of all this brightness only the sand seems to hold a shadow. The towns that surround it or flank it, Portici . . . Resina, Torre del Greco, Torre dell' Annunziata, of which, in passing, one can pick out the porticoes and peaked roofs, have, despite the intense sun and the typical color of Mediterranean plaster, something Plutonian and rusty about them, like Manchester and Birmingham; the dust is black, and an imperceptible smudge attaches to everything. One can feel that the great forge of Vesuvius heaves and smokes only a few steps away. The three friends descended at the station of Pompeii, laughing among themselves at the mixture of scholarly and modern that leaps to the eyes in reading these words: "Pompeii Station." A Greco-Roman city and a railroad station!

They crossed the cotton fields, a white puff floating here and there, separating the railway station from the area of the excavated city, and hired a guide at the inn built outside the ancient walls, where, to be perfectly accurate, a guide engaged them. A calamity hard to avoid in Italy.[2]

The site also began to attract overnight guests with the enticing prospect of a visit after dark. The old Rapillo tavern began catering to a more refined clientele, some of whom arranged dinner parties within the ruins, as flickering shadows conjured up fantasies of ancient ghosts. Gérard de Nerval describes this arresting combination of modern train travel and antiquarian reverie in his 1854 story, *Isis:*

> Before the opening of the railway line from Naples to Resina, an outing to Pompeii was a whole voyage in itself. [Now] it takes day to visit the sequence of Herculaneum, Vesuvius—and Pompeii, two miles farther on; often one stays on in the area until the following day, in order to wander through Pompeii during the night, in moonlight, and thus to create a complete illusion.. Everyone can pretend, in effect, that, defying the course of the centuries, they have suddenly been allowed to wander the streets and squares of the sleeping city; the gentle moon may well be more becoming than the blazing sun for these ruins, which suddenly excite neither admiration nor surprise, and where antiquity shows itself, one might say, in a modest state of undress.[3]

More fastidious visitors still toured the site by making a brief day trip from Naples. Two of these were grumpy Anglo-Saxon writers Charles Dickens (1845) and Samuel Langhorne Clemens (1867), whom we will meet again in the next chapter.

For people who loved art more than archaeology, a more charming, less challenging Pompeii could be experienced in greater comfort and concentration in Naples, where the royal collection of antiquities had been moved from Portici in 1777. The Royal Museum, including the Farnese collections of paintings, gems, and statuary, occupied an enormous palazzo just outside the old city wall, which began its life in 1577 as the viceregal stable (placed so that mounted troops could pour into the city at the slightest sign of unrest). In 1615, however, Viceroy de Lemos decided to remodel the building to house the University of Naples, which up to then had shared quarters with the Dominicans, the Inquisition, the Dominican College, and the Accademia degli Oziosi in the spacious but crowded convent of San Domenico Maggiore. The revamped palazzo was known as the Palazzo degli Studi, or simply the "Studi." The colossal building's final transformation into the Royal Museum took more than four decades, from 1777 to 1818; evidently the continuous political upsets of 1799–1817 interrupted work on a regular basis. With the abolition of the monarchy in 1946, the Royal Museum became what it is today: the National Archaeological Museum. It took a building the size of an ancient Roman bath to house the statues that the Farnese family had harvested from the ancient Roman Baths of Caracalla, together with the Bourbon family's gleanings from Pompeii and Herculaneum.[4] An 1841 guidebook describes the museum's collections in detail (using an ornamental final "j" rather than "i" for words like "Studj" and "Carraccj"):

THE STUDJ

This extensive building was erected in 1577 by the viceroy Duke d'Ossuna on the plans of Julius Fontana and destined for a university. It was enlarged by the Count de Lemos and by Charles III, but once the colleges had been transferred to S. Salvatore, Ferdinando I dedicated it to the Academy of Sciences and Fine Arts instituted in 1780. The collection of objects of art and science deposited in this establishment, named the Museo Borbonico, is divided into five classes.

1. The statues forming the inheritance of the Farnese family, at Rome, and those discovered in the excavations of Herculaneum and Pompeii.

2. The papyrus manuscripts found in these two ancient cities, and the ingenious mechanism employed in unrolling them.

3. The library composed of 150,000 printed volumes and of 3,000 manuscripts.

4. The picture gallery containing a beautiful annunciation by Pinturicchio and some fine paintings by Carracj, Schidone, and Coreggio.

5. A collection, unique for its number and beauty, of vases called Etruscan, medals, sculptures and other objects in bronze; antique glass wares and provisions found at Herculaneum and Pompeii; paintings from the excavations of those cities, cork models of the ancient theatre of Herculaneum and of the temples at Paestum.

The most remarkable statues are the Farnese Hercules by Glico the Athenian, the Flora, highly esteemed for its drapery, the Farnese bull by Apollonius and Andriscus who have represented in this admirable group the mystic Dirce at the moment of her rescue from the bull to whose horns she had been tied; these works were found at Rome in the thermae of Caracalla.

Our guide is misinformed about the gigantic statue group known as the Farnese bull; Dirce is being tied to the creature, not rescued, and the bull will drag her to her death. She was the wicked stepmother of the two young brothers who devised this cruel revenge. He has less difficulty identifying some of the smaller statues: "We shall also notice a beautiful Venus Callipyge [Greek for 'pretty bottom'; this Venus is caught in the act of admiring her own backside as she lifts her skirts, no underwear in sight], an Adonis, a statue of Aristides found in the theatre of Herculaneum, two gladiators full of expression, a Venus and Cupid found at Capua, a Venus and Hermaphrodite at Pompeii, equestrian statues of Balbus, numerous busts of Roman emperors, inscriptions and architectural fragments of the best times of the art."[5]

The paintings, which have been moved to the former royal palace at Capodimonte, make up one of the world's most stunning collections, though here again our guidebook is not entirely reliable. The painting identified in its text as a fine Pinturicchio *Annunciation* is nothing of the sort; it shows Ulysses and his fellow sailors returning to Ithaca from the Trojan War. Ulysses, in colorful hose, is greeting his wife, Penelope, who looks up from her loom as her splendid tiger cat plays with a ball of yarn. There are no angel wings or doves of the Holy Spirit in sight.

10

Charles Dickens and
Mark Twain

The life of a cicerone was never an easy one. They were working-men compelled to barter their time and knowledge for other people's money. Of necessity, they knew several languages, whereas their customers might know only one, and a vulgar version at that. Much was invariably lost in translation between the guide and his clients (in those days the cicerone was always a man), including, all too often, compassion, humor, and any true communication. Strict distinctions of class almost always divided the well-heeled tourist from the shabby cicerone, one of whom desperately needed the money the other could spend without compunction. Clients were often physically or psychically demanding, only marginally interested in the details of history or the beautiful objects that provided the cicerone the only joy of his thankless profession. His customers were almost always snobs, like William Thomas Beckford, who called his cicerone "the savage" simply because the man was Italian. Or the client might be a wag, like the energetic American with the bushy hair and bushier moustache, Samuel Langhorne Clemens, who came to Pompeii in 1867, two years after the end of the American Civil War and seven years after Naples joined the unified Italian state.

Clemens was a brash, young journalist from Missouri who had built a following in California with his tales of the American West; his last article before setting out for Europe had been "The Celebrated Jumping Frog of Calaveras County." He had never written a book. His editors at the San Francisco *Alta California* decided that it might be amusing for readers to follow this pure specimen of a Yankee to the Holy Land on board the SS *Quaker City,* a newly refitted warship, and Clemens, as Mark Twain (a name that drew on his experience aboard a paddle steamer on the Mississippi), wrote a series of long, chatty, and slightly fictionalized letters back home at every stage of the journey. These he gathered, rewrote, and published in 1869 as *The Innocents Abroad.* Naples and Pompeii were important stops en route to the Levant, and we have already heard Twain on the Grotta del cane.

Like every company of travelers, from the pilgrims of Chaucer's *Canterbury Tales* to the tour groups that swarm over Pompeii today, the passengers on the *Quaker City* developed their own private jokes, funny only to those people in those circumstances; for Twain and his friends, it was to call all their guides by the name "Ferguson" after their experience in Paris with a man whose real surname, Billfinger, struck them as "atrocious."[1]

Strangely, two of the most socially compassionate writers of the nineteenth century, Mark Twain and Charles Dickens, were so disconcerted by the foreign setting of southern Italy that the dead of Pompeii became more manageable for them than the living population of Naples. Dickens had come to Pompeii more than twenty years earlier than Twain, in 1845, but his evocation of the ancient city and the human poignancy of its calamities in *Pictures of Italy* (1845) is virtually timeless:

Stand at the bottom of the great market-place of Pompeii, and look up the silent streets, through the ruined temples of Jupiter and Isis, over the broken houses with their inmost sanctuaries open to the day, away to Mount Vesuvius, bright and snowy in the peaceful distance; and lose all count of time, and heed of other things, in the strange and melancholy sensation of seeing the Destroyed and the Destroyer making this quiet picture in the sun. Then, ramble on, and see, at every turn, the little familiar tokens of human habitation and every-day pursuits; the chafing of the bucket-rope in the stone rim of the exhausted well; the track of carriage-wheels in the pavement of the street; the marks of drinking-vessels on the stone counter of the wine-shop; the amphoræ in private cellars, stored away so many hundred years ago, and undisturbed to this hour—all rendering the solitude and deadly lonesomeness of the place, ten thousand times more solemn, than if the volcano, in its fury, had swept the city from the earth, and sunk it in the bottom of the sea.[2]

The press of living people around him on the chaotic streets of Naples posed a far greater mystery:

Why do the beggars rap their chins constantly, with their right hands, when you look at them? Everything is done in pantomime in Naples, and that is the conventional sign for hunger. A man who is quarrelling with another, yonder, lays the palm of his right hand on the back of his left, and shakes the two thumbs—expressive of a donkey's ears—whereat his adversary is goaded to desperation. Two people bargaining for fish, the buyer empties an imaginary waistcoat pocket when he is told the price, and walks away without a word: having thoroughly conveyed to the seller that he considers it too dear. Two people in carriages, meeting, one touches his lips, twice or thrice, holding up the five fingers of his right hand, and gives a horizontal cut in the air with the palm. The other nods briskly, and goes his way. He has been invited to a friendly dinner at half-past five o'clock, and will certainly come. . . . All over Italy, a peculiar shake of the right hand from the wrist, with the forefinger stretched out, expresses a negative—the only negative beggars will ever understand. But, in Naples, those five fingers are a copious language.[3]

Dickens was unable to read Andrea De Jorio's treatise on Neapolitan gestures; that pioneering volume was not translated into English until 1999. But then again, he might have been repelled by the Neapolitan canon's attempt to ground the present-day realities of southern Italy so firmly in the ancient world. Antiquity always remained magically idealized for nineteenth-century Europeans despite the cruelty of the arena games, the boundless promiscuity, and the inescapable paganism of cities destroyed in the earliest years of Christianity. Ultimately, Dickens found more chance of human redemption in the slums of London than under the cheerful skies of Campania:

All this, and every other kind of out-door life and stir, and macaroni-eating at sunset, and flower-selling all day long, and begging and stealing everywhere and at all hours, you see upon the bright sea-shore, where the waves of the bay sparkle merrily. But, lovers and hunters of the picturesque, let us not keep too studiously out of view the miserable depravity, degradation, and wretchedness, with which this gay Neapolitan life is inseparably associated! It is not well to find Saint Giles's so repulsive, and the Porta Capuana so attractive. A pair of naked legs and a ragged red scarf, do not make *all* the difference between what is interesting and what is coarse and odious? Painting and poetising for ever, if you will, the beauties of this most beautiful and lovely spot of earth, let us, as our duty, try to associate a new picturesque with some faint recognition of man's destiny and capabilities; more hopeful, I believe, among the ice and snow of the North Pole, than in the sun and bloom of Naples.[4]

Part of the problem that Naples posed for Protestant visitors was its exuberantly theatrical and ubiquitous Catholicism. In Naples, moreover, this Catholicism took the form of a cult of the Souls in Purgatory, which involved caring for the bones, especially the skulls, of the dead in the belief that they might repay this affectionate attention by interceding on the caretaker's behalf with the forces of heaven; Purgatory was a whole step closer to God than the everyday world.

Dickens learned about this Neapolitan cult of the dead when he visited the catacombs beneath the Baroque church of San Pietro ad Aram (Saint Peter at the Altar), an impressive building in the center of Naples. San Pietro stands over a triple-vaulted crypt, and although this space was not definitively revealed as an early Christian church until 1930, its hoary antiquity was never in doubt. The catacombs are also early Christian, from the fourth century, and Dickens was sure that the living guardians of the place must have been nearly as old themselves:

> The old, old men who live in hovels at the entrance of these ancient catacombs, and who, in their age and infirmity, seem waiting here, to be buried themselves, are members of a curious body, called the Royal Hospital, who are the official attendants at funerals. Two of these old spectres totter away, with lighted tapers, to show the caverns of death—as unconcerned as if they were immortal. They were used as buryingplaces for three hundred years; and, in one part, is a large pit

FROM POMPEII

full of skulls and bones, said to be the sad remains of a great mortality occasioned by a plague. In the rest there is nothing but dust. They consist, chiefly, of great wide corridors and labyrinths, hewn out of the rock. At the end of some of these long passages, are unexpected glimpses of the daylight, shining down from above. It looks as ghastly and as strange; among the torches, and the dust, and the dark vaults: as if it, too, were dead and buried.[5]

In many ways, then, nineteenth-century Pompeii often seemed more alive to foreigners than Naples itself despite the lush vitality of the Campanian climate. But Dickens was not entirely pessimistic about Naples or Italy. He was writing only a few years before the whole of Europe exploded in a series of republican rebellions, and the Naples he saw was the Naples of a fading Bourbon dynasty. His diagnosis of the peninsula's ills, however, could have been written yesterday:

[Italians are] a people, naturally well-disposed, and patient, and sweet-tempered. Years of neglect, oppression, and misrule, have been at work, to change their nature and reduce their spirit; miserable jealousies, fomented by petty Princes to whom union was destruction, and division strength, have been a canker at their root of nationality, and have barbarized their language; but the good that was in them ever, is in them yet, and a noble people may be, one day, raised up from these ashes. Let us entertain that hope! And let us not remember Italy the less regardfully, because, in every fragment of her fallen Temples, and every stone of her deserted palaces and prisons, she helps to inculcate the lesson that the wheel of Time is rolling for an end, and that the world is, in all great essentials, better, gentler, more forbearing, and more hopeful, as it rolls![6]

Mark Twain, on the other hand, came to Italy in the midst of its painful, bloody process of unification. By 1867 Naples had joined the united Italian nation-state, but Rome was still its own temporal power, ruled by Pope Pius IX, the onetime liberal turned sourly conservative after being attacked and exiled in the course of the revolutions of 1848–1849. The Eternal City would finally fall to Italian Bersaglieri (Targeteers) on September 20, 1870. Mark Twain knew all about unification movements; by 1867 his own country had barely begun to recover from a far bloodier civil war and the assassination of a president. Oddly enough, John Surratt, one of the conspirators involved with John Wilkes Booth in a plot to kidnap (though not to kill) Abraham Lincoln, escaped from the United States to fight for Pius IX among the Papal Zouaves.[7]

It may not be surprising, then, to see Twain's caustic wit trained full force on the cult of San Gennaro:

> In this city of Naples, they believe in and support one of the wretchedest of all the religious impostures one can find in Italy—the miraculous liquefaction of the blood of St. Januarius. Twice a year the priests assemble all the people at the Cathedral, and get out this vial of clotted blood and let them see it slowly dissolve and become liquid—and every day for eight days, this dismal farce is repeated, while the priests go among the crowd and collect money for the exhibition. The first day, the blood liquefies in forty-seven minutes—the church is crammed, then, and time must be allowed the collectors to get around: after that it liquefies a little quicker and a little quicker, every day, as the houses grow smaller, till on the eighth day, with only a few dozens present to see the miracle, it liquefies in four minutes.[8]

This writer, who laid bare the injustices of his own society, was appalled by the injustices he saw in Naples and by the gulf between rich and poor. Like the Mozarts a century before him, he made the afternoon promenade down the Riviera di Chiaia. He did so, however, in a far less tolerant mood than the two Austrian musicians, despite the fact that the Riviera now boasted a large public park, a pioneering marvel of urban planning meant for the entire population, not just the elite:

> In the thoroughfares of Naples . . . things are all mixed together. Naked boys of nine years and the fancy-dressed children of luxury; shreds and tatters, and brilliant uniforms; jackass-carts and state-carriages; beggars, Princes and Bishops, jostle each other in every street. At six o'clock every evening, all Naples turns out to drive on the "Riviere di Chiaja" (whatever that may mean); and for two hours one may stand there and see the motliest and the worst mixed procession go by that ever eyes beheld. Princes (there are more Princes than policemen in Naples—the city is infested with them)— Princes who live up seven flights of stairs and don't own any principalities, will keep a carriage and go hungry; and clerks, mechanics, milliners and strumpets will go without their dinners and squander the money on a hack-ride in the Chiaja; the rag-tag and rubbish of the city stack themselves up, to the number of twenty or thirty, on a rickety little go-cart hauled by a donkey not much bigger than a cat, and they drive in the Chiaja; Dukes and bankers, in sumptuous carriages and with gorgeous drivers and footmen, turn out, also, and so the furious procession goes. For two hours rank and wealth, and obscurity and poverty clatter along side by side in the wild procession, and then go home serene, happy, covered with glory![9]

The crowds and smells of Naples dismayed most travelers, but Twain had a way with words that few of them could match when it came to describing the *lazzaroni*:

They crowd you—infest you—swarm about you, and sweat and smell offensively, and look sneaking and mean, and obsequious. There is no office too degrading for them to perform, for money. I have had no opportunity to find out any thing about the upper classes by my own observation, but from what I hear said about them I judge that what they lack in one or two of the bad traits the canaille have, they make up in one or two others that are worse. How the people beg!—many of them very well dressed, too.[10]

Remarkably, however, Twain had words of sincere admiration for the Dominican friars who plunged into the Neapolitan slums as missionaries to the urban poor:

Having grown calm and reflective at length—I now feel in a kindlier mood. I feel that after talking so freely about the priests and the churches, justice demands that if I know any thing good about either I ought to say it. I have heard of many things that redound to the credit of the priesthood, but the most notable matter that occurs to me now is the devotion one of the mendicant orders showed during the prevalence of the cholera last year. I speak of the Dominican friars—men who wear a coarse, heavy brown robe and a cowl, in this hot climate, and go barefoot. They live on alms altogether, I believe. They must unquestionably love their religion, to suffer so much for it. When the cholera was raging in Naples; when the people were dying by hundreds and hundreds every day; when every concern for the public welfare was swallowed up in selfish private interest, and every citizen made the taking care of himself his sole object, these men banded themselves together and went about nursing the sick and burying the dead. Their noble efforts cost many of them their lives. They laid them down cheerfully, and

FROM POMPEII

well they might. Creeds mathematically precise, and hair-splitting niceties of doctrine, are absolutely necessary for the salvation of some kinds of souls, but surely the charity, the purity, the unselfishness that are in the hearts of men like these would save their souls though they were bankrupt in the true religion—which is ours.[11]

We shall be meeting these Dominicans again in Chapter 12.

For Mark Twain, as for Dickens, Pompeii was easier to bear than Naples itself, not least because he could reshape the ancient city in his own imagination:

The sun shines as brightly down on old Pompeii to-day as it did when Christ was born in Bethlehem, and its streets are cleaner a hundred times than ever Pompeiian saw them in her prime. I know whereof I speak—for in the great, chief thoroughfares (Merchant Street and the Street of Fortune) have I not seen with my own eyes how for two hundred years at least the pavements were not repaired!—how ruts five and even ten inches deep were worn into the thick flag-stones by the chariot-wheels of generations of swindled tax-payers? And do I not know by these signs that Street Commissioners of Pompeii never attended to their business, and that if they never mended the pavements they never cleaned them? And, besides, is it not the inborn nature of Street Commissioners to avoid their duty whenever they get a chance? I wish I knew the name of the last one that held office in Pompeii so that I could give him a blast. I speak with feeling on this subject, because I caught my foot in one of those ruts, and the sadness that came over me when I saw the first poor skeleton, with ashes and lava sticking to it, was tempered by the reflection that maybe that party was the Street Commissioner.[12]

Twain was genuinely moved in particular by the story of the Steadfast Soldier, a Pompeian legend that grew up after early excavators uncovered the arched, oblong tomb of a man named Marcus Cerrinus Restitutus next to the Herculaneum Gate. A skeleton was found beneath the arch, clearly some unfortunate fugitive who ducked under the arch to take shelter from the hail of lapilli and died shortly thereafter in a pyroclastic surge. Quickly, however, fertile imaginations turned the fleeing Pompeian cowering in a convenient shelter into a soldier who stood firm in his guard box, awaiting orders to evacuate that never came. The English archaeologist William Gell fixed the story for English-speaking readers in his *Pompeiana* of 1819: "An arched recess, around and without which seats are formed. . . . Within this recess was found a human skeleton, of which the hand still grasped a lance. Conjecture has imagined the remains of a sentinel, who preferred dying on his post to quitting it for the more ignominious death, which, in conformity with the severe discipline of his country, would have awaited him."[13]

The Steadfast Soldier reflected the same moral values as those presented in the story of Giocante Casabianca, the young boy who was spotted on the deck of his father's ship, *L'Orient,* in 1798, as Lord Nelson's cannons pounded away at Napoleon's fleet in the Bay of Abou Kir. To the British sailors' amazement and then regret, young Casabianca steadfastly held his position until a shot struck the vessel's powder magazine, and it sank in an inferno. In 1826, three years before writing "The Image of Lava," Felicia Hemans immortalized the brave youth in a poem that rivaled Bulwer's *Last Days of Pompeii* for popularity well into the twentieth century, "Casabianca." Mark Twain knew the poem, like most people, by its opening line, "The boy stood on the burning deck"; one of Tom Sawyer's classmates recites it on Examination Day, just after Tom's recitation of Patrick Henry's "Give me liberty or give me death."

By Twain's own day, the Steadfast Soldier had become as real a figure as Giocante Casabianca, the Boy on the Burning Deck, especially for travelers from England and the United States, with their military and governmental traditions so explicitly modeled on the example of ancient Rome.

In 1865 the English painter John Edward Poynter immortalized the soldier's martyrdom in a painting called *Faithful unto Death* (Figure 10.1). The low, shallow, blind arch of the tomb has become a tall postern gate in the city wall; Poynter's display of archaeological knowledge admits some adjustment of detail for the sake of drama. The soldier's deep-set eyes and anguished look are taken from ancient Roman sculptures in the National Museum, and they are exactly right for the tastes of imperial Rome at the time of the eruption; the twentieth-century excavations at the seaside villa of Tiberius in Sperlonga, just off the Appian Way between Rome and Naples, would reveal that emperor's preference for this emotional style, associated with the ancient Greek sculptor Scopas.[14]

As Mark Twain walked through the streets of Pompeii, he reflected on this blameless, anonymous (and as we now know, fictitious) hero, memories of the Civil War too fresh for him to mock military virtue:

> But perhaps the most poetical thing Pompeii has yielded to modern research, was that grand figure of a Roman soldier, clad in complete armor; who, true to his duty, true to his proud name of a soldier of Rome, and full of the stern courage which had given to that name its glory, stood to his post by the city gate, erect and unflinching, till the hell that raged around him burned out the dauntless spirit it could not conquer.[15]

We never read of Pompeii but we think of that soldier; we can not write of Pompeii without the natural impulse to grant to him the mention he so well deserves. Let us remember

10.1.   Sir Edward John Poynter (1836–1919), *Faithful unto Death*, 1865 (oil on canvas). Walker Art Gallery, National Museums Liverpool / The Bridgeman Art Library.

that he was a soldier—not a policeman—and so, praise him. Being a soldier, he staid,—because the warrior instinct forbade him to fly. Had he been a policeman he would have staid, also—because he would have been asleep.[16]

For another American writer in these same years, Pompeii meant something radically different from the Steadfast Soldier. Secreted away in her home in Amherst, Massachusetts, Emily Dickinson read avidly about volcanoes and found in them a perfect metaphor for human emotions. For her, as for Sigmund Freud several decades later, Pompeii meant the human psyche, a buried city of fiery passion:

> I have never seen "Volcanoes"—
> But, when Travellers tell
> How those old—phlegmatic mountains
> Usually so still—
>
> Bear within—appalling Ordnance,
> Fire, and smoke and gun,
> Taking Villages for breakfast,
> And appalling Men—
>
> If the stillness is Volcanic
> In the human face
> When upon a pain Titanic
> Features keep their place—
>
> If at length the smouldering anguish
> Will not overcome—
> And the palpitating Vineyard
> In the dust, be thrown?
>
> If some loving Antiquary,
> On Resumption Morn,

Will not cry with joy "Pompeii"!
To the Hills return![17]

For Mark Twain, taking the last train out of Pompeii was as exotic an experience as it had been for Théophile Gautier, the same mixing of ancient and modern in the unsettling experience of a disoriented, hopelessly foreign visitor:

We came out from under the solemn mysteries of this city of the Venerable Past—this city which perished, with all its old ways and its quaint old fashions about it, remote centuries ago, when the Disciples were preaching the new religion, which is as old as the hills to us now—and went dreaming among the trees that grow over acres and acres of its still buried streets and squares, till a shrill whistle and the cry of "All aboard—last train for Naples!" woke me up and reminded me that I belonged in the nineteenth century, and was not a dusty mummy, caked with ashes and cinders, eighteen hundred years old. The transition was startling. The idea of a railroad train actually running to old dead Pompeii, and whistling ir-reverently, and calling for passengers in the most bustling and business-like way, was as strange a thing as one could imagine, and as unpoetical and disagreeable as it was strange.[18]

Being the cicerone for this bright but profoundly restless man cannot have been an easy task. But the Grand Tour to the Holy Land effected all the transformations in him that earlier genera-tions had counted on undergoing. Both the man, Samuel Lang-horne Clemens, and the literary figure, Mark Twain, could now measure themselves against a much wider world and know that they could hold their own. A private letter written during the trip simply says, "I like Italy," and Twain would eventually settle there for a period at the end of his life.[19]

Experience as a Grand Tourist and a popular writer increased his social confidence as well as his ambition. In December of 1867, on his return from the Holy Land, he met an attractive, lively young woman from New York society named Olivia Langdon and courted her successfully. The self-consciously Western writer was already working toward a more universal viewpoint and a more universal identity even in transforming his original letters into his first book. *The Innocents Abroad* turned out to be one of the most popular travel books of all time, and Mark Twain was well on his way to becoming a great American author. When Samuel Clemens returned from his long, roundabout journey to Pompeii, he was more than ready to inhabit that role.

11

Giuseppe Fiorelli, the "Pope" of Pompeii

When Mr. Freeman visited Herculaneum in 1751, he was convinced that most of the inhabitants had escaped from the town before it was buried. The buildings still stood upright, the valuable metals seemed to be gone, and the cataclysm seemed to have left no bodies: "It is said, some human bones were found, tho' few; which perhaps might belong to some miserable bedridden wretch or other, who could not escape, or of a person dying suddenly of fright; which I think is not difficult to imagine, when one considers what a scene of horror they must have had before their eyes."[1]

It would take nearly another two and a half centuries to discover how many people had died in Herculaneum; the victims turned out to be huddled in a mass along the shoreline, waiting for rescue from the sea. Their last refuge was not uncovered until the early 1980s.[2] Still, Mr. Freeman's basic line of reasoning was correct: Vesuvius had sent out early warnings of its displeasure, and many people had taken those warnings seriously enough to evacuate.

From the beginning, the excavations of Pompeii revealed traces of the dead. The rain of volcanic lapilli from Vesuvius miraculously spared and preserved the city's solid, durable objects, but it destroyed living things and their organic derivatives by a quick process of baking at high temperatures: trees, plants, food, clothing, animals, people. (By contrast, the pyroclastic flow that buried Herculaneum left its wooden shutters and half-timbering carbonized but intelligible). Gradually, these fragile bodies and objects decomposed, so that the earliest excavators found nothing more of Pompeii's people than skeletons and the occasional imprint, like the famous breast of "Arria Marcella," and the suggestively placed "steadfast soldier," who so moved Mark Twain.

The skeletons were haunting enough, but in the 1860s, the ingenious director of the excavation, Giuseppe Fiorelli, showed how careful digging could reveal a wealth of information about the victims of the eruption. Fiorelli was the very first director of excavations to serve the newborn Kingdom of Italy.[3] He had first been appointed in 1848, when Naples still ruled the Kingdom of the Two Sicilies, thus serving the House of Bourbon as a royal official, but he lost his position almost immediately amid suspicions of republican activity. His sympathies certainly lay in that direction, and when Naples joined the state of Italy in 1860, Fiorelli came back to his post as director of excavations at Pompeii, unified Italy's most famous archaeological site.

The director's revolutionary interests involved more than politics; Fiorelli was one of the first archaeologists to excavate stratigraphically, that is, by removing layers of earth from the top down, following the subtle changes of color and texture that distinguished one floor level or surface from the one beneath it. The first excavators had simply dug holes in the ground around Civita to see what they could find (and Domenico Fontana simply dug a ditch right through the area before filling it with water). Weber and La Vega revolutionized excavation at Pompeii by recovering the street plan as they dug, but this meant that they entered buildings by channeling trenches in from the street. Fiorelli's workers, however, removed the blanket of lapilli layer by layer, taking care to preserve the buildings and their decoration as they went. Examining the stratigraphy told them how the eruption must have struck the city. The careful pace also gave Fiorelli and his team time to spot oddly shaped bubbles in Pompeii's ash cover. When these were injected with liquid plaster and allowed to dry, out came the solidified silhouettes of everything from bread to woodwork and, most affectingly, the forms of animals and people, captured as they struggled, hopelessly, against the rising levels of pumice and the noxious fumes.

From old finds like the imprints of bodies in the Villa of Diomedes, Fiorelli could see how Pompeii's organic material had decomposed without disturbing the dense layer of compressed ash that surrounded them on all sides, including the ground itself. Thus the outlines of door and window frames, the shapes of bodies, the roots of trees and shrubs, all the organic remains of the town survived as hollow voids within the pumice. It took a clever strategist to devise a way to recover these lost shapes, but Giuseppe Fiorelli was nothing if not clever. He was also energetic and overbearing, so domineering a figure that when he rose to national prominence, his colleagues in Tuscany called him the "Pope" behind his back.[4]

Fiorelli's casts still survive, some of them displayed in the places where they were found (and far too many of them moldering away in storerooms). They include the famous dog; an old man in his underwear wearily shielding his face as he lies down for eternity, too weak to move any farther; a couple embracing as the lapilli bury them. The skeletons of all of these individuals still survive within the plaster and sometimes show through where the plaster itself has deteriorated; bone was sturdy enough to withstand what was essentially a process of baking in hot ash.

Fiorelli called these plaster ghosts *calchi* (plasters), the same word used for the plaster casts made of classical sculpture that were so much in vogue at the same time. Today, the *calchi* remain the most eloquent witness to the real horror of the eruption, catching the volcano's victims at their moment of supreme vulnerability, the margin between life and death, and in many cases the immediate aftermath of death.[5] The tortured poses of many *calchi*, including the dog, are the result of postmortem muscle contractions, a response to the searing heat of the pyroclastic waves rather than the living experience of intense pain. Though visitors like Madame de Staël and Mark Twain felt that Pompeii had been interrupted in the middle of normal life, archaeology tells a different story: under the layers of ash, we really see a town that has been mortally wounded and living things that were already dead.

It is the intimacy of our view that has made the bodies of Pompeii so compelling for visitors (typically, I was fascinated by them on my first visits, but now, looking at them seems an intolerable intrusion on their private agony, including the dog's).

As a Neapolitan himself, Fiorelli knew that his *calchi* fit into the region's long and varied list of strangely preserved bodies, a list that included the relics of San Gennaro, the skulls and mummies in the catacombs of San Gaudioso, and the bodies under San Pietro ad Aram. The bodies of Pompeii, however, belonged to people who had been surprised by death, whereas the mummies and relics of Naples had been carefully tended by the living. But Fiorelli's Naples had also been visited by sudden death—in the form of cholera, a disease that sometimes struck so violently that people lost all of their bodily fluids in one devastating rush and died on the spot. The epidemic of 1866, recalled by Mark Twain, occurred while Fiorelli was working in Pompeii. The victims were piled into the cemetery at Poggioreale (see Chapter 4) and the ancient quarry of Fontanelle, which we will investigate in Chapter 18.

The *calchi* have inevitably changed the way that visitors respond to Pompeii; at one moment a well-preserved ancient building can seem vibrant with life, like the marketplace in the forum, with its circular fish stall standing in the center like a rustic temple, or the spacious, beautifully stuccoed courtyard of the Stabian baths. And then the sight of a *calco* interrupts the reverie with its agonized posture and its insistence on a different Pompeii, a Pompeii of flaming skies, of hot stone hail, of panic. A house near the amphitheater, like many on its block and those of its neighbors, encloses a substantial (and productive) vineyard within its garden walls. In the shed at the very back of the vineyard, already mentioned in Chapter 1, thirteen people lie side by side, eleven adults and two toddlers. They were discovered in 1961 by Excavation

11.1.   Pompeii, antiquarium (destroyed 1943). Adoc-photos / Art Resource, NY.

Director Amedeo Maiuri (see Chapter 17), and the little private vineyard is now called the "Garden of the Fugitives" *(Giardino dei fuggiaschi)*. The *calchi* in the Garden of the Fugitives preserve the general shapes of bodies, clothing, and facial features but not details. One couple lies in a loose embrace, the male—man, youth?—tenderly shielding the much smaller female—girl? woman?—who leans her head into his chest. They could be lovers, or brother and sister, or father and daughter. All we know is that they have found some kind of peace in the middle of the inferno. Meanwhile, the vines grow and thrive under the Pompeian sun, and beyond the walls of their ruined house looms the profile of Vesuvius.

Fiorelli also established a museum in Pompeii itself. His request for a separate building in 1861 was denied for lack of funds; the new state had war damage to repair. Instead, Fiorelli set up a little antiquarium (Figure 11.1) inside a vaulted space next to the seaward city gate, the Porta Marina, which had become (and remains) the main entrance to the site. The *calchi* lay stretched out in glass cases in the center of a series of rooms lined with shelves full of amphorae, vases, and other finds. The *calchi,* however, along with a statue of Venus reaching for her gilt sandal and clad only in a painted-on gold net brassiere, were always the main attraction, the real people in real anguish who drove home the tragedy of Pompeii.

12

Bartolo Longo

When Bartolo Longo's train pulled into the station of Pompei Scavi, "Pompeii Excavations," on an October morning in 1872, the thirty-one-year-old lawyer was relieved to see the silhouette of the ancient amphitheater protruding above the umbrella pines.[1] It was the same station where the combination of ancient and modern had so amused Théophile Gautier twenty years earlier and Mark Twain much more recently; there, in between stations serving two modern towns, Torre Annunziata and Scafati, was a railroad station with the name of a city that had lain buried for eighteen centuries.

Bartolo Longo may have been relieved to see the outline of Pompeii's amphitheater as he stepped down from the train, but that relief vanished when he saw the pair of sunburned riflemen who introduced themselves as his escorts for the day. In the first place, the three of them could barely communicate with each other. Longo spoke a local dialect of Puglia, a region on the opposite coast of the Italian peninsula, as well as the florid academic language of a respectable professional lawyer. The illiterate riflemen, on the other hand, spoke only an impenetrable local version of Neapolitan, with its wealth of Spanish loanwords and its lilting rhythms. Sometimes, however, the men's failure to communicate stemmed not so much from the words they used as from the different meanings they ascribed to the same vocabulary. The word "bandit," for example, produced roughly the same effect in Longo's companions that saying "Mafia" might have had on certain Sicilians. Their conversation made such an impression on him that he recalled it nearly verbatim years later:

As we hiked along the provincial highway toward the inn, I turned to them at a certain point. And the dialogue I report here, with a thousand interruptions, because we barely understood each other, gave me an immediate sense of the state of this land and its inhabitants. "What's wrong? We can't even walk safely along the highway?"

"Oh, when you come with us," one of them answered with a swaggering air, "there's nothing to be afraid of."

"What? Are there bandits?"

"Oh, bandits!" . . .

"Well, why go around with weapons?"

"Eh," he repeated with an ironic smirk, "for the bad guys."

"Bad guys?" I replied, raising an eyebrow. "Thieves on the highway? What about the Carabinieri?"

"No Carabinieri barracks here." And reaching with his right hand for the rifle he carried on his left shoulder, he continued, "We have to take care of ourselves."

And with that, our merry company reached the point near the Amphitheater where the road is hemmed in by great piles of pumice and ruins.

"Here's the Valley Pass" (Passo del Valle), said the other peasant. "Here you always need to pay attention because this is where the robberies and holdups usually happen."[2]

The riflemen, as Longo knew perfectly well, belonged to the Camorra, the Neapolitan version of the Mafia. Like the Mafia in Sicily, the Camorra had developed in Naples to provide a variety of rough justice where the Spanish viceroy, the Bourbon monarchy, and generations of feudal landlords had provided virtually none. The Camorrista in charge of escorting Bartolo Longo had put the situation plainly enough to his guest, "We have to take care of ourselves." Longo, in turn, was too canny to use the word "Camorra" in conversing with his well-armed hosts; "bandits" was a more neutral term, and it allowed him to confirm the suspicions he must have had long before he boarded the train from Naples. The land along the River Sarno, the Pompeii Valley, was in the hands of the gang, not the government, and Bartolo Longo was bound for the lawless land outside the excavation, not the archaeological site.

Longo, intense and high strung, had come to the Pompeii Valley as estate manager for the Neapolitan aristocrat who owned much of the land in the area, Countess Marianna Farnararo De Fusco di Lettere (the excavation itself, as a royal domain, belonged to the Kingdom of Italy). In theory, most of the thousand-odd souls who lived in the Pompeii Valley were her tenants, but the area was so dangerous that no landlord had ventured near it for decades. These dangers included mosquitoes as well as the Camorra and freelance bandits, for the area had been malarial ever since Alfonso Piccolomini's botched attempt to divert the course of the River Sarno toward his water mills in 1659. But the Countess De Fusco and Avvocato Longo were ready to face down both thugs and mosquitoes; they belonged to a group of energetic Catholic philanthropists who regularly charged into the slums of Naples with the Dominican fathers to do good works. They knew all about disease, indifference, inertia, and the Camorra.

Longo's tour of the Pompeii Valley was part of his general effort to put the contessa's financial affairs in order. Officially, he had come with the idea of improving her ability to collect the rent for these neglected properties. Yet what he saw in the next few days shocked him deeply even after years of study and social work in the center of Naples. Instead of devising new ways of extracting money from the residents, he began wondering how he could help them rather than exploit them more efficiently. At first he may have been excited at the prospect of seeing the ruins of ancient Pompeii as part of his tour of the valley. But the two Camorristi guided him into a situation that shifted his focus abruptly from past to present and, even more emphatically, prompted a vision of how he might shape the future.

Bartolo Longo is now known largely as a religious leader, but he was much more than that: he was a phenomenal organizer and an urban planner, and, as such, he was an exemplary nineteenth-century social reformer (Figure 12.1). In a matter of fifteen years, between 1872 and 1887, he created a new city in what had been a desolate valley, centered on a new pilgrimage site as well as the ancient ruins. Since the late nineteenth century, every single

12.1. Bartolo Longo at the age of fifty. Old postcard.

visitor to Pompeii, ancient site or modern city, has benefited from the work of this remarkable man.

By the time he met his rifle-toting escorts in the Pompeii Valley, Bartolo Longo had already lived several different lives in his thirty-one years. His personal struggles mirrored the gigantic changes that transformed Italy in the mid-nineteenth century as a motley collection of republics and monarchies fought and bargained themselves into a unified nation-state. In this process of unification, southern Italy, the former Kingdom of the Two Sicilies, would suffer the greatest losses, and Longo himself, as a southerner, would fall victim to some of the changes.

From his birth in 1841 until 1860, when the Kingdom of the Two Sicilies merged into the Kingdom of Italy, Bartolo Longo had led a relatively tranquil life. He belonged to a wealthy landowning family from Latiano, a small town that lay along the ancient track of the Appian Way near its endpoint, at Brindisi. Like most members of his social class, he was sent away to a boarding school (in his case run by the Scolopian Fathers) at the age of five and then was tutored privately in the nearby city of Lecce until he earned the equivalent of a teaching certificate. He had never come near a public institution or a university. With unification, however, this southern Italian tradition of private instruction came under particular fire from the new national Ministry of Education. Longo's degree, because it had was privately earned, lost its validity in the new nation. In 1863, therefore, he enrolled as a law student in the state University of Naples.[3]

A law degree was something quite different from a teacher's certificate; Longo took this apparent setback to his career as an opportunity to shift his ambitions sharply upward. In Puglia, he had taught a bit and focused his thoughts mostly on dancing, riding, and fencing. From this comfortable life in the provinces, he now moved into the maelstrom of Naples, the city he had always considered his capital. In 1860, however, Naples had been abruptly stripped of that status. Turin, far in the north, was the capital of Italy now, and Naples just one of several large Italian cities. If Bartolo Longo felt lost as a new arrival in Naples, so did many Neapolitans who had been there all their lives. Many of those who had worked for the Crown were now unemployed; if, like Giuseppe Fiorelli, they had managed to keep their jobs, they answered to a government in Turin packed with northerners.

The University of Naples, which rivaled Paris, Salerno, and Bologna as the oldest in the world, was feeling its own sense of loss and displacement. The educational reforms instituted by the new Kingdom of Italy had been devised by northern Italian friends of the court, mostly Piedmontese from Italy's extreme northeast. The Ministry of Education, like most of the national government, was run by these same people, who had a long bourgeois tradition and close cultural ties to France. To many Piedmontese Italians, the former Kingdom of the Two Sicilies, with its strong Spanish heritage and its feudal aristocracy, seemed corrupt and backward (an attitude that has yet to change). Resentful of the supercilious directives that issued from the newly founded Ministry of Education, the University of Naples fought hard to establish itself on its own terms as a modern institution in a modern nation, employing famously republican professors like the firebrand Luigi Settembrini, condemned to death by the Bourbon king for his liberal ideas (in the nineteenth-century sense of that word) but now an honored senator of Italy. (An excerpt from one of his letters appears in Chapter 1 and is posted just outside the Garden of the Fugitives, mentioned in the previous chapter.)

Settembrini was one of the professors who had the greatest influence on the student Bartolo Longo, who, for the first time in his sheltered, piously Catholic life, encountered the free exchange of ideas in a public institution. After his close-knit community in Latiano, the freewheeling, heated atmosphere of the university and Naples both excited and confused him. Like most students, he plunged into passionate discussions with his classmates, gathering in favorite haunts like the Café de Angelis, on the corniche of Chiaia (where well-off Neapolitans still gather in the cafés of the Piazza dei Martiri to ponder the same mysteries of existence). There was also the daunting chaos of Naples itself, more densely packed with humanity than any other city in Italy.

Like many students then and now, Longo gradually dropped some of the religious rites that had regulated his life up to that point. The Scolopian Fathers had trained him to recite a daily Rosary and five Hail Marys, but he discontinued this habit, though he still attended Mass with some regularity. Then one of his friends recommended a new French novel, Ernest Renan's *La vie de Jésus*, which presented Jesus as an entirely human figure rather than the Son of God. Renan wrote compellingly enough to shake the very basis of the faith that had always governed the most basic rhythms of Longo's life.

In this vulnerable state of mind, one May evening in 1864 Longo followed some of his friends from the Café de Angelis to a Spiritualist séance, where the medium, doing what was then called "magnetic sleepwalking" (we might define the sleepwalking as hypnosis), asked the aspiring lawyer whether he had any questions. "Is Jesus Christ God?" he asked. "Yes," the medium replied. "Are the Ten Commandments true?" "All but the sixth."[4] Reassured, Longo decided to become an initiate, pledging to attend the group's nightly séances, to read about Spiritualism, and to subject himself to experiments that would test his own ability to communicate with the spirit realm.

Perhaps because of its large English population, midcentury Naples had become a center for nineteenth-century Spiritualism (*spiritismo* in Italian), a movement that began in New York in the 1840s and spread rapidly thereafter to the rest of the world. Soon legions of middle- and upper-class Europeans and Americans were rushing to consult their Ouija boards and conduct séances to communicate with the dead. Normally the deceased spoke from the beyond through a human medium, but Spiritualist sessions also routinely featured flying objects, rapping noises, slamming doors, and mysterious gusts of wind. Believers included illustrious figures such as Charles Dickens, biologist Alfred Russel Wallace, and Sir Arthur Conan Doyle. Nor was Wallace the only scientist to be attracted by the possibilities of communication beyond the grave: Marie and Pierre Curie attended séances conducted in Paris by the Neapolitan medium Eusapia Palladino, who began her career as a child and may have met Longo himself on one occasion; he writes about attending a séance with a young girl as the medium.

In 1864, as Longo progressed through law school, he kept up with his Spiritualist exercises. His Neapolitan cohorts turned out to be a more ascetic group than most. He would later come to see their sessions as satanic, but his questions to the medium at his first séance show that, like many Spiritualists, he continued to consider himself a Christian and that initially he saw the movement as a progressive and scientific means of spiritual enlightenment. One of his fellow lodgers at his Neapolitan boardinghouse was a Calabrian Catholic priest who also participated faithfully in these Spiritualist meetings.

The movement may have found this fertile ground in Naples so hospitable because nineteenth-century Neapolitans were quite accustomed to "communicating" with the dead by a variety of means; Spiritualism, with its magnetic sleepwalking and its socially progressive membership, seemed more modern and scientific than lavishing care on anonymous skulls or embalmed bodies, and no one who engaged in any of these practices felt any less Christian for doing so.

Longo's personal guide to the spirit world, at least as he saw it in 1864, was the Archangel Michael, and to Saint Michael the young man finally pledged his allegiance when he was invested as a medium in his own right, thereby rising to the role of priest within his Spiritualist circle. But like many cults, the Spiritualists put greater and greater demands on the members who became involved with the organization. As Longo rose within the Spiritualist ranks in Naples, both the archangel and the human adepts around him began to require an increasingly rigorous regimen of fasting, as well as nightly séances that took their toll on his studies. Despite unrelenting pressure from the spirits and his peers, Longo earned his law degree in December of 1864, a step that only freed him to devote more and more attention to his Spiritualist exercises. His private income meant that for the time being he could survive in Naples without working as a lawyer; the newly minted Avvocato Longo's eventual plan was to return to Puglia and set up a practice, but in the meantime the spirits claimed nearly all of his energy.

After a year of sporadic meals, incessant consultation with Michael and his angelic legions, and no regular work, Longo, always high strung, had become a nervous wreck. Half-starved, sleepless, and frantic, he was also racked with stomach cramps from lifelong digestive problems. He would always blame his poor digestion on the fact that, as a young man, he had lived on nothing but potatoes for a year to save up the money for a harpsichord. His sufferings may have had another cause, sounding as they do like a stomach ulcer, but the story of the potatoes indicates the fierceness of Longo's will even in what he regarded as his own indolent youth.

When a séance called up the ghost of Longo's late father in this agitated period, adding nostalgia to his list of seething emotions, he broke down. Yearning for a father figure, he called on an old family friend in Naples, Professor Vincenzo Pepe, and poured out all of his troubles, physical and existential, mixed with his new Spiritualist convictions.

Alarmed by the young man's physical state and perhaps even more by his nightly contact with the spirit world, Pepe, a pious

FROM POMPEII

Catholic, recommended talking with a good friend of his, a Dominican friar named Alberto Radente. In fact, Radente was a good deal more than a Dominican friar; he was the former prior of the convent of San Domenico Maggiore, the same convent where Thomas Aquinas had lived and taught in the fourteenth century, where local barons and the friars fomented rebellions against Spain in the sixteenth and seventeenth centuries, where the Inquisition had shared quarters with the heretics Giordano Bruno and Tommaso Campanella, and where Viceroy Osuna had founded the Accademia degli Oziosi. In 1864 San Domenico Maggiore was still a force to be reckoned with despite the fact that the friars had been ejected from their convent in 1860 by the new Italian state. At this point Rome was still the capital of an independent papal state run by Pope Pius IX, and unified Italy was fiercely anticlerical. Father Radente, therefore, was now operating from a private house, but he was still an authority figure. In 1866, in the midst of the cholera epidemic, it was Radente's Dominicans whose courageous work would come to the notice, and earn the praise, of Mark Twain.

Despite his energetic engagement in concrete projects for social welfare, Radente drew on a mystical vision of religious faith, and this mystical bent, along with an authoritative personality, helped convince Bartolo Longo to change his views about spiritual longing and how best to fulfill it. For the whole month of June 1865, by a process that closely resembled modern "deprogramming," Padre Radente weaned Longo away from Spiritualism, redirecting his energies toward orthodox Catholic prayers and focusing the agitated lawyer's scattered attention by urging him to recite the Rosary a hundred times over if that was what it took to calm him.

Radente's own former convent, the majestic Gothic San Domenico Maggiore, had been a center for devotion to the Rosary for several centuries. The devotion involved repeating a short prayer to the Virgin Mary while contemplating, in succession, fifteen mysteries of Catholic faith; thus the ritual provided a concise catechism along with a comforting rhythm of prayer and, when recited in church, the companionship of other worshippers. In the case of Bartolo Longo, the combination of the determined friar's spiritual guidance, the fatherly friendship of Vincenzo Pepe, and the formalized prayers of the Rosary (not to mention some much-needed food and sleep) lent a welcome structure to his troubled life. Eager as ever to progress in life, Longo, with Radente's encouragement, became a Dominican tertiary, taking vows of poverty, chastity, and obedience but opting to live outside a convent—not that there was a convent to join at that moment in Naples. In his enthusiasm, Longo also tried to convert his Spiritualist friends to his rediscovered Catholic faith, but they only laughed at him.

For a brief time in 1866 Longo even attempted to return to the kind of life he had led before coming to Naples. He moved back to little Latiano, proposed marriage to a local girl from a suitably aristocratic family, and prepared to settle into a genteel legal career. He returned to Naples to buy his fiancée the most stylish necklace he could find as a bridal gift, heading straight for the Via Toledo, the most fashionable shopping street in the whole Kingdom of Naples. He also stopped in to see Vincenzo Pepe and Father Radente for old times' sake. The fierce old Dominican reprimanded him; had he not taken vows of poverty, chastity, and obedience? What was he doing buying vanities rather than spending that money for the poor? He was meant for a heavenly purpose, not a worldly life. And so Bartolo Longo changed his plans; he broke off the engagement and resolved to stay in Naples to help Father Radente with his work in the Neapolitan slums. Through the friar, he met Countess Marianna Farnararo De Fusco, a wealthy, attractive twenty-seven-year-old widow with vast properties, five children, and great need of a qualified person to help her manage her estate. In 1867 Avvocato Longo took on the dual role of managing her properties and acting as tutor for her children, living in an apartment in her Neapolitan palazzo. Though both counted as landed gentry, Longo, a minor provincial aristocrat, was regarded as the social inferior of a Neapolitan countess, especially when he was working as her employee. (In fact, Marianna Farnararo came from Puglia and its local aristocracy, just like Bartolo Longo; her superior status derived from her marriage to the late Count De Fusco. But once a countess, she was forever a countess.)

To outsiders, there was always a certain ambiguity to their relationship, given that they were young, vigorous, and good looking, as well as living under the same roof. Yet there were also strong forces keeping them apart: their vows of chastity, their discrepancy in social standing, and Countess Marianna's volcanic temper. However, they could also work together with amazing efficiency, and their deepest bond was certainly one of love.

This, then, was the bearded man with the burning eyes who stepped off the train in Pompei Scavi in October of 1872. If his encounter with his armed escort had given him pause, his meeting with the contessa's tenants would prove positively surreal. The friendly Camorrista riflemen marched him from the station to the Rapillo inn (which also served as the local post office and employment agency), on past the amphitheater to the strictly local (and presumably Camorra-ridden) Taverna di Valle, where Longo left his luggage, and then another mile or two down the Royal Road to the parish church of San Salvatore. Founded in 1093 to serve a flourishing community, "Holy Savior" was now an isolated chapel in the depopulated countryside. This is how Longo describes what he found:

What a church! An altar of worm-eaten wood, where the insects nested undisturbed and the rats sucked away at the oil in the votive lamp. . . . The locals were ignorant of even the simplest prayers or the most rudimentary ideas of the catechism, not to mention the sacraments. Their religion was a mixture of superstition and folk tradition. . . . For every necessity they went to the witch, the enchantress, the fortune-teller to obtain charms and spells. Most of the population never went to Mass or heard a sermon: ignorant, uncared-for souls.[5]

He resolved on the spot to take care of those neglected souls. Rather than returning to Naples, he set himself up in the little two-story Taverna di Valle and began thinking about what he could do to better their lives. His answer would turn out to be an extraordinary mixture of Catholic mysticism and nineteenth-century social reform in a period when the Catholic Church and the Kingdom of Italy were sworn enemies. Bartolo Longo, how-ever, bridged the gap between church and state, carefully and deliberately combining the new nation's ideas of progress (what patriots called the Risorgimento, the "resurgence") with traditional Catholic faith.

The mystical solution to the valley's problems came first. Sev-eral days after his arrival, wandering in an isolated field, Longo heard a voice call out: "If you spread the Rosary, you will be saved!" just as the noon Angelus bell rang out from the dilapidated tower of San Salvatore. Kneeling down in the dirt in his finely tailored suit, he resolved to build a new chapel to the Rosary on the site and make it the focal point of a "pious society," a religious club. Religious clubs, confraternities, sodalities, and Rosary societies were standard features of Italian social life, and thus Longo's idea had its practical as well as its spiritual aspect. As the Dominicans had discovered among the urban slum dwellers of Naples, devo-tion to the Rosary was, in fact, a practical way to provide disad-vantaged people with a capsule catechism and help to insert them, through more active participation in conventional church life, into society at large. The national government might be anticlerical in its orientation, but the church had been entrenched in Italian society since the first days of the Roman Empire. It was not going away anytime soon. A Rosary club in the badlands of the Pompeii Valley would bring benefits to its isolated, ignored, and ignorant residents.

However, Longo had no intention of restricting his efforts to founding a Rosary club. He also meant to bring education to the valley, as well as prosperity and the essential elements of modern life: sanitation, communication, transportation. On his return to Naples, he told the contessa of his vision, and together they began campaigning for contributions to build a new church in the Pompeii Valley, one dedicated to the Madonna of the Rosary. Cleverly, Longo requested a modest sum, "a *soldo* a month" (a silver coin, small change along the lines of the American March of Dimes) from a broad range of contributors, while the countess pressed her aristocratic peers for more substantial donations. By 1876 these revenues, bolstered by a large contribution from Countess De Fusco herself, were enough to begin building a sizeable church. A professor of architecture at the University of Naples, Antonio Cua, supplied the design. The land for the project already belonged to the countess. Longo chose a site near the place where he had had his first epiphany, a short distance from the ancient amphitheater of Pompeii—right in the heart of that bandit-ridden area, the Passo di Valle. Civilization, in the form of the Rapillo inn and the railroad station, stood within easy reach. For a pilgrimage site, it was a brilliant choice: a standing challenge to the Camorra, a safe distance from the swampy Sarno, reasonably close to all of the modern lines of communication.

No church, as Longo knew, would be complete without an altarpiece. In San Domenico Maggiore, devotees of the Rosary probably prayed at one time before Caravaggio's *Madonna of the*

Rosary (it was subsequently sold to the Habsburgs and is now in Vienna), and Longo's original plan had been to provide the luckless peasants of the valley with something truly beautiful to contemplate. He began searching for a good painting among the art dealers on the Via Toledo, the same elegant street where he had gone looking for a bridal necklace only a few years before. Once again Father Radente interfered in his shopping expedition: the father had just donated an old painting of the Madonna of the Rosary to a community of Dominican nuns on the Via Medina, and the sisters would be delighted if Longo would take it as their gift to the new church in Pompeii.

It was not an offer that Longo felt he could refuse, but the painting itself was a disaster:

> When I first saw it, my heart sank. Not only was it a worn-out old canvas, but also the Madonna's face, rather than that of a benevolent Virgin full of sanctity and grace, seemed to belong to a rough, coarse housewife. In my heart I felt that the poor Pompeiians would have a hard time concentrating on their prayers faced with such an ugly image. In addition to her misshapen, disagreeable face, a few inches of canvas were missing above her head; her whole mantle was cracked and deteriorated by time, riddled with worm holes, and because of the cracking, flakes of paint had fallen off here and there. About the ugliness of the other figures there is little to say. Saint Dominic on the right looked not like a saint, but the village idiot; and on the left was Saint Rosa, with the gross, rough, vulgar face of a peasant, crowned with roses.[6]

The presence of Saint Rosa was unconventional; normally the Madonna handed out rosaries to Saint Dominic and Saint Catherine of Siena (who had been a Dominican tertiary). On the other hand, the gift, however unprepossessing, came with the best of wishes from the best of people, and the ancient mother superior was persuasive as only an insistent nun can be—backed, formidably, by the stern specter of Father Radente.

And so, on May 8, 1875, the homely, dilapidated painting was bundled off the train from Naples and loaded onto a peasant's cart, already heaped high with a full cargo of dung for the fields. As the dung cart pulled up before San Salvatore (the church of the Madonna was still under construction), the little congregation looked at their dark, deteriorated altarpiece with the same dismay that Longo had felt. A Neapolitan painter, Federico Maldarelli, offered to perform a quick "restoration" that was really a redecoration; as directed, he cleaned and repaired the damaged canvas, but he also repainted the faces of the figures and the background architecture.[7] The image, suddenly a good deal more attractive, hung for the time being in the church of San Salvatore as builders began construction on its real home, the church of the Madonna of the Rosary of Pompeii.

Whatever its aesthetic shortcomings, the Madonna soon earned a reputation for working miracles: healing the sick, protecting worshippers from accidents, granting couples healthy babies. Pompeii began to attract pilgrims to the Madonna as well as visitors to the excavations.

Miracle-working Madonnas have been a part of Italian spiritual life for centuries. Some of them are truly ancient icons from the end of the Roman Empire. Many more were painted in the thirteenth century, and many in the fifteenth. Some are sculpted, at least one (in Syracuse, Sicily) is made of modern plastic. They have appeared in trees and at crossroads, or they simply begin answering prayers with particular efficiency from a high altar. The story of the Madonna of Pompeii, a dilapidated old painting brought to a blighted valley in a dung cart, is unusual among them for the unrelieved humility of its beginnings.

Still more unusual, though, was Bartolo Longo's vision for the Valley of Pompeii. It was a quintessentially nineteenth-century vision, for Longo always envisioned the church of the Rosary set within a thoroughly modern infrastructure. He was inspired to some extent by the recent example of Lourdes, but for the most part his thinking reflected his own local experience as an estate manager in Naples and his convictions as a citizen of modern Italy, and the result was totally original. From the outset, Longo wanted to benefit the local tenant farmers of the valley at least as much as he wanted to attract pilgrims from outside, and so he envisioned setting up institutions to address the valley's particular problems: a grievous lack of employment, education, and connection to the rest of the world. Around the church of the Madonna of the Rosary, therefore, he meant to create a little city, complete with its own train station, post office, telegraph office, schools, charitable institutions, and hotels, a new living Pompeii, a middle-class Pompeii to flank the city of the dead. He would even add a scientific institute to the mix.

He could never have done it all without the help of the Countess De Fusco, who had the status, the social connections, and the sheer force of will to insist that the government set up the post and telegraph offices and build a brand-new train station on a long axis with the new church, thereby creating the basic skeleton for the new town plan. In 1884 the sanctuary of Pompeii obtained its own stop on the rail line from Naples to Salerno. Bartolo Longo could then echo travelers like Gautier and Mark Twain by reciting the stops along the route, but with his own particular perspective:

> [The traveler's] thoughts go back to the life and the houses of a people that has been snuffed out. He imagines seeing Roman ghosts moving across those housetops. And beneath those stones, still standing after eighteen centuries, his imagination descends to the deserted streets, amid that web of

long, narrow, incinerated, melancholy alleyways. . . . But those homeowners will never return again! All that pagan grandeur ended then and there. . . . Barely five minutes have passed, and the locomotive's whistle startles him, and lets him know that he has left *the Pompeii that is dead,* and the approaching station is *the Pompeii that rises again.*[8]

In 1885, on the advice of Pope Leo XIII, who absolved them both of their vows of chastity, Bartolo Longo and Marianna De Fusco were married in Naples, thus putting an end to two decades of gossip. He was forty-four, she forty-eight; they had been working together for twenty years. Longo still called his wife "Contessa"; marriage did not change her sense of their uneven social status. Her children were already grown, and one daughter, Giovanna, worked for the sanctuary together with her mother and her former tutor. Life with the countess was never easy, but Longo took it in stride; in fact, his ability to put up with her temper added to his growing reputation for holiness.

In 1887, fifteen years after his first trip to the valley, Longo finally presented New Pompeii to the world, presiding over a ceremony that has been repeated annually ever since: the *supplica,* a formal, public prayer by the city of Pompeii to the Madonna of the Rosary, which took place (and still does) at noon on May 8 (an earlier, less formal version of the *supplica* was launched in 1884). Longo wrote the text of the *supplica* himself and issued a pamphlet to describe these inaugural festivities, printed by the press he had set up in one of his charitable institutions, a school for the sons of prisoners.

These children of prisoners were regarded as a terrible social problem in late nineteenth-century Naples; Longo's solution was to give them food, lodging, training in a trade, and respect. The first boys were admitted to his "hospice" in 1884, but by 1891 work had begun on a huge school building across the street from the railroad station. It was these boys who printed the pamphlets for the first *supplica* in 1887, and all the *suppliche* that followed.

For the inaugural festival in 1887, two special trains brought visitors and what Italians still call "the authorities" in an hour from Naples to the new Valle di Pompeii station to participate in the three-day celebration, as the *armoniosa banda municipale* of Torre Annunziata played its heart out, a gift from the mayor of that city to his new neighbors. Longo describes the festivities with suitably flowery rhetoric (including *armoniosa banda municipale*):

> The first hour of the New Pompeii, of a city that rises again next to the ruins of the famous ancient pagan city, was struck on the memorable day of May 8, 1887. On that day a people that rises again had its baptism. And from that day began the history of this people that, illuminated by Religion, is born again to the benefits of modern civilization.
>
> A post office, a telegraph, railroad, printing press, newspapers, schools, nursery schools, a shelter for abandoned maidens, economical workers' houses, halls of labor, crafts, arts, painting, sculpture, bronze, marble, gilding, aqueducts of hygienic water, streets shaded by eucalyptus and plane trees, fountains, piazzas, behold the beginnings of civil life in a resurgent city.[9]

Longo's use of the word "resurgent" echoes the word that Italians used for unification: resurgence, *risorgimento*. His days as a student with Luigi Settembrini and the other founding fathers of the new Italy continued to shape his ambitions for the new community:

> Religion and Civilization, forever in agreement about their admirable intentions, to produce moral and material prosperity for the classes that are not so much disadvantaged as

FROM POMPEII

indigent, to fly to the aid of the weak, to take care of the education of abandoned innocence: this is the idea that informs the whole movement of the new things that outfit the New Pompeii; this is the idea that animates every one of our programs, whether it be new institutions or festivals.

For us, the Church is like a center of light that sheds its beneficent rays to illuminate the straight path that civilization should take. The rich man and the poor man, the artisan and the farmer, the newsman and the tradesman, in short, the people who rise up toward greater civility, in the light of the faith that comes from the Church, becomes naturally *moral* [the emphasis is Longo's].

And the proletarian, who sits at his poor table with his modest little family, comforted by the charity inspired by religion, educates his children to work, to patience, to morality, to faith, to the love of family, to the true love of country.[10]

Longo also puts the whole development of New Pompeii into a long historical perspective by comparing the feudal arrogance of the hapless landlord Alfonso Piccolomini with modern standards of good government, building on the historical ideas of Giambattista Vico, the remarkable eighteenth-century Neapolitan scholar who exerted great influence on the makers of the Italian Risorgimento:

In the seventeenth century, Alfonso Piccolomini, Prince of Valle, planted palisades in the River [Sarno] to power his mills at Scafati; these, along with blocking navigation, produced the stagnation of the waters, and hence malaria in all the villages of the Sarno, so that many settlements went extinct, including the ancient manor of Valle, first built in the first century at a kilometer's distance from the place in which the new Sanctuary arises.

Behold the give and take of the generations, of the ages, of the epochs, according to Vico. Who would ever have been able to imagine that this historic water of the Sarno, which fed the baths, fountains, buildings and squares of the ancient city of luxury, after 18 centuries would come down to quench the thirst of new Pompeiians, to beautify the Christian Pompeii that rises again, to enliven her fountains, which we inaugurate today, and refresh our Workers' Houses, our workshops, our Halls of Labor, and our Nursery Schools and our Orphanage?[11]

The economical workers' houses (visible at left in Figure 12.2) were another of Longo's remarkable innovations, inspired by contemporary experiments in Berlin and by contemporary efforts in Naples at *risanamento,* the city's "restoration to health" after successive epidemics of cholera, an urban renewal project that involved tearing down many of the city's worst slums and replacing them with houses that were spacious, airy, and well served by plumbing.[12] The original urban plan for New Pompeii called for five of these three-story, thirty-family apartment buildings, but only one was ever completed. Its five housing blocks are arranged in a quincunx pattern, originally with one large apartment and two smaller ones on each floor, every apartment equipped with its own kitchen and bathroom and supplied with running water, a rarity at the time. Furthermore, the tenants could apply their rent toward eventual purchase of the apartment; by this means, Longo envisioned transforming a group of day laborers into property owners.

In the 1930s the pairs of small apartments were all consolidated into single units, so that the economical workers' houses could hold only twenty families rather than thirty, but they were thus able to live in less cramped conditions. Structural damage from the 1980 earthquake forced evacuation of the building in 1985,

Valle di Pompei - Terme Valpompeiane "Fonte Salutare,,

12.2.   New Pompeii, Fonte salutare, Hotel Fonte Salutare, and economical workers' houses at left. Old postcard.

and it now stands empty as the city decides how and whether to renovate its interior. By contemporary standards the apartments are tiny; they were designed, after all, for "the proletarian, who sits at his poor table with his modest little family."

The remains of an ancient Pompeian laundry *(fullonica)* emerged from the foundation trench of the economical workers' houses, and Longo insisted that they remain visible after the building had gone up. In order to include modern science among the activities of New Pompeii, Longo also created a "Vesuvian observatory" as one of his benefactions.[13] His own "villino" near the archaeological site had a tower room with a splendid view of the volcano; its upper story is now a museum of volcanology and is named after the observatory's first curator, Giovanni Battista Alfano.[14] Longo's townhouse was torn down to expand the piazza in front of the sanctuary.

The establishment of New Pompeii had an immediate effect on the archaeological site, just at the time that mechanized transport began to increase the numbers of visitors exponentially. The old Rapillo inn was replaced by a modern hotel, the Diomede, named, of course, for the ancient suburban villa that still topped the list of things to see in Old Pompeii. Financed by two Swiss entrepreneurs, a rival establishment, the Hotel Suisse (Figure 12.3), went in across the main road to Naples, the Strada Reale ("Royal Road").[15] Wilhelm Jensen's 1904 novelette *Gradiva* describes the two inns as "the Dioscuri, Hotel Suisse and Hotel Diomed, which measured their power of attraction in a ceaseless, silent, but ferocious struggle."[16] However, the Hotel Suisse quickly earned a reputation as the best accommodation in town (it still survives as a restaurant for tourist groups). The Hotel del Sole

12.3.   Pompeii, Hotel Suisse, May 2013. Photo by author.

went up opposite a new entrance near the amphitheater, poised to serve both "Scavi" and "Santuario," the two poles of the new town. Not to be outdone, Longo himself sponsored the construction of a hotel directly across from the sanctuary. Not surprisingly, he called it the Albergo del Santuario.

In keeping with his own sense of history, personal as well as general, Longo put the sanctuary and its orphanage for abandoned girls under the protection of Saint Michael. He had long since decided that the angel who had guided him in his Spiritualist days had been a satanic figure, but for those two years in Naples, Longo might be better described as an eclectically Christian Spiritualist or an eclectically Spiritualist Christian who swore allegiance in good faith to Saint Michael and continued to attend Catholic Mass. After that, although he was a Dominican tertiary, institutionally Catholic, he continued to harbor Risorgimento ideas about politics and society. For all the complexities of his character and all the dramatic changes in his life, Longo held on to certain ideals with great consistency, including his devotion to Saint Michael and to the ideals of the Risorgimento and modern Italy.

In 1901 Pope Leo XIII declared the sanctuary of the Madonna of Pompeii (Figure 12.4) a major pontifical basilica, which turned it from a parish church in the Diocese of Nola into an extraterritorial property of the Vatican. With this elevation of the sanctuary to international status, Longo's triumph, and the triumph of his bold, progressive vision, must have seemed complete. But a change in popes would drastically alter the philanthropist's fortunes.

Leo's successor, Pius X, found the close connection between the sanctuary and its founder deeply suspicious. Money was pouring into Pompeii, and the pope wondered how much of it actually went to the benefit of the Madonna of the Rosary and Pompeii's other charitable institutions. In part, the pontiff's doubts involved matters of church authority. Longo was a layman, not a priest, and it was almost unheard of for a layperson to wield as

Pompei dall'aereo - Panorama generale

12.4.   New Pompeii, Sanctuary of the Madonna of the Rosary from the air, with ancient amphitheater in the background. Old postcard.

much power as he did over so extensive a group of religious institutions. Furthermore, in the opening years of the twentieth century, the church and the Italian state still operated as bitter adversaries. Writing as late as the 1940s, when Italy was supposedly one of the Allied powers, Longo's militantly Catholic biographer,

Luigi Spreafico, lists respect for the United States Constitution as one the pernicious ideas bandied about by the young Bartolo Longo's professors at the University of Naples. Like many Christian Democrats in Italy, Spreafico regarded the rigorous separation of church and state as anathema. Bartolo Longo's freedom of activity in the region of Pompeii struck Pius X as similarly suspect.

In part, the pope's animosity toward Longo was also a matter of regional prejudice; as a Venetian, Pius regarded southerners as far more corrupt than other citizens to the north (and this attitude is prevalent in Italy even today). In part, Pius was also reacting against the authority wielded in the sanctuary by the countess, who had taken charge of administering its finances in 1894. If a powerful layman invited suspicion, a volatile laywoman was even more doubtful. Finally, the sanctuary of New Pompeii was as subject as any human institution to the kinds of pressures to which institutions are always prone: gossip, jealousy, and intrigue. An unhappy associate had been only too delighted to report his dissatisfactions to an already wary pope. In 1905 Pius removed the founder and his wife from any association with the sanctuary's administration and subjected them to an official investigation run by three northern Italian cardinals who shared the pope's dim view of southerners in general and Bartolo Longo in particular. The name for this kind of inquiry was "inquisition." The sanctuary's administration reverted directly to the Vatican; in effect, Pius took it over.

For Longo, sensitive and high strung as ever, the inquisition was an agonizing ordeal that lasted until March of 1906, when he and the countess signed over the sanctuary and all of its institutions to the Vatican and were received at last by Pope Pius in Rome. The inquisition exonerated Longo entirely. The countess had clearly given generous amounts of money over the years to her two troubled sons, but she was a wealthy woman who had a great deal of her own money to give without dipping into the revenues of the sanctuary, where her daughter Giovanna worked as tirelessly as the countess and her husband had always done. The couple may have been exonerated by the inquisitors, but they were no longer in charge of the sanctuary. Since 1906 it has belonged to the Vatican in order to remove it as much as possible from local politics.

Longo's enemies came not only from the ranks of the church. In 1902 the Neapolitan archaeologist Antonio Sogliano, soon to become director of excavations for "old" Pompeii, wrote a scathing denunciation of his predecessor, Fiorelli, blaming him for "supine neglect of Pompeii's future," specifically for having allowed hotels to be constructed around the site and having listened more to Bartolo Longo than to his own superiors in the ministry (imagine listening to a charismatic philanthropist rather than to government bureaucrats!).[17] The expansion of New Pompeii, Sogliano thundered, was blocking and encroaching upon the excavation of ancient Pompeii and especially of its suburbs; Longo's discovery of a fuller's shop underneath his economical workers' houses is a case in point. The settlements of the living were hemming in the city of the dead, as we can see from a photograph of the sanctuary in Figure 12.4, where the amphitheater is visible just behind the huge church of the Madonna of the Rosary. Thus some archaeologists began to agitate for the dead.

Meanwhile, the list of New Pompeii's attractions increased once again. In 1900 Count Francesco De Fusco, the contessa's second son, dug a well behind his Art Nouveau villa on New Pompeii's main square. Workers dug down through ninety-six meters of soil and three successive layers of volcanic deposit before striking a trickle of water, enough, but only barely, to supply the household. An earthquake in 1906 must have shifted something underground and opened up a long-blocked artesian spring because on the afternoon of August 26, 1907, the feeble well behind the Palazzo De Fusco suddenly became a gusher twenty-five meters high, spouting at first shells, coral, sand, and soil and then a geyser of pure mineral water. Pompeii added another amenity for the enjoyment of its visitors: a mineral-water spa, the Fonte Salutare, the "Healthful Fountain." In 1914 the Palazzo De Fusco was turned into the Albergo Fonte Salutare (described in the 1926 revised edition of August Mau's guidebook to the site as "very good and clean," "sehr gut und sauber"). As Figure 12.2 shows , it was an elegant establishment, and guests could also admire the progressive architecture of the economical workers' houses in the next block.

Although they no longer administered the sanctuary of the Madonna of Pompeii, Bartolo Longo and the contessa continued their philanthropic work in Pompeii until their deaths, she at eighty-eight in 1924 and he at eighty-four in 1926. His last foundation was a home for the daughters of prisoners. In 1928, two years after the founder's death, New Pompeii was incorporated as its own city.

By that time, the number of pilgrims to the Madonna of Pompeii had become so numerous that work was undertaken from 1934 to 1938 to expand the basilica to its present dimensions; huge subsidiary buildings included the massive hotel that appears at left in Figure 12.4. Unusually for the time, it was executed in a neo-Baroque style that once again asserted its independence, artistic as well as social, political, and religious. In 1980 Pope John Paul II conferred on Bartolo Longo the title of "Blessed," the first step toward canonization. His onetime adversary, Pius X, had already been proclaimed a saint by Pope Pius XII in 1954.

Today the sanctuary of the Madonna of Pompeii not only is a magnet for pilgrims; situated in the exact center of town, it also provides a focus for modern Pompeii's social life in what is now called the Piazza Bartolo Longo.[18] The same earthquake that crumpled a wall of the House of the Vettii in Old Pompeii and undermined the stability of the economical workers' houses in New Pompeii also shifted the artesian channels that fed the Fonte

Salutare. A routine inspection in 1987 revealed that the principal spring was now contaminated by E. coli bacteria (probably from contact with fertilizer), while a second well, drilled when the spa was expanding its clientele, had begun to spew forth poisonous gases. No longer healthful, the Fonte Salutare was closed as a health hazard, its huge marble basin, stained red by years of contact with the iron-rich waters, now looming dry and silent in the center of a dilapidated public park. The Fonte Salutare Hotel had already been turned into the city hall in 1974, when a plan to expand the hotel and the facilities around the mineral spring fell through.[19] The Hotel del Santuario on the piazza's west side is still in operation.

Pompeii's charitable institutions have modified their mission with changing levels of education and prosperity, laws, and social norms. Nineteenth-century philanthropists favored putting disadvantaged children into institutions, and size was taken as an indication of success. At their peak, Longo's schools and children's homes housed 600 pupils. In the 1990s, however, Italian law maintained that smaller institutions were more effective and ordered the decentralization of existing orphanages so that none would have a population in excess of forty and most would become "case famigilia," houses that mimicked a family home as closely as possible. In 2000 the law changed again, this time to recommend keeping troubled children at home whenever possible. This meant the end of institutions like the gigantic, austere Istituto Sacro Cuore, the successor, built in the 1950s, to Bartolo Longo's home for the daughters of prisoners, founded at the end of his life. An orphanage and school for 180 pupils, managed by Dominican nuns, the Istituto Sacro Cuore sits directly opposite the amphitheater entrance to the archaeological site of Pompeii.

Now the property of the Italian government, the building is maintained by the Superintendency of Archaeology, though it is not easy to see how its forbidding institutional architecture can easily be adapted to any other purpose. The hostel for the sons of prisoners has become the Istituto Bartolo Longo, a private Catholic school under direct papal sponsorship and open to all students. Various other organizations share its spacious premises and make use of its theater. The institute's architecture, unlike the Soviet-style Sacro Cuore, is expansive in the traditional Neapolitan neoclassical style without being overbearing; it fits comfortably into the urban fabric of a city in which it was one of the very first important buildings. The Sanctuary of the Madonna of Pompeii continues to sponsor smaller institutions for young people, managed from a huge network of subsidiary buildings that back up to the archaeological site, as well as scattered projects throughout the larger urban area of Pompeii; Longo's concerns for the residents of the valley have not been forgotten.

For visitors, the two faces of Pompeii, "Scavi" and "Santuario" (the two terms that classify Pompeian licenses for souvenir booths) are two poles along the axis that was once called Strada Reale and is now called Via Plinio. Most of the visitors who come for the *supplica,* for example, also visit the archaeological site. Many of the people who come to the archaeological site also eventually wander into the town of Pompeii. No longer simply a side trip from Naples, Pompeii has become a destination in itself, and this is to a great extent due to the work of a lawyer named Bartolo Longo, who remembered the humanity of his tenants when they were dirty, poor, and uneducated and within a generation turned them into middle-class citizens of a united Italy. Because of him, Pompeii today is full of living people as well as the plaster ghosts of the dead.

13

The Social Role of
Tourist Cameos

Bartolo Longo was not the only person to think about ways to improve living conditions around the Bay of Naples in the nineteenth century. In 1805 a carver of coral and shell from Marseille, Paul Bartholomé Marin, set up a shop in Torre del Greco.[1] At the time, Torre del Greco was best known for ribbons of pasta and vats of tomato sauce drying in the sun, and the best cameos were made of carved agate in Germany. Shell was much easier to carve than stone, and in those days before industrial pollution the Bay of Naples had shells and coral in abundance, many of them visible on mosaics from Pompeii. Marin's business went well enough that he hired a Roman assistant, Pasinetti, and soon they were training their neighbors in Torre del Greco as specialized artisans. By the 1880s, thanks to their cleverly carved shell cameos and corals, the citizens of Torre del Greco had transformed themselves from subsistence farmers and fishermen into a whole range of participants in the new cameo trade: sculptors in miniature, jewelers, sales personnel, and shopkeepers, adapting skillfully to the nineteenth-century trends that broadened the aristocratic

Grand Tour into the bourgeois Cook's Tour.[2] A state-sponsored cameo and coral school was set up in Torre del Greco in 1887 to handle many of the same social problems that Bartolo Longo's institutions addressed in the Pompeii Valley.[3] The story of Torre del Greco and its cameos is an inspiring tale, but it is now, sadly, a tale with an uncertain ending. Environmental degradation has polluted the Bay of Naples, destroying its coral beds and the marvelous profusion of sea life that we see on Pompeian mosaics and hear about in eighteenth-century Neapolitan songs. The coral fishermen of Torre del Greco once brought up a seemingly endless supply of raw material; the fleet of little boats numbered in the hundreds. Now the artists on the Bay of Naples use shells and coral from the coast of Sicily and Asia. Cameo carving is an exacting art, but it does not pay particularly well except at the very top of the profession. Young people are reluctant to enter it. For people who cannot tell the difference between a real coral or cameo and its plastic imitation, made anywhere in the world but most probably China, the two-euro souvenir is more appealing than the one that costs two hundred. The myths depicted on the most elaborate cameos are no longer as familiar to the general public as they once were. But these cameos are not only souvenirs of Pompeii and the Bay of Naples: they are also memorials to and promoters of culture, art, history, and enlightened social policy. They, too, are a resource of inestimable value.

By the later nineteenth century, every stop on the Grand Tour of Italy had its own souvenir jewelry: Venice featured mosaics of tiny bits of Murano glass, set into filigree frames of gold or silver wire; Florence produced inlays of the hard stones known as *pietre dure,* an ancient art rediscovered by Florentine artisans in the sixteenth century; in Rome, micromosaics pictured Roman ruins or Saint Peter's; and the Bay of Naples specialized in carved coral, shell, and lava cameos. In every case the original inspiration came from a combination of ancient art (or Byzantine art, in the case of

Venice) and local artistic tradition, but the path from antiquity to the modern era has seldom run straight.

Souvenir jewelry has also tended to mimic the jewelry of the rich and powerful. In the case of Torre del Greco and its shell cameos, two elite models inspired artisans and tourists when the industry began to pick up speed: Queen Victoria, who ordered a cameo bracelet in 1861 to commemorate Prince Albert and started the fad in Britain; and the engraved gems of the royal collection in Naples. The royal cache of antiquities included both the Farnese gem collection and the treasures gleaned from the buried cities: a loaf of charred bread with a baker's mark from Herculaneum, metalwork, including what that early visitor Mr. Freeman called "a beautiful mascharron of metal, having the face of a cat, with a mouse in her mouth," ivories, glass, and wall paintings. However, as Mr. Freeman lamented:[4] "There are many other valuable curiosities, which I could not see, being lock'd up in the king's closet, and private apartments: such as medals, intaglia's, and cameo's." In 1751 another English visitor also noted that Herculaneum had yielded "a few good intaglios and cameos," but whether he saw them he does not report. He was much more exercised, as noted in Chapter 3, by the strange, uncouth quality of Roman wall painting.[5]

Almost all of these ancient "cameos," like the intaglios, were cut gems rather than cut shell and coral. The excavations at Pompeii also yielded a spectacular vase of blue and white cameo-cut glass, very much like the famous Portland Vase, which was known to Mr. Freeman and his contemporaries in Rome as the Barberini Vase (discovered in Rome, it did not come to England until 1784). Both "intaglia's" and "cameo's," whether carved in hard stone or softer glass and shell, required the special manual skill and sharp eyes of a miniaturist.

The Italian word *intaglio* simply means "cut in," and Italians apply the term both to wooden inlay work (which they also call *intarsia)* and to gems or cheaper glass imitations, whose design is carved into their surface, producing a negative image. Intaglio was already popular among the ancient Babylonians, who used the technique to decorate rings and the cylindrical seals they rolled across the clay of their bureaucratic documents as an official signature. From Babylon, the art of intaglio spread to the Minoan Cretans and Mycenaean Greeks in the Bronze Age, passing later on to the Etruscans, Greeks, and Romans. In all of these cultures, intaglio gems continued to serve as signets, pressed into clay or hot wax to provide official validation for documents or shipments of goods.

Cameos are carved in precisely the opposite way; they are raised positive designs rather than sunken negatives, and theirs is a much more recent history, just over two millennia. Many ancient gems are sculpted in a single color, like carnelian, prized for its deep russet shade and its ability to take a high polish. Cameos, intriguingly, were carved from hard stones that are naturally layered in contrasting colors, especially agate, with its strata of brown and white or brown and red. By carving through a variegated stone's contrasting layers, artists could produce striking color effects in bas-relief, and the Romans loved the result; they were as smitten with miniatures as they were by colossi.

Like so many of ancient Rome's luxury arts, the cutting of cameos seems to have been invented in Alexandria. Ancient Egyptian artisans had carved beautiful bowls from agate and other hard stones, but it was the Ptolemaic rulers of Hellenistic Alexandria and their refined courtiers who seem to have invented the idea of multicolored carved gems. From the beginning, the cameo technique seems to have been used especially for portraits, and there is some connection between the imagery of cameos and coins, which were an equally popular venue for miniature sculpture. Coins, by their very nature, were public images that circulated through every level of society, whereas gem portraits, tiny and personal, would have been visible only to the subject's closest associates. The Romans observed the same distinction between public and private imagery as the Ptolemies when they began commissioning cameos on their own. No Roman in the age of Julius Caesar or Augustus would have dared to portray himself as a god in Rome itself: as Caesar discovered on the Ides of March, it was dangerous enough to be suspected of wanting to be king. In Cleopatra's Alexandria, however, Marc Antony felt free to commission a cameo of himself as the ram-headed Egyptian god Zeus Ammon.[6]

In effect, contemporary shell cameos continue the same tradition by portraying a young woman in profile as a goddess: usually Venus or Flora, occasionally the virgin goddesses Diana or Minerva, all flattering references to the divine beauty (or in the case of Minerva, intelligence) of the women who will eventually wear them. The ideal profile of these carved goddesses has changed over time. Cleopatra may have been legendary for her charm and intelligence but not, Plutarch tells us, for her physical beauty, and her portraits bear out that assessment: Cleopatra's aquiline nose, above her receding chin, could charitably be called "important." It was rather her low, melodious voice, the biographer reports, which seduced everyone who heard her speak in the eight languages she commanded with ease, including ancient Egyptian and pointedly not including Latin.

When the first shell cameos began to be mass-produced in the Bay of Naples, the gods and goddesses on the gems and monumental sculpture of the royal collection provided a general guideline for classical beauty: a rounded, oval face; a long, straight nose; a small, Cupid's-bow mouth; and masses of elaborately dressed, curly hair. Nineteenth-century fashion favored a squarer, more robust face than the ancients admired, with a firm jaw and a slightly shorter, still straight nose rather like the features of the *Electra* statue in the Royal Collection. Cameos from the 1920s suddenly sported short, feathery, flapper hairstyles and upturned "French" noses, making their images of goddesses seem much more like charming human girls than immortal women. Some cameos were "dressed," *habillé*, in tiny necklaces, with marcasite or diamond pendants.

Other cameos reveled in their status as souvenirs by featuring dramatic eruptions of Vesuvius, with clouds of ash spilling over the Bay of Naples or the ruins of Pompeii.

The most ambitious cameo artists looked to two ancient works in Naples as a challenge to their skill. One was the cameo-cut glass vessel pulled from the earth in Pompeii. The other work, though ancient, has almost certainly spent its entire life above ground, passed reverently from owner to owner for more than two millennia. This is the agate cup now known as the Tazza Farnese, created, in all probability, as a diplomatic gift from Alexandria to Rome (that is, from a Ptolemaic ruler to some member or members of the Senate) as the fates of those two cities became more and more closely entwined in the second century B.C.

Significantly, the Farnese cameo collection also includes "modern" sixteenth-century shell cameos showing people in contemporary dress. These were probably carved in Rome, where the Farnese family had begun gathering its own stable of talented sculptors specializing in miniatures in a variety of media, ranging from the hard substance of gemstones and rock crystal to softer materials like glass and shell. With their ancient form and modern content, these Farnese cameos may well draw their inspiration from a famous series of stuccos in the Vatican Palace, executed by Raphael and his workshop for Pope Leo X, the former Cardinal Giovanni de' Medici, in 1518 and restored by Pope Paul III, the former Cardinal Alessandro Farnese, in 1534.

The Farnese cameos, the Tazza Farnese, the Farnese Casket, and the rest of the Farnese collection came to Naples in 1734 with Charles III, who had inherited it all, statues, paintings, gems, textiles, and decorative arts, from his mother, Elisabetta Farnese. His archaeological excavations began shortly thereafter, and as new "intaglios and cameos" emerged from the soil of Herculaneum and Pompeii, they were funneled into the royal collection at Portici; visitors, needless to say, hoped to see both the old Farnese treasures and the new finds.

Eighteenth-century visitors to the buried cities often took real antiquities home with them, as did many a nineteenth-century visitor, especially in the early decades of the century. William Hamilton supplemented his meager income by supplying collectors with "Etruscan vases." It was much more difficult, however, to make off with finds from Herculaneum or Pompeii, which were royal property. Until there was a town of Pompeii, the Rapillo inn was the only place to buy souvenirs near the site, and Torre del Greco made the most of that lack. Today the vendors outside the site of Pompeii itself (the ones with "scavi" licenses) purvey both real cameos and plastic Chinese imitations and will still gladly tell gullible tourists that what they have on display are real Etruscan vases, just as Norbert Hanold, the love-struck protagonist of Wilhelm Jensen's 1904 novelette, *Gradiva,* is convinced that the proprietor of the Hotel del Sole has sold him a golden brooch snatched from the very ruins of Pompeii (see Chapter 18). For the archaeologist he purports to be, Hanold is comically clueless; his beloved, Zoë Bertgang, takes one look at the piece and assures him that "it probably did not exist until this year."[7]

14

Pierre-Auguste Renoir

In October 1881 Pierre-August Renoir had just turned forty. For nearly twenty years he had struggled to make a career for himself as a painter in Paris, with only indifferent success. It was time, he decided, to pay a visit to Italy.[1] A self-taught artist from a humble background, Renoir was a far cry from the average Grand Tourist. It was far too late for an Italian journey to succeed in putting a veneer of refinement on his eccentric behavior or his rough manners; the man was what he was. Furthermore, to most contemporary eyes, his modern way of painting flew in the face of the classical tradition. Unlike the painters, sculptors, and architects who studied in Rome at the École des Beaux-Arts and showed their work in the Parisian salons, Renoir avoided portraying scenes from classical mythology or great moments in history; he turned his attention instead to ordinary people doing ordinary things, to ordinary objects. He made these people and things extraordinary by building up their forms in thick daubs of paint, layer upon layer of brilliant, unexpected colors piled on in curious combinations, and this, too was a far cry from what Parisians regarded as classical procedure. His Beaux-Arts colleagues perfected their classical figures with the help of transparent glazes and minute brushstrokes, trying to make their work look as if human hands had never touched it. But Renoir created big, coarse-textured canvases. What possible response could a person like this have made to the Old Masters and ancient art of Italy except to repeat what the great neoclassical sculptor Antonio Canova said when he finally beheld the marbles Lord Elgin had stripped from the Parthenon: "The naked figures are real flesh, in all its beauty"?[2]

Yet beneath the large-grained, everyday surface of Renoir's paintings was a strong classical current. It showed in the careful placement of his figures; his great daubs of paint might look random, but they were put down with consummate care. Renoir had taught himself painting by studying the Old Masters, copying the great works in the Louvre until he understood how an almost imperceptible slash of red across the white shirt of Baldassare Castiglione jolted Raphael's gray-toned portrait to life; how Nicolas Poussin knit his colors together into a web of reflections, so that every human figure had a minute spot of paint on its nose that matched whatever it was wearing; how Titian could make big slabs of paint resolve magically at a distance into forms in space. When Renoir adapted the Impressionists' experiments with color to his own layered method of painting, he continued to observe a rigorous classical harmony among his colors and forms that was worthy of the Old Masters. Artistically, in fact, Renoir wanted to be neither a standard academic salon painter nor what he termed a "revolutionary," and least of all an Impressionist. A tour around Italy might well give his individual style an added touch of classical cachet to drive a further wedge between himself and the "revolutionaries" and thereby increase the value of his work on the Parisian market. In addition, it might provide this keenly intelligent but odd man another point of contact to help him fit into the higher reaches of French society, where the best hopes for future commissions lay.

However carefully Renoir may have thought out the potential social and financial repercussions of his trip, he could never have predicted what would happen once he relocated from a dark, rainy Paris winter to the light of Italy, with only a swift journey by train to separate the two realities. For a man who lived through his eyes, the colors of Italy, right from the beginning, were pure ecstasy. His letters speak rapturously about the sunlight, both the real sunlight that saturated the landscape and the sunlight that shone forth in Italian paintings from every era.

When he finally saw Raphael's frescoes in Rome, this experience, like his experience of Italian light, caught him completely by surprise. His letters from Venice suggest that he still nourished a certain amount of skepticism about Raphael, who was, after all, the idol of Parisian academic painters. But then he saw the work: "I'm like the kids at school . . . and I'm 40 years old. I have seen Raphael in Rome. The work is quite beautiful and I should have seen it long before now. It is full of knowledge and wisdom. He never tries, like me, to do the impossible. But the work is beautiful. I love Ingres more for oil painting. But the frescoes! They are amazing for simplicity and grandeur."[3] Somehow it is hard to believe that he could ever have looked at Raphael's *Portrait of Baldassare Castiglione* in the Louvre in quite the same way once he returned to Paris.

From the mists of Venice and the golden light of Rome, Renoir went on to Naples. He painted the Riviera di Chiaia one resplendent morning and then again in the evening (Figure 14.1); in his joyous hands, even the gray, solemn mass of Vesuvius glows a benign lavender over a tranquil pastel bay.

When he first saw the ancient frescoes from Pompeii in the National Museum in Naples, Renoir would use the very same terms, *grandeur* and *simplicité,* that he had used for Raphael— he now understood, in an immediate, physical way, the intimate

14.1. Pierre Auguste Renoir (1841–1919), *The Bay of Naples with Vesuvius in the Background,* 1881 (oil on canvas). Sterling and Francine Clark Art Institute, Williamstown, MA / The Bridgeman Art Library.

connection between ancient Roman art and the art of the Renaissance master. As he wrote from Naples:

> Here I can do what will be impossible once I come back to Paris. I have perpetual sun and I can erase and begin again as often as I like. There is nothing to do here but learn, and in Paris one simply has to content oneself with a little. I have studied the Naples Museum a lot; the paintings from Pompeii are extremely interesting from every point of view, and otherwise I stay in the sun, not to make outdoor portraits, but by driving myself and keeping watch on myself, I think I will achieve that grandeur and simplicity that the ancients have. Raphael cannot have worked without having studied

the sun because his frescoes are filled with it. And so by looking at the outdoors I end up not seeing anything but the grand harmonies, and worry no longer about the little details that tinge the sun rather than setting it afire.[4]

What Renoir discovered in Italy, therefore, was the way that classical style was saturated in light and color, working together in ways he could never have imagined in the oblique northern sunlight of Paris. Moreover, because he drew and painted as he traveled, reveling in the sunlight, his work began to reflect at first his bedazzled impressions and then his considered thoughts about color, painting, composition, and the enigma that had driven him to Italy in the first place: the human figure.

Even something as simple as a Pompeian still life (Figure 14.2) excited him, allowing him to commune artist to artist with the ancients, like Raphael four hundred years before him, as if the

14.2.   Still life from Pompeii. Museo Nazionale, Naples. Photo by author.

14.3. Pierre Auguste Renoir, *The Onions,* ca. 1881 (oil on canvas). Sterling and Francine Clark Art Institute, Williamstown, MA / The Bridgeman Art Library.

passage of millennia meant nothing. Who better than he could appreciate both the immediacy of the Pompeian painters' humble subject matter as well as their ingenious application of color? Ancient painters often worked in diagonal sweeps of the brush, building up their figures by cross-hatching that ran through a surprisingly large range of colors as they modeled up from dark to light. Renoir had always painted in thick layers of widely varying hue. Now he tried applying the same diagonal technique to a handful of onions and garlic arranged on a crumpled paper in his room (Figure 14.3). As a result, Fronia Wissman observes, "these onions are bursting with three-dimensionality."[5] They also contain a whole rainbow of colors, just like the Pompeian still-life paintings that share Renoir's same sense of juicy vitality—the Italian term for this genre, *natura morta,* "dead nature," has nothing to do with the plump, brilliant fruits and vegetables we see on Pompeian walls and on Renoir's delectable canvas.

Renoir's background has a "distressed" look as if it, too, has undergone the eruption of Vesuvius and spent two millennia underground, whereas the vegetables have been gathered moments before. But then the Pompeian paintings present the same enigmatic contrast between worn wall surface and what still looks, after all these centuries, like fresh, succulent food, still tempting us to reach for it as birds were said in ancient times to peck at the painted grapes of the Greek artist Zeuxis.

Vegetables, of course, could be made to sit still without complaining. People were another challenge altogether (as Zeuxis, the great painter of grapes, well knew). A significant source of Renoir's income had come from portraits, but he found them difficult. In the years before his Italian trip, he had tried to adapt the Impressionists' scintillating surfaces from landscapes to bodies, both in portraits and in figure studies, but the results must not have satisfied him. Now Italy gave him important new stimuli— Raphael and the ancients might be long dead, but they spoke to him, painter to painter, through their work. By looking closely at the ancient paintings in the Naples Museum, Renoir could see how a lattice of tiny brushstrokes, the same technique he saw in ancient still lifes, could still add up to create a substantial figure (Figure 14.4). In the case of Raphael, who combined rigorous training in the traditional craft of Italian painting with an unusual openness to ancient technique, Renoir could see that same combination of oblique strokes and crosshatching brought to its pinnacle of proficiency.

According to Renoir's son Jean, the *Blonde Bather* of 1881 (Figure 14.5) was painted in Naples, its subject the artist's traveling companion during the Italian trip and thereafter: his future wife (and Jean's mother) Aline Charigot.[6] Now, at last, the restless Frenchman found a way to combine luminous color with a weight and a presence that are almost sculptural. The contrast between the definite shadow cast by the bather's arm and the soft texture of the arm

14.4.   Diagonal painting on an ancient Roman wall painting from Pompeii. Museo Nazionale, Naples. Photo by author.

itself (not to mention the misty, "impressionistic" background) shows how the new "Pompeian" Renoir melded with the old Parisian Renoir.

Another quality of this nude also seems to reflect its author's direct contact with ancient painting: its radiance. The final touch for Pompeian wall decoration involved impregnating the painted plaster with melted wax and then polishing the surface of the wall to the sheen of a mirror. Two thousand years and one volcanic cataclysm later, many of these walls still survive remarkably well, as smooth and cool to the touch as polished stone.

14.5. Pierre Auguste Renoir, *Blonde Bather,* 1881 (oil on canvas). Sterling and Francine Clark Art Institute, Williamstown, MA / The Bridgeman Art Library.

To the paint itself, this encaustic treatment lends a supernal glow, especially to light flesh tones. The painted goddesses of Pompeii often seem to beam as brightly as the moon (Figure 14.6), and it is not surprising to find the same technique used for early Christian images of the Madonna, like the "Imago antiqua" in

14.6. "Radiant" encaustic painting from Pompeii. Museo Nazionale, Naples. Photo by author.

the Roman church of Santa Francesca Romana, a sixth-century encaustic painting whose sublime color still gleams through all the damage of time and overpainting.

Renoir achieves his luminosity in a radically different way, by applying linseed oil to a rough surface rather than rubbing tallow into smoothed and polished plaster, but in the end his *Blonde Bather* glows as brightly as a Pompeian Venus.

But Pompeii is not the only influence on this beautiful figure. She also reflects Renoir's dazzled response to two Italian Renaissance artists. Aline's Titian hair and buxom figure clearly hark back to the great Venetian (and to another later admirer of both Titian and women, Peter Paul Rubens). However, the painting's radiant modeling also owes a profound debt to Raphael, especially after the latter's own exposure to ancient painting in Rome.

For the wealthy banker Agostino Chigi, a brilliant merchant with an equally sharp eye for attractive women, Raphael painted the nymph Galatea (Figure 14.7), scudding over the waves on a shell pulled by dolphins, caught at the very moment when the cupids are shooting at her with the arrows of love. Agostino was a Sagittarius; the more arrows the cupids aim at her heart, the merrier. Galatea herself clearly descends from ancient Roman images of Venus on the half shell, like the goddess who lends her name to Pompeii's House of the Marine Venus.

As the Marine Venus and the patroness of Pompeii, she protects both the owners of this wealthy house and their city, lavishing fertility on the garden and affection on the household. She often spread her beneficent influence over private spaces like this, either opulent gardens like her domain in Pompeii or more modest, more public spaces like a little paved courtyard on Rome's Caelian Hill, preserved when the whole little neighborhood was built over by a fourth-century Christian church.[7]

Neither Raphael nor Renoir saw the House of the Marine Venus; it was excavated in the 1960s. We do not know which Marine Venus or Venuses Raphael saw in the ancient ruins of Rome, but he must have seen them, just as Renoir must have stopped in to see Raphael's Galatea during his visit to Rome. Renoir's letters do not mention the paintings on the walls of Pompeian houses, but only the paintings preserved in the archaeological museum; it would not have been hard for him to reach Pompeii, but we cannot know for certain what piercing,

14.7. Raphael, *Galatea*. Rome: Villa Farnesina, 1512. Alessandro Angeli, 2003 for Art Resource, NY.

ancient ultramarine blue inspired his own piercing cobalt blues. The same goes for the voluptuous vision of women and water. Unlike Raphael and the artists of Pompeii, who designed and executed large-scale frescoes, Renoir had less of an opportunity to "consult" with Roman painters about how to lay out a painted

14.8.   Pierre Auguste Renoir, *The Large Bathers,* 1884–1887 (oil on canvas).
Philadelphia Museum of Art / The Mr. and Mrs. Carroll S. Tyson Jr.
Collection, 1963 / The Bridgeman Art Library.

wall as if it were a work of architecture, but he certainly knew
how to lay out a canvas with a rigor of composition that was almost architectural.

Seven years after his short, life-changing Italian trip, Renoir
returned to the theme of women bathing in a landscape (Figure
14.8). Mary Cassatt decried these figures in 1913 as "abominable
paintings" of "enormously fat red women with very small heads"—
that is, with perfect classical proportions. Later critics have
echoed her opinion. Nonetheless, Renoir's *Bathers* of 1887, luxuriating amid the vibrant cobalt tones of the water and the lushness
of the landscape, deserve a more insightful analysis than Cassatt's
summary dismissal, which has been seconded by more recent
critics like Kirk Varnedoe and Linda Nochlin (whereas Picasso,
another visitor to Pompeii, owned a big Renoir nude and painted

his own *Bather* in 1921). These *Bathers* not only reveal a remarkable experience of paint and the act of painting but also echo a complex, ecstatic memory: of Pompeii, of Naples, of Titian, and of Raphael's *Galatea,* herself the echo of an ancient Roman Venus on a half shell.

15

The Legacy of August Mau

By the late nineteenth century, Pompeii had begun to outstrip
Naples as a tourist destination (the 1884 cholera epidemic in Naples, which killed 14,000 people, may also have helped tilt the
balance). John Murray's 1892 *Handbook for travellers in southern
Italy and Sicily,* for example, recommended that visitors spend six
days on the Bay of Naples in order to see all the "Principal sights,
when time is limited." The first day is devoted not to Naples itself
but to an excursion to Pompeii. The guidebook assumes that the
traveler will take the train:

The entrance to the ruins faces the stat[ion]. Adm[ission].
2 fr[anc]s., which includes the attendance of an official compulsory guide. On Sundays free, without a guide. After the
first visit, the traveller who wishes to explore the ruins at his
leisure will find it best to go alone. No attention should be
paid to officious persons who offer their services outside.
Tickets of admission for a month, with permission to sketch,
copy, measure, &c. can be obtained by artists, or bonâ fide

students of art, at the secretary's bureau in the museum, on application to the director, Signor Ruggiero. . . . The gates close at sundown.[1]

As for recommended reading, the *Handbook* is a creature of its own era: "For a graphic description of the life of the city, and the eruption which destroyed it, there is nothing like Bulwer's 'Last Days of Pompeii.'"[2] The phrasing "there is nothing like Bulwer" is artfully diplomatic. It offers no judgment of quality whatsoever.

With its recommendation that the visitor to Pompeii be steeped in historical fiction rather than sober scholarship, Murray's *Handbook* is evidently written for an English-speaking Cook's tourist rather than a Grand Tourist, for whom the Italians are perhaps even more of an alien race than they were to the Dilettanti of the eighteenth century. It recounts the history of the House of the Centenary (the home of the painting with Vesuvius and Bacchus clothed in grapes) with almost anthropological detachment:

On the 25th of Sept. 1879, the Neapolitans, with a somewhat grim sense of humour and more than questionable taste, celebrated the eighteen hundredth anniversary of the destruction of this unfortunate city by a fête amidst the ruins. A gay crowd of nearly 7000 persons circulated in the streets, and bazaars and refreshments were served by maidens dressed in the supposed costume of Pompeian times. Several houses were excavated in honour of the occasion, the most interesting of which is the Casa del Centenario in the Strada di Nola, where the [statue of the] Faun and Wineskin was found. Another excavation revealed the shop of a seed merchant and dealer in singing birds. It contained cages with drinking cups, skeletons of various warblers, and carbonized remains of seed. The expense of this singular exhibition vastly exceeded the sum realized by entrance fees.[3]

German tourists, on the other hand, could arm themselves with a guidebook written by August Mau, who knew as much about the site as anyone in the nineteenth century. Originally trained as a theologian, Mau received a doctorate in theology from the University of Kiel in 1863, but poor health led him to leave Germany for Rome in 1872. There he took a position at the German Archaeological Institute, where he began studying Pompeian inscriptions with the great Theodor Mommsen (the only historian to have won the Nobel Prize in literature for his scholarly work). This research took Mau to Pompeii itself, where he worked closely with the "Pope," Giuseppe Fiorelli, carefully recording the graffiti, inscriptions, and wall paintings that emerged with progressive excavation of the site. Unlike many of his contemporaries, especially in Germany (where the Greeks were regarded as a variety of proto-Germans), Mau was convinced that Roman art had developed as an independent tradition in its own right rather than as an unthinking imitation of Greek originals. To illustrate this contention, he published a magisterial study of Pompeian wall painting, *Geschichte der dekorativen Wandmalerei in Pompeji* (History of Decorative Wall-Painting in Pompeii) in 1882, followed by *Pompeji in Leben und Kunst* (Pompeii in Life and Art) in 1900, a vivid reconstruction of daily life in the buried city. His *Führer durch Pompeji* (Guide through Pompeii), first published in 1893, became one of the standard guides to the site.

Under Fiorelli's directorship, Pompeian paintings and mosaics were no longer removed to the royal collection but left in situ so that scholars and tourists alike could drink in the atmosphere of a whole series of ancient houses, all of them somewhat alike but each one also engagingly different, imbued with its own personality. Fiorelli also removed the famous "Cave canem" ("Beware of the Dog") mosaic from the archaeological museum and restored to its original site in the entrance of the House of the Tragic Poet, where it quickly became one of the most popular attractions in

Pompeii. By this time, moreover, modern viewers had made their peace with ancient Roman artistic style.

They were helped in this endeavor by the enduring popularity of the ancient architectural writer Marcus Vitruvius Pollio, a Campanian catapult maker for Julius Caesar, who went on to receive a pension from Augustus's sister Octavia and may have served as the head of waterworks for the city of Rome. In his old age, Vitruvius wrote a comprehensive treatise on his profession and dedicated it to Augustus, including a detailed written account of the Roman painting technique, which he discusses in the seventh of his *Ten Books on Architecture.* Wall painting, to his mind, was as important to the design and construction of a house as its walls, floors, doors, and roofing. As a true architect, he begins his instructions with the proper way to prepare a wall, thus allowing his readers to follow the creation of an ancient Roman painting from the first rough undercoat of plaster to the wax fixative that gave painted walls their final gleaming finish. Here, as often, the standards that Vitruvius imposes for good workmanship are far higher than what Roman builders usually put into practice. A truly durable wall, he insists, requires one layer of rough plaster, three of sand mortar, and three of marble plaster before the painters start their work; most Roman builders settled for a good deal less.

The plaster itself was made of lime and water mixed with sand, powdered gypsum, crushed terra cotta, and powdered travertine or marble dust, and the pasty mixture was spread over an underpinning of reeds tied together in bundles. Vitruvius, never one to spare any expense in writing for an emperor, prefers horsetail for the reeds and silk for their ties and strongly recommends marble over gypsum to give plaster walls a bright white sheen.

Vitruvius also tells us that the ancient Romans applied their color to fresh, wet plaster; their wall paintings, then, were true frescoes, although the way that painters went about their work was somewhat different. He supplies instructions for making pigments, which were derived for the most part from powdered minerals and plants. He also tells us plainly what we can see by observation: that the most prized color for paint in the ancient Roman world was a brilliant red made from powdered cinnabar. This ore, mercury sulfite, is the secret ingredient that produced the famous "Pompeian red," a deep, rich scarlet that delighted eighteenth-century visitors as much as it had delighted their forebears in imperial Roman times. Cinnabar was rare and expensive, found in an iron-rich region near Ephesus in Asia Minor and in Spain. The stone bled beads of mercury whenever miners struck it with their pickaxes; when they baked it in kilns, drops of mercury clung to the steam that escaped. Once separated from its content of quicksilver, Vitruvius asserted, the stone was "tender and feeble," eager to drink up every drop of moisture when it was applied to wet plaster and create a powerful bond with the mortar. But its glorious color could not bear direct exposure to sunlight without turning black. Hence the practical Vitruvius recommended that homeowners use it "as sparingly as medicine" and only for interior rooms. For open, exposed spaces like courtyards and dining rooms he instead recommended red ochre, which produced a less intense but cheaper and more durable hue.

The other elements Vitruvius describes as part of the ancient painter's palette are also the predominant colors we see in Pompeian painting. Black could be made from charred resin mixed with glue or, barring that, ash from a combination of wood shavings and pitch pine. White came from lead oxide. True blue (what he calls "Armenian blue") was made from powdered lapis lazuli and cost nearly as much as cinnabar red. Another blue derived from "Indian indigo." The best green came from powdered malachite. Yellow ochre occurred widely in central Italy; it could be powdered or baked until it turned red (the same hue modern painters know as "burnt sienna"). When vinegar was added, it turned purple. A number of the red walls in Pompeii today were probably yellow to begin with; their yellow ochre pigment turned red in the last pyroclastic surges that struck the city. The original proportion of red to yellow walls was probably about fifty-fifty, and only the best of these were cinnabar red.

Many homeowners, however, opted instead for cheaper colors, like the blue made from copper sulfate, which eventually turns green. We can see the results of their economizing in the occasional brackish tones of painted seas and skies. Weld, a plant, yielded a cheaper yellow for dyers and painters, and the northern European herb called woad provided another kind of cheap blue.

Vitruvius also divulges the secret of the glossy finish that survives on so many Pompeian walls, their painted surface as smooth and reflective as colored marble: he tells us that the painted plaster wall was sealed with melted wax in a technique he called "encaustic," a Greek word for "burning in"; we continue to use the same term today.

Vitruvius, however, may be less concerned with the technique of painting than he is with its purpose. Just after he has presented the basic principles of plasterwork and before he turns to grounds and pigments, he devotes a chapter and a half of his seventh book to "correctness in painting." He follows Aristotle's lead in declaring that the task of art is to imitate nature, but he does more than this: he insists that such imitation and therefore art have a moral effect on artist and viewer alike. Art that imitates nature's sovereign principles is good for the eyes and the soul; art that strays too far into fantasy, on the other hand, is aesthetically and morally pernicious, and modern art, to his mind, has veered dangerously into the realms of uncontrolled imagination (Figure 15.1): "For monsters are now painted in frescoes rather than reliable images of definite things. Reeds are set up in place of columns, as pediments, little scrolls, striped with curly leaves and volutes; candelabra hold up the figures of aediculae, and above the pediments of these, several tender shoots, sprouting in coils from roots, have

15.1. "Depraved" Pompeian painting in situ in Pompeii. Photo by author.

little statues nestled in them for no reason, or shoots split in half, some holding little statues with human heads, some with the heads of beasts."[4]

As with every subject Vitruvius covers, there is method in this outburst about modern art. By his own admission, he wrote the

Ten Books on Architecture to supply Emperor Augustus with firm criteria for judging art and architecture at a time when Rome faced several challenges at once: influence from a host of sophisticated cultures, huge advances in building technology, and, as a direct result, enthusiastic experimentation in every field from construction to literary style.[5] His own book is one long experiment in which he tests the possibilities of elevating architecture from a craft to a liberal art, of writing about his subject in a comprehensive, philosophical way, of applying the Latin language to a theoretical treatment of a subject, architecture, which had never received a theoretical treatment on such a scale ever before—in any language. But experiments, Vitruvius contends, must have their limits, too, and that is why he has set down those for good painting: "Minds beclouded by feeble standards of judgment are unable to recognize what exists in accordance with authority and the principles of correctness. Neither should pictures be approved that are not likenesses of the truth, nor, if they are made elegant though art, is that any reason why favorable judgment should immediately be passed on them, not unless their subjects follow sound principles without interference."[6]

The fact that Vitruvius took such pains to opine on modern art suggests that a larger discussion of the subject must have been taking place in his own time, two generations before the eruption of Vesuvius. In fact, we can see evidence of how these two contrasting styles, the "good" old realistic style and the "depraved," fantastic modern style, developed in the paintings of Pompeii. August Mau would eventually identify four different, chronologically ordered, styles of Pompeian painting, and his system is often followed today.[7] Mau's work is one of the supremely important moments in the study of Pompeii, but after a century of scrutiny his scheme has been shown to present two major problems. First, because it is restricted to Pompeii, it ends with the eruption of Vesuvius, whereas the Romans continued painting for centuries, and the Pompeian tradition is not in fact any different from the tradition of Rome because the same artists were often at work in both cities. Furthermore, the lines between Mau's Second, Third, and Fourth Styles are not always clear and ultimately become a matter of individual judgment; in fact, as we will soon see, Vitruvius includes Mau's Second and Third Styles in a single category. Mau devised his system of stylistic analysis to help determine the age of Pompeian buildings; now there are more accurate methods to do so, including chemical analysis and analysis of the paintings' underlying masonry.

A room in the big, opulent House of the Faun (Figure 15.2) provides a perfect example of what Vitruvius describes as the

15.2.   First Style wall decoration from the House of the Faun, Pompeii. Photo by author.

15.3. Second Style wall decoration from the House of the Faun, Pompeii. Photo by author.

oldest kind of interior décor (what Mau would call the First Style, dating from the Hellenistic period and ending somewhere around 150–125 B.C.): "The ancients who established the beginnings of painting plaster first imitated the varieties and placement of marble veneers, then of cornices and the various designs of ochre inlay."[8] The room seems, in fact, to be decorated with colored marble panels rather than plaster. At the time, a real inlaid wall would have been prohibitively expensive; in the later years of the Roman Empire, the trade in colored marble had become so widespread that the wealthiest houses (and of course the imperial family) could boast real inlay decoration, called *opus sectile,* or "cut work."

FROM POMPEII

Most of the rooms in the House of the Faun and in many other Pompeian houses (including, famously, the dining room of the Villa of the Mysteries) are painted in what looks like the next stage in Vitruvius's historical scheme: "Later they entered a stage in which they also imitated the shapes of buildings, and the projection into space of columns and pediments, while in open spaces like exedrae [elaborate public benches], because of the extensive wall space, they painted stage sets, in the tragic, comic or satiric style, and adorned their walkways, because of their extensive length, with varieties of landscape . . . with the likenesses of the gods or the skillfully arranged narrations of myths, such as the Trojan battles, or the wanderings of Ulysses."[9]

Mau classifies systems of fictive architecture and landscapes as typical of the Second Style, dating from 150 B.C. to about 30 B.C. (Figure 15.3), and relegates the more extravagant theatrical effects to a Third Style, which prevailed from the time of Augustus up to the earthquake of 63 (Figure 15.4).

Pompeii also preserves abundant examples of the "depraved" style that Vitruvius so vocally deplores. Like his decadent contemporaries, modern viewers have usually found the most fanciful compositions the most irresistible, what Mau defined as the fourth Pompeian style. What would Vitruvius have thought, for example, about the exquisite little miniatures sketched on Pompeian walls (Figure 15.5) or the little black-background friezes from the dining room of the House of the Vettii, with butterfly-winged Psyche figures shopping for wine, flowers, and perfume, flirting with storekeepers who are all little cupids? "Now these things do not exist nor can they exist nor have they ever existed," Vitruvius thunders, but in fact they do exist—we can see them!—and they are captivating.

As a guide to Pompeii, however, August Mau was as thorough and correct and scholarly as could be. He would not have recommended Edward Bulwer for a graphic reconstruction of

15.4. Third Style painting from Pompeii. Naples, Museo Nazionale. Photo by author.

the ancient city; in fact, he provided for that need himself with his six-hundred-page, richly illustrated *Pompeji in Leben und Kunst.*

For visitors who wanted a more portable reconstruction of ancient Pompeii to take around the site with them, Luigi Fischetti, a professor of architecture at the University of Naples, provided "then" and "now" visions of the site's buildings in 1907, described in a disarming, largely (but not completely) correct English:

After having roamed for several hours among the wonderful and immense ruins of unburied Pompeii, it often happens

15.5. Fourth Style miniature from Pompeii. Museo Nazionale, Naples. Photo by author.

to the hurried visitor to abandon them, wearied out and not wholly satisfied. His mind becomes almost confused among such a mass of remains which speak nevertheless so powerfully to the mind of the learned: he found it difficult, in a flying visit, even if assisted by an eloquent cicerone, to pause a while in order to reconstruct ideally on the heaps of stones before him, monuments, temples, and ancient edifices, and to imagine the customs and life carried on therein.

The house of the Wettii [for Italians, *w* is really a double *v*] is among all the houses of Pompeii the one that attracts in a special manner the visitor's attention, and justly so, because even if the atrium and the misting part of the portico have not been reconstructed as would have been the case, had the excavations been done in our days, it is so coquette, so full of life and the freshenend and variety of ist decorations as to produce the illusion of our being transported back to the life lived there two thousand years ago and we imagine we must meet some of its wealthy and gay citizens in peplum and rich toga.

FROM POMPEII

16

Crown Prince Hirohito
of Japan

When Crown Prince Hirohito of Japan sailed into the port of Naples on July 10, 1921, he arrived aboard a 16,000-ton battleship. The *Katori* was the flagship of the Japanese imperial fleet, and this choice of transport was designed not only to make an impression on European heads of state, though that was certainly part of the plan. It was also designed to address serious concerns about the young man's safety. As in the rest of the world, modern ideas had begun to penetrate into tradition-minded Japan, including doubts about the emperor's immortality and about monarchy itself as a form of government. (He would escape an attempted assassination not long after this trip.) Furthermore, Hirohito's father, Yoshihito, the Taishō emperor, had begun to show signs of serious physical and mental instability; to preserve the myth of an imperial house descended from the sun goddess herself, a quick succession from incapacitated father to young son might have to take place. In pressing the international trip on the empress, who resisted sending her son off to the West, the influential courtier Matsukata Masayoshi put as positive a face as he could on a deeply troubled—and troubling—situation: "There may never be another time like this to inquire into the reasons for the popular movements and intellectual unrest that are occurring right before our eyes. This is a great chance for the crown prince to observe personally, at first hand, the rise and fall of the power of many states."[1]

Italy would be Prince Hirohito's final European stop on a journey that had already included Singapore, Ceylon, Cairo, Malta, Gibraltar, 24 days in Britain, 26 in France, 5 in Belgium, and 5 in the Netherlands. Importantly for the imperial image, the stop in Gibraltar had included an appointment with an agent of the Savile Row tailor Henry Poole and Co., who wired the prince's measurements ahead to London so that Hirohito could be met on arrival in England with a set of uniforms (lieutenant colonel in the Japanese navy and major in the Japanese army), tweed golfing suits, white flannels, and dinner suits (Figure 16.1). Hence, when the twenty-year-old prince strode down the gangplank in Naples, he did so impeccably styled "to the English fashion" like all of the most refined visitors.[2]

In Rome, King Victor Emmanuel III took his young colleague in hand and personally escorted the young prince around the Forum as he noted that Italy's own Caesars had also been regarded as divine. Victor Emmanuel knew all too well that his family enjoyed no such privilege; the country had long since become a hotbed of anarchy, and three insurgents had tried to assassinate his father, Umberto I, the last of them successfully. The diminutive king hosted the Japanese entourage in his vast Quirinal Palace, where he proudly displayed his collection of medals. In the Vatican, not yet pacified with the Italian state, Pope Benedict XV received the crown prince twice, and Hirohito was delighted to climb the dome of Saint Peter's basilica as far as the gilded bronze ball at the top of the cupola, which is still the highest point in the city—an inscription at the base of Michelangelo's

16.1.   Prince Regent Hirohito in an English suit, ca. 1921. Bridge-man Fine Arts.

gigantic dome still proudly notes that he ascended into the bronze ball twice. He also took in the cascading fountains and beautiful views of Villa d'Este in Tivoli, as well as a sporting event staged by the Italian army, already, like the king, strongly attracted to Benito Mussolini's new Fascist movement.

The crown prince's visit to Pompeii came on his last day in Europe, July 18, 1921. Dressed in his naval uniform, Hirohito declared himself impressed with the ruined city, but Vesuvius was another matter; its blackened, asymmetrical peak, blown apart in 1631 and riddled with small secondary cones from the eruptions ever since, could scarcely compare with the perfect cone of Mount Fuji.[3] A procession through Naples in an open carriage ended at the fifteenth-century seaside castle that acted as City Hall; by 3:30 p.m., the prince had returned aboard the *Katori,* where the mayor of Naples presided over a farewell ceremony, and at 4:30 p.m. Hirohito put out to sea, bound for home.

Of all the sights the future emperor saw on his global Grand Tour, London apparently impressed him the most, from the comparative informality of the British monarchy's manners to the strength and lengthy history of the country's parliamentary tradition. However, that favorable impression would not be enough to alter the course of future events in Japan, Europe, and the world. Hirohito would succeed his father as the Showa emperor in 1926, and on that Chrysanthemum Throne he would preside over the military adventures that led to Japan's brutal invasion of Manchuria and its participation on the Axis side in World War II. Victor Emmanuel, for his part, would receive Benito Mussolini as prime minister in October of 1922 and shortly thereafter acknowledge his assumption of a new office, Duce, "leader." By 1937 the list of foreign visitors to Pompeii and Vesuvius included officers of the German Luftwaffe, who can be seen in a short film scrambling up the slopes of the smoking volcano with a local priest. One of the party struts about in his lederhosen as if they are in the Bavarian Alps rather than climbing a Campanian volcano.[4] Luftwaffe head and future Reichsmarschall Hermann Göring made repeated visits to the buried city not only out of interest but also to establish German—not Italian—possession of Europe's cultural heritage. Göring and his SS would pay similarly close and publicity-minded attention to the Athenian Acropolis.

Hirohito's brief visit to Pompeii, however, left a more positive legacy than Göring's. He was the first Japanese monarch ever to leave his country, and that openness began to have a profound effect on Japanese culture as a whole. In 1967, half a century after Hirohito's international tour and a quarter century after the end of World War II, a Japanese student, Masanori Aoyagi, enrolled in the Department of Art History at the University of Rome. He returned to Italy in 1974 to begin research in Pompeii as a young professor. In 2001 Aoyagi, by now a distinguished figure in Japan and head of Tokyo's Museum of Western Art, decided to turn his attention to the other side of Vesuvius, in an area known as Starza della Regina. Here a Fascist-era excavation had turned up a villa from the age of Augustus, first identified, in the flush of nationalist fervor, as the residence of Augustus himself, for the emperor was said by all of the literary sources to have died in his villa at nearby Nola. Aoyagi was more prudent in his conclusions; he would admit that the "Villa Augustea" belonged to the right era, but without any solid evidence, the identity of its owner must remain uncertain.

One member of the Japanese team, archaeologist Akira Matsuda, decided to focus his research on the present rather than the past, studying the impact of the excavation and the Japanese presence in general on the local community. Jobs have always been too scarce in populous Campania; did people resent having a foreign team, especially a group from Asia, work among them? When the site declared two "open days" for visitors in 2005, Matsuda distributed more than six hundred questionnaires to the people who came to the site. His question was simple: "What do you think of the fact that it is Japanese archaeologists who are doing the excavation of the Villa? Please answer honestly."

The responses, as it turned out, were overwhelmingly positive, and Matsuda, writing in English, cites some of the comments in his final account of the experience, translating from his respondents' Italian. The language definitely is Italian; unlike the impoverished peasants of the nineteenth century, the new generations of Campania, because of factors like compulsory education and national television, have a command of the national language as well as their regional dialect:

> I'm pleased. Whether it's Japanese or Italians [does not matter to me]. In fact, Italians work in Egypt. There is a museum run by Italians there. They too are happy with this museum. It's international cultural heritage, isn't it? So whether it is done by Japanese or Italians, for me, it doesn't change anything.

> Great pleasure. Well, great pleasure. . . . Each people bring in new things of their culture to these excavations. It's something very nice.[5]

A century and a half after Bartolo Longo first ventured into the lawless badlands along the River Sarno, these Japanese scholars found neighbors who were far more than literate: they were people who saw themselves as part of a global community with a global heritage. For all that still seems changeless about the region around Vesuvius, a great deal has changed in a very short time, including the conviction that this unique local landscape, with its unique history, somehow belongs to the entire human race rather than just one part of it, just as Mount Fuji has become a worldwide symbol of Japan.

Here is another example of this swift, globalizing change: Hirohito's visit to Italy, like the rest of his journey, had been planned with the utmost precision. His elderly advisors had considered extending the itinerary to include the United States, but two factors decided them against it: the precarious situation at home and the rough habits of the Americans, too unrefined for a future emperor's company. Exactly seventh-three years later, between July 8 and 10, 1994, a Japanese president rather than an emperor came to Naples on another official visit, this time as part of the summit conference known as the Group of Seven (G7), a meeting of the heads of the world's seven most powerful nations: Canada, Italy, the United States, Japan, France, Britain, and Germany. On the site of devastating Allied bombings and bloody battles between Allies and Axis, the former mortal enemies of World War II now pledged to work together rather than to destroy each other. On this occasion, no less than for Hirohito's visit in 1921, every movement of the Canadian, Italian, Japanese, and British prime ministers, the German chancellor, the presidents of France, the United States, and the European Commission and their wives (in 1994, all of these officers were men) had been carefully arranged months in advance, but then the First Family of the United States threw these well-laid plans into chaos. The Clintons wanted to see Pompeii, but Pompeii was not on the itinerary.

As the presidents gathered in the Royal Palace, at the center of a gleaming, optimistic Naples (its brief "Neapolitan renaissance" still a hope rather than a promise betrayed), their wives were to be swept off to Herculaneum. Compact, beautifully preserved, easy to guard, close to Naples, and less thronged with tourists, all of whom would have to be displaced for the diplomats and their entourages, Herculaneum was perfectly suited for a short, informative archaeological excursion. But Hillary Clinton would have none of it. She and her daughter, Chelsea, she announced, would see Pompeii and nothing but Pompeii. Seventy years after Hirohito's visit, the manners of Americans could still strike Japanese and Europeans as rough edged. (The adjective used by one eyewitness for Mrs. Clinton on this occasion was "*volitiva*"—"determined.")

The First Ladies' designated guide on this crucially important political occasion was, appropriately, the highest official in the local archaeological hierarchy: Baldassare Conticello, the superintendent of antiquities—for both Pompeii and Herculaneum. For the dapper Conticello, there was no acceptable diplomatic solution to the split contingent of First Ladies except to be in two places at the same time or to come as close to that condition as possible. His wife, the archaeologist Marisa de' Spagnolis, quickly turned their own house on the site of Pompeii into a shower facility and dressing room for the two Clintons, mother and daughter, while Conticello himself raced down the autostrada between his distinguished contingents, only to be joined shortly thereafter by another unexpected guest and logistical headache: President Clinton himself, apparently as eager to see Pompeii as the rest of his family.

Dottoressa de' Spagnolis recalls the whole itinerary for the impromptu state tour, including its limitations:

> After breakfast the guided tour began, following an itinerary that took in the most important buildings: the Forum, the House of the Faun, the House of the Vettii, the House of the Chaste Lovers, Via dell'Abbondanza, the Amphitheatre. Before allowing the First Lady to enter any space, an American security officer [a Secret Service agent] inspected it, evaluating its appropriateness. In the House of the Vetti, Mrs. Clinton was prevented from entering the *Venerio,* a room in which the owners of the house dedicated themselves to trysts with their maids. In that room, in fact, there was a statue of the god Priapus, endowed with a phallus of enormous dimensions. A photo in that space, next to that statue, would have been truly embarrassing for the Presidentessa and would have gotten around the whole world![6]

The House of the Vettii, indeed, has always presented a problem for distinguished visitors; its paintings are famous, exceptionally rich, and exceptionally well preserved (especially before the earthquake of 1980), but the two unmarried Vettius brothers shared a passion for fertility images with outsized penises. When Queen Elizabeth of England made her state visit in 1980 (a month before the quake), the painting of Priapus in the Vettius brothers' entrance vestibule had just been freed from the locked metal screen that had hidden it from view for years (Figure 4.2; the clamps that secured the screen are still visible in the picture). In the old days, a guard could be persuaded to unlock the screen with great ceremony and then stand poker faced as the visitor gaped at the garden god weighing his monumental phallus against a cornucopia-load of ripe fruit, a sign of fertility so potent that any evil spirit with plans to enter the House of the Vettii would be cowed into impotent submission.

Now, however, in the enlightened year of 1980, the screen was gone. Instead, Prince Phillip stood in front of the provocative picture (with the same impassive expression the guards used to affect) as his wife made a brisk transit through the vestibule into the atrium. The fact that this mother of four and owner of countless dogs and horses might have had a certain familiarity with phallic realities as well as phallic symbols was beside the point; royal majesty, as Dottoressa de' Spagnolis notes about presidential dignity, would have dictated avoiding the possibility of any compromising photographs.

17

Don Amedeo Maiuri

Crown Prince Hirohito's guide through Pompeii, Superintendent Vittorio Spinazzola, had been appointed to his position in 1911. Using horse-drawn carts, he had already begun conducting an extensive excavation campaign along the city's main street, the Via dell'Abbondanza, where his painstaking methods would enable him to preserve many of the buildings he uncovered all the way up to their second story, complete with the graffiti that seem to have covered most public walls in Pompeii. Spinazzola also expanded the range of organic forms that could be reconstructed in plaster by casting what remained of the root balls of the plants in Pompeian gardens. This technique would be continued with remarkable success in the later twentieth century by Wilhelmina Jashemski, whose researches at Pompeii and Oplontis in the later twentieth century helped turn the history of gardens into its own scholarly discipline.[1] Thanks to her discoveries, many of the ancient Roman houses of Pompeii and elsewhere in the Bay of Naples have been replanted with the same species that were present in antiquity. But Spinazzola, despite his extensive archaeological skill, ran into trouble with the advent of Fascism in 1922; not only was he opposed to the regime, but he was also married to a Jewish scholar, Alda Levi Spinazzola (and the anti-Semitic policies of the Fascists had already begun to make themselves felt long before the racial laws of 1938). In 1924 the inconvenient director was removed from his position by the Mussolini government and replaced by Amedeo Maiuri, who had been working up to then at the Italian excavations in Rhodes.

Maiuri was an alumnus of Rome's famous Liceo Visconti, the public secondary school that has occupied the rooms of the old Jesuit College since 1870. He attended class, therefore, in Athanasius Kircher's old haunts and must have seen what remained of Kircher's museum and perhaps used some of the same scientific instruments as Kircher himself, many of which still exist in the science laboratories at Liceo Visconti. Maiuri then earned a degree in Byzantine literature at the University of Rome before going off to do fieldwork in Greece. An appointment as archaeological inspector in Naples brought him back to Italy, but he returned to Greece in 1913 as director of the archaeological museum in Rhodes, as well as the island's superintendent of antiquities. On the strength of his administrative abilities and several successful excavation campaigns in Rhodes and Asia Minor, he came at last to Naples in the double position of superintendent of antiquities for Naples and southern Italy and director of the National Archaeological Museum in Naples. From the beginning of his career, "Don Amedeo" was an imposing presence, energetic and authoritative, as well as a poetic writer who became the virtual embodiment of Pompeii for much of the twentieth century. When talking about the site, he liked to use words like "magic" and "mystery," and he himself became Pompeii's chief "magician" for an enthusiastic public. He would serve in his position at Pompeii for thirty-seven years, retiring in 1961 at the age of seventy-five, at a moment when Italy itself was cresting on a wave of optimism and prosperity.

Maiuri was the first excavation director at Pompeii to make routine use of mechanical earth-moving equipment, which allowed workers to clear extensive tracts of the city with unprecedented speed. The soundings they took revealed a plethora of new houses, new artifacts, new paintings, and new bodies and showed how significantly modern technology could further a better understanding the ancient world.[2] In 1931 Don Amedeo continued the excavation of the suburban Villa of the Mysteries, first uncovered in 1909–1910, with its superb, enigmatic paintings of the wine god Bacchus and his initiates, a fitting magical episode in the magician's public career, but this magic was always firmly wedded to technology.

When Maiuri's classic guidebook to Pompeii discusses the myths despicted on the walls of its houses, "Don Amedeo" enters completely into the story; he could be a native Pompeian himself: "In an exedra to the left are three little pictures representing episodes from the taking of Troy, an epical triptych: the Horse of Troy being drawn into the city through a breach in the walls by the festive crowd, whilst Cassandra tries in vain to dissuade the Trojans from the fatal mistake; the meeting of Menelaus and Helen in Priam's palace, whilst Cassandra, closely pursued by Ajax, embraced the Palladium as a last refuge; the death of Laocoon [sic] and his sons."[3]

Maiuri necessarily found a way to live with Fascism: he joined the Italian Academy, the honorific society that replaced the centuries-old Accademia dei Lincei in 1929, when Mussolini dissolved it because of its high proportion of Jewish members. As superintendent, Maiuri once delivered a speech in Rome praising the work of Italian and German culture in combating "Oriental" (that is, Jewish) influence. However, his chief allegiance was always to the site of Pompeii, not to any ideology. He decried the outbreak of World War II as "bleak and unnatural" *("funesto e innaturale")* and began sandbagging parts of the archaeological museum as early as 1942 to protect the collections from bombs and bullets. Small objects were removed to remote locations for safekeeping (sadly, one of these places, Montecassino, was later ravaged by Allied bombs). With the Allied invasion of Italy in 1943, Maiuri began pleading with the German occupation troops to move away from the excavations to protect them for the future, but his request was refused; Pompeii was a coastal city, and the Allies were preparing to attack Italy by sea (as they did at Salerno, Anzio, and Sicily). The Germans intended to maintain their watch along the Italian coast, and that was that. In hopes of saving Pompeii from damage during the war, Maiuri unfurled every bit of his famous eloquence to capture the attention of the media on both sides of the conflict. However, the German presence around the ancient site meant that the Allies moved in as relentlessly as the Germans had held their ground. They mistakenly believed that German troops might be hiding among the ancient buildings (a mistake the Allies repeated at Montecassino, destroying that magnificent monument in the erroneous belief that Germans were concealed there).

The first wave of bombs fell on the night of August 24, 1943; Maiuri would point out that this was the same date as the fateful eruption of Vesuvius in 79 (though some scholars opt for November, as we saw in Chapter 2). The strafing of Pompeii continued throughout the month of September. In the end, 162 bombs struck the site, destroying the little museum in the Porta Marina and irreparably damaging a number of houses. The Albergo del Sole, which housed a number of German officers but not an entire garrison, was obliterated.

The war made civilian transportation extremely difficult and extremely dangerous. In September, unable to take a car on the roads, Maiuri tried to bicycle to Naples, but he was struck on the ankle by machine gun fire in Torre del Greco and confined to a hospital bed in that little town for two months. The Allies finally entered a shaken New Pompeii on September 29, 1943. Maiuri returned to Old Pompeii in mid-November, still limping.

Allied soldiers eagerly toured the excavations, and in their presence Maiuri was prudent in his complaints about the bomb damage. Like Italy itself, he had changed sides with his government from the Axis to the Allies in 1943 and afterward devoted his tremendous talents to the tasks of rebuilding and restoration rather than recrimination. Amedeo Maiuri was the voice of postwar Pompeii as he had been the voice of prewar Pompeii and wartime Pompeii, as steadfast in his defense of the ancient site as the steadfast soldier of Pompeian legend. And like the steadfast soldier, he also had to deal with an erupting volcano, for at the same moment that American B-17 Flying Fortresses and B-25 Mitchell bombers began buzzing over Italy, San Gennaro's blood failed to liquefy, and Vesuvius added its voice to the rumblings of war.[4] The volcano began to spew smoke on August 12, 1943, but most of the violent explosions occurred in February and March of the following year.

Norman Lewis, a young British officer stationed in Naples, left a vivid account of the eruption in his diary:

> Today Vesuvius erupted. It was the most majestic and terrible sight I have ever seen, or ever expect to see. The smoke from the crater slowly built up into a great bulging shape having all the appearance of solidity. It swelled and expanded so slowly that there was no sign of movement in the clouds which, by evening, must have risen thirty or forty thousand feet into the sky, and measured many miles across. The shape of the eruption that obliterated Pompeii reminded Pliny of a pine tree, and he probably stood here at Posillipo across the bay, where I was standing now and where Nelson and Emma Hamilton stood to view the eruption of their day, and the shape was indeed like that of a many-branching tree. What

FROM POMPEII

took one by surprise about Pliny's pine was that it was absolutely motionless, not quite painted—because it was three-dimensional—but moulded on the sky; an utterly still, and utterly menacing shape. This pine, too, trailed uncharacteristically a little tropical liana of heavy ash, which fell earthwards here and there from its branches in imperceptible motion. At night the lava streams began to trickle down the mountain's slopes. By day the spectacle was calm but now the eruption showed a terrible vivacity. Fiery symbols were scrawled across the water of the bay, and periodically the crater discharged mines of serpents into a sky which was the deepest of blood reds and pulsating everywhere with lightning reflections.[5]

The eruption showered Pompeii with ash but did not rebury it. Maiuri cleared the volcanic debris away along with the rubble of war.

18

Roberto Rossellini and Ingrid Bergman

When film director Roberto Rossellini set out for Naples in his bright red Lancia in February of 1953, his passionate, scandalous romance with Ingrid Bergman was already showing signs of strain. Everyone knew the story: after seeing a Rossellini retrospective in Stockholm in 1948 she had written him a letter. The two forth-right Scandinavian sentences were supposed to be lighthearted and mildly flirtatious, but to an Italian, accustomed to more elaborate circumlocution, they would have sounded like serious business:

Dear Mr. Rossellini,

I saw your films *Open City* and *Paisan,* and enjoyed them very much. If you need a Swedish actress who speaks English very well, who has not forgotten her German, who is not very understandable in French, and who in Italian knows only "ti amo," I am ready to come and make a film with you.

Ingrid Bergman[1]

Rossellini replied, and Bergman flew to Rome. He met her at the Rome airport and swept her off in his Lancia for a tour of southern Italy. Both were married, and Rossellini had another lover, but within a week a paparazzo caught them holding hands, and soon afterward Bergman turned out to be carrying Rossellini's child. Robertino Rossellini was born in 1950, the year in which the couple married, followed by the twin girls Isabella and Ingrid Isotta in 1952. Marriage and children cooled the public scandal somewhat, but the partnership itself was always a collision of two powerful personalities from two different cultures.

Their first film together, *Stromboli* (1950), had been designed first for Rossellini's lover Anna Magnani, whose reaction to Bergman's letter had rivaled Vesuvius for sheer explosive power. They followed with *Europa '51* (1951). Neither film was a great success, and disappointment with their professional partnership only intensified their discomfort with one another as Rossellini prepared for their next film. His original idea had been to transpose a 1934 novel by Colette, *Duo,* about an unhappy married couple on the brink of divorce, a subject that seemed to express the state of his own marriage. Just before he began filming, however, Rossellini learned that the rights to *Duo* had been sold.[2] With his cast already in place in Naples, he began to write another screenplay. No one knew where the new script might lead, including Rossellini himself. The definite elements were the unhappy married couple (that much he could keep from *Duo* without incurring charges of plagiarism), the actors (Ingrid Bergman and George Sanders), and the Neapolitan setting. As it turned out, the eventual meaning of the film would hinge on the episode that takes place in Pompeii, but no one, including the director, planned it that way. It simply happened.

When *Viaggio in Italia (Journey to Italy),* finally came out in 1954, it received the same tepid response as Rossellini's earlier films with Bergman. Gradually, however, it has come to be seen as his masterpiece for the very reasons that disturbed its early critics, for *Viaggio in Italia* revolves, in a pioneering way, around atmosphere rather than action.

That atmosphere, from the very beginning, is one of alienation and disorientation. Bergman and Sanders, as Alex and Katherine Joyce, a wealthy and unhappy English couple, speed down the Appian Way in their dark, shiny Bentley, continually forced to slow their pace on the two-lane highway to make way for bicycles, motorbikes, horse-drawn carts, and herds of cattle. They are foreign to Italy and to each other. The suavely handsome Sanders was even more out of his element than Bergman on the set; back in Hollywood, his marriage to Zsa Zsa Gabor was breaking up, he had never lived in Italy (he was actually born in Russia), and in between takes he spent inordinate amounts of money phoning his analyst in Los Angeles. And he knew even less about the screenplay than his leading lady. Both Sanders and Bergman were professional actors accustomed to working from scripts, whereas Rossellini had made his reputation by improvising with nonprofessional actors. As a result, the Italian director and his two northern European leads were hopelessly at odds with each other—but they did have the wits to pour all of that tension and uncertainty into the film itself.

Rossellini spent the first two weeks of production shooting Ingrid Bergman as she visited the National Archaeological Museum in Naples, a movie goddess set among the ancient divinities of marble and bronze. As she would reveal later, she did not know what her husband had in mind; the whole enterprise seemed to her like a tremendous expenditure of time and money to no apparent purpose. If she looks gloriously confused on screen, it is because she was in life.

At the same time that Ingrid Bergman was confronting perplexity in Naples and Pompeii, another cinematic goddess was also filming in Naples: a nineteen-year-old Sophia Loren, at work

18.1.   Sophia Loren in the Rione Materdei, Naples. Still from Vittorio De Sica's *L'oro di Napoli* (1954). The Kobal Collection at Art Resource, NY.

on Vittorio di Sica's *L'oro di Napoli (The Gold of Naples),* filmed, like *Viaggio in Italia,* in 1953 and released in 1954 (Figure 18.1). If Bergman moves through Rossellini's Naples like a beautiful alien, Loren strides through the streets of the rough, tough neighborhood of the Rione Materdei as if she owns the place. But then the former Sofia Scicolone was Neapolitan herself, born in Rome but brought up in Pozzuoli, the site of San Gennaro's martyrdom, from early childhood. De Sica had signed her up for *L'oro di Napoli* shortly after meeting her, impressed by her spirit as well as her stunning, thoroughly Neapolitan beauty. Ironically, after filming briefly as Sofia Lazzaro, she had just settled on a stage name,

Sophia Loren, which was meant to sound vaguely Swedish. But her role in De Sica's film was as a voluptuous young woman who makes fried pizza in Materdei and sells it on credit; it was no role for a Swede.

If the teenaged Sophia Loren could move through neighborhoods like Materdei and Sanità looking like an ancient statue from the National Archaeological Museum suddenly come to life, the streets of Naples presented an entirely different face to Rossellini, born and bred to the comfortable bourgeois society of Rome's northern suburb, Parioli. In many ways Naples was no less alien to him than to his Swedish wife, and the adjoining neighborhoods of Materdei and Sanità present the city in its most concentrated form, an unbelievable number of people crammed into towering buildings, from marvelous Baroque concoctions (two by Ferdinando Sanfelice, the architect of the Villa d'Elbeuf in Portici) to the hovels of modern cave dwellers, hollowed into the golden volcanic rock on which the city rests. Joaquin Murat constructed a viaduct in 1809 that allowed him to pass over this area altogether when he moved from his seaside palace to the hilltop palace of Capodimonte. Vittorio de Sica, on the other hand, plunged right in with *L'oro di Napoli;* the Rione Sanità was the birthplace of Sophia Loren's costar Antonio de Curtis, better known as Totò, the greatest comic actor of Italian cinema.

If George Sanders was a typical movie star of the era, tall, dark, handsome, foreign, and formal (if not quite gentlemanly) in his manner, Totò, with his lopsided face, beaked nose, and prognathous jaw, would never qualify as an Adonis. He did, however, claim aristocratic descent, and there was certainly something regal about the way he moved both his body and his incredibly expressive face, not to mention his hands, ceaselessly engaged in the whole repertory of Canon De Jorio's Neapolitan gestures, with a few more of his own added to the mix. If ever a living human being embodied that archetypal theatrical rogue Pulcinella, it was the self-styled Prince Antonio de Curtis. Today, Totò's boyhood apartment in a precipitous palazzo of the Rione Sanità is one of the area's landmarks.

One of the most important scenes in *Viaggio in Italia* also occurs in this remarkable district as a kind of prelude to the visit to Pompeii, when we, and Rossellini's fictitious heroine, Katherine Joyce, are taken into one of strangest places in Naples, the Fontanelle Cemetery, while her husband Alex gallivants with a group of sophisticates on the island of Capri, contemplating adultery.

Like the neighboring catacombs of San Gennaro and San Gaudioso (the latter beneath the church of Santa Maria della Sanità, the church that gives its name to the Rione Sanità), the huge underground halls of the Fontanelle Cemetery have been carved into bedrock just beyond the perimeter of the ancient city. Because it is so riddled with catacombs, the area has been known for centuries as the Valle dei Morti, the Valley of the Dead. Beneath Naples itself, the first Greek colonists began to carve out a system of vast underground tunnels as they quarried stone for building. Some of these tunnels eventually served as cisterns; others simply continued as quarries, like those that lined the slopes above the Valley of the Dead. As the city's population expanded in the seventeenth century, people began to settle in the valley and along its steeply sloping sides. The Rione Sanità occupies the slopes, but the valley floor attracted the most desperate of settlers because the area was remote from the city center, outside its protective walls, and the valley floor turned into a torrent whenever rain came sluicing down from the steep volcanic hills. In ancient times this position outside the city walls and alongside a stream had ideally suited the Valley of the Dead for a graveyard, for running water was thought to wash away the taint of death. But making a home there meant living among the deceased; hence the valley's residents numbered among the city's poorer *lazzaroni,* one step up from the lowest of the low, who lived out their lives in the street. When a hospital was established near the church and catacombs of San Gennaro in the seventeenth century, it was called San Gennaro dei Poveri, "San Gennaro of the Poor." Two other local churches, named Santa Maria della Sanità, "Our Lady of Health," and Santa Maria dei Miracoli, "Our Lady of Miracles," suggest how desperate the conditions of their congregations must have been. When epidemics struck Naples, it was often the citizens of the densely packed Sanità district who suffered disproportionately. And it was during a particularly terrible outbreak of the plague, in 1636, that the vast ancient quarry called the Fontanelle in the Valley of the Dead was designated as mass grave for the epidemic's victims (Figure 18.2).

The seventeenth century also saw the rapid growth in Naples of a cult dedicated to the Anime nel Purgatorio, the Souls in Purgatory; these were normal, redeemable sinners whose penance in Purgatory would eventually admit them to heaven. Throughout the city streets, little shrines have been hollowed into the stone walls of buildings by private citizens, each stocked with little terra cotta statues of the souls burning in waist-high flames (the flames of hell reach all the way up), often adoring the cross as they pray their way into the earthly paradise and then, they hope, on to heaven (Figure 18.3).

Because of their holy penance, the Souls in Purgatory were believed to have some ability to intercede on behalf of the living, and in the seventeenth century Neapolitans began praying to them as if they were all potential saints. Eventually the residents of the Valley of the Dead began to realize that the plague cemetery provided a gigantic treasure trove of candidates for Souls in Purgatory, and they devised a special form of prayer to involve these "uncared-for souls," to borrow Bartolo Longo's evocative phrase. Just as Longo cared for the living, these humble Neapolitans, the poorest of the poor, cared for the neglected dead. People went

18.2.   Fontanelle Cemetery, Naples, November 2012. Photo by author.

into the old quarry, picked out a skull, and began to lavish affection on it, renaming it, decorating it, caressing it, bringing it gifts, asking it to intercede with God, the Madonna, Jesus, and the saints. A skull that heard a prayer was thought to grow moist; if the prayer was answered, the skull was rewarded with its own

18.3.   Street shrine to the Souls in Purgatory, Naples, Rione Sanità. November 2012. Photo by author.

little shrine, a tiny temple or a Rosary crown (Figure 18.4). In the meantime, the old quarry continued to act as a mass grave, taking in the people buried under the floors of Neapolitan churches as standards of sanitation changed. Here the city also deposited the cholera victims during the 1825 epidemic (including, probably, the great poet Giacomo Leopardi, the author of "La Ginestra"; see Chapter 1), as well as the bodies unearthed in 1935 by Mussolini's urban renewal and other construction projects that opened old burial sites.

In 1969, in the aftermath of the Second Vatican Council, Pope Paul VI officially banned the cult of the Fontanelle and shut down the old quarry, but intrepid worshippers still managed to get into the Fontanelle to tend to their skulls. The cult persists even today—in the fall of 2011, offerings to what seemed to be the

18.4. Skull shrines, Fontanelle Cemetery, Naples. November 2012. Photo by author.

cemetery's most efficacious skull included a ticket to a Team Napoli soccer game from 2010.

There were other skull cults in Naples, too: within the city, for example, at the church of San Pietro Ad Aram, where Charles Dickens met the two Methuselahs who guarded the tombs (see Chapter 10). Although it shocked Dickens and Twain, among other visitors, the Neapolitans' preoccupation with the Souls in Purgatory has something touchingly compassionate about it. In the Fontanelle, an area on the margins of the city in every possible physical and social sense, it has often been the neediest people who have provided attention and affection, if only posthumously, to the neglected and forgotten of the past. Today, the Sanità district bursts with all of the same contradictions that marked it in the seventeenth century; it is still a dense slum, vibrating with life, buzzing with motor scooters, potentially dangerous, and full not only of Camorra gangsters and gorgeous old artistic treasures but also of exciting new artworks and cultural associations created right in the area.

For Rossellini, a filmmaker with international ambitions and an international cast, the Fontanelle Cemetery, so specifically, strangely Neapolitan, can only serve as another experience to increase Katherine Joyce's feelings of alienation. The endless piles of skulls and the tiny little ladies who minister to them are so bizarre that the Englishwoman can scarcely make sense of them. Their significance finally becomes clear only when the film moves on to another graveyard, this time one with universal resonance: the ruins of Pompeii. Alex and Katherine arrive, as usual, in their Bentley, slinging barbed comments or glaring at one another in surly silence; Sanders, with his offstage reputation as a *cafone,* a boor, is particularly good at this art. A still from the film (Figure 18.5) shows Ingrid Bergman sitting alone on an upturned column capital in the bleak ruins of the Temple of Venus, her face a picture of confusion and despair. In the company of a guide, a descendant of generations of Neapolitan *ciceroni,* they come to an area where archaeologists are testing for buried bodies by tapping on the solidified volcanic cover; whenever the excavators hear a hollow sound, they inject liquid plaster into the void, wait for it to dry, and then dig. (In 1953, during the fimling of *Viaggio in Italia,* the charismatic Don Amedeo Maiuri was superintendent and was carrying out precisely this kind of activity in the *praedia* of Julia Felix; see Chapter 7.) As Alex and Katherine look on, workers uncover the plaster bodies of a Pompeian man and woman from nineteen centuries ago, resolved to face the volcano's fury in a loving embrace. As the plaster cast of the couple emerges from the earth, Katherine, overcome, rushes out into the ancient street. Alex follows her to see what is the matter. "Life is so short," she blurts through her tears. "That's why we should make the most of

18.5.   Ingrid Bergman at the Temple of Venus, Pompeii. Still from *Viaggio in Italia* (1954). Mary Evans Archive.

it," Alex replies with pat assurance, but for once there is a hint of uncertainty in his pontificating tone.

On the written page, this brief exchange sounds impossibly superficial, but in the movie it resonates as memorably as Rossellini meant it to. The colors of Pompeii are reduced in the old black-and-white film to blacks and silvers, but they are blacks and silvers of luminous brightness; we can feel the heat of the Campanian sun. The tragic tranquility of the ghostly plaster bodies makes the sparring of the living couple seem all the more trivial and all the more pointless by lifting the scene out of melodrama

Roberto Rossellini and Ingrid Bergman

and suggesting a potential repetition of tragedy. The disaster that struck Pompeii is too great, and strikes too close to home, to brook an instant response, even from that bored sophisticate, Alex Joyce. Unlike his wife, and the viewers of *Viaggio in Italia*, he has not seen the piles of skulls and desperate poverty of the Fontanelle Cemetery; he was partying on idyllic Capri rather than coming face to face with human mortality.

Years later Isabella Rossellini, the daughter of Ingrid Bergman and Roberto Rossellini, described her own responses to *Viaggio in Italia* in an interview:

> And mother, little by little in the film, looks at the monuments, and thinks: "Oh, how beautiful, how rich, how interesting." But all of a sudden, it dawns on her, they were people; these are messages they have left for us. And when she finally goes to Pompeii and sees a couple dead in their embrace, she breaks down and cries. Because all of a sudden it isn't the Italy of tourism, the strength of Italy is its history, that under our feet, where we walk, there are millions of people buried, literally buried, some of them mummified. And that consciousness is what's so strong in *Viaggio in Italia,* which I didn't understand as a child but only as a grown-up. At the end of the film, it ends with this miracle of the couple realising how lost people are in this universe, and they are separated by a crowd, and in that moment of panic they find each other and they embrace.[3]

And this is how *Viaggio in Italia* ends: Alex and Katherine have finally resolved to divorce and are going home to England to start the proceedings. As they leave Naples for the north, a village procession surrounds their Bentley and forces it to stop. Rossellini shot the scene in the picturesque streets of Maiori, a village on the Amalfi coast (south, not north of Naples), sacrificing geographical accuracy for the sake of an evocative setting. Because Alex and Katherine cannot move the car, surrounded as it is by the religious parade, they step out to watch the people go by. Suddenly the crowd of tiny, stocky Italians sweeps the tall couple away and parts them. In a panic, they look around wildly, and suddenly they catch sight of each other again, each of them towering over the crowd that swarms around them. When they finally find their way back together again and embrace, it is because they have suddenly truly seen each other; their boredom and irritation have been lifted away and carried off by the pageant. And so the little statue of the Madonna and the half-pagan village procession have wrought their miracle on the foreign sophisticates as well as the faithful locals. Alex and Katherine's *Journey to Italy* has brought them what such journeys to Italy have always been supposed to provide: a return home, a return to the self. The catalyst of it all is Pompeii, which, with its intertwining of life and death, inscrutable foreignness, and universal humanity, has done its part to perform the age-old miracle, as reliable in its own way as San Gennaro himself and his liquefying blood.

For a surprising number of visitors to the Bay of Naples, real as well as fictitious, the experience of Pompeii provided its own peculiar therapy for whatever ailed them. The mild climate, the volcanic vapors, and the artesian waters of Campania were all regarded as physically healthful in themselves, but immersion in the life of the buried town added a spiritual and an emotional dimension to the Neapolitan segment of the Grand Tour.

The streets of Pompeii provided insights not only into nature's might but also, piercingly, into the real extent of human fragility. The beauty of the artifacts extracted from the strange volcanic soils of Pompeii and Herculaneum was hard to reconcile with the savagery of the mountain's revenge on the inhabitants of its slopes. Sometimes a face stares out from an ancient painting so intently that a person still seems to be living behind it, like the elderly man with the luminous eyes whose label in the Naples National Archaeological Museum calls attention—unusually—to his "expressive face" (Figure 18.6). He could, in fact, be the remote ancestor of Totò.

Théophile Gautier and his Octavien, as we have already seen (Chapter 9), fantasized about another evanescent glimpse of a human being: the imprint of the breast and arms of "Arria Marcella." The novelette *Arria Marcella,* in turn, must have helped to inspire German writer Wilhelm Jensen to conceive his gently witty archaeological fantasy, the short novel *Gradiva.* Immensely popular in its day and still a delight to read, *Gradiva* caught the

18.6.   The man with the expressive face. From Pompeii. Naples, Museo Nazionale. Photo by author.

FROM POMPEII

attention of Sigmund Freud because of its inherent charm and its effectiveness in illustrating his own growing conviction that the human psyche was itself a kind of archaeological site. The story tells of a studious young German classicist, Norbert Hanold, who becomes obsessed with a relief sculpture he has seen in Rome (the sculpture is in the Vatican Museum). When he returns to Germany, he installs a cast of the relief in his study and gives it the fanciful name "Gradiva," "the stepper," because of her lovely striding posture.

Like many an archaeologist, Norbert dreams of meeting Gradiva, and with this obsession dominating his mind, he makes a summer tour to Rome, Naples, and Pompeii. When he reaches Pompeii, he is amazed to spot Gradiva herself, stepping prettily down an ancient street. He follows her into the atrium of a house and calls out to her in Latin. She turns and tells him that if wants to converse with her, he had better speak to her in German. Flustered, he asks to meet her again in the same place at noon the next day.

Norbert is so confused that he wanders off to the opposite edge of Pompeii, near the amphitheater, and encounters a typical Pompeian spiel for gullible tourists:

> Buried in thought, he did not notice the mistake until he had come right up to a building which was neither the Diomed nor the Suisse. In spite of that it bore the sign of a hotel; nearby he recognized the ruins of the large Pompeiian amphitheater and the memory came to him that, near this latter, there was another hotel, the Albergo del Sole, which, on account of its remoteness from the station, was sought out by only a few guests and had remained unknown to even him. The walk had made him hot; besides, the cloudy whirling in his head had not diminished; so he stepped in through the open door and ordered the remedy deemed useful by him for blood-congestion, a bottle of lime-water.

The room stood empty except, of course, for the fly-visitors gathered in full numbers, and the unoccupied host availed himself of the opportunity to recommend highly his house and the excavated treasures it contained. He pointed suggestively to the fact that there were, near Pompeii, people at whose places there was not a single, genuine piece among the many objects offered for sale, but that all were imitations, while he, satisfying himself with a smaller number, offered his guests only things undoubtedly genuine.[4]

The hot and bothered, fantasy-stricken Norbert buys a brooch the host swears he has taken straight from the body of a Pompeian girl; in his heart, Norbert just knows that it must have been Gradiva. When he finally meets the girl again in the atrium, he presents it to her, and in short order the mystery of the German-speaking apparition is revealed: this walking, talking, Germanic "Gradiva" is no more antique than the brooch she recognizes as "made yesterday"; she is his childhood friend and neighbor, Zoë Bertgang (a meaningful name: Greek for "life" and German for "beautiful walker"), with whom he lost touch when adolescence turned him into a reclusive scholar with his head in the clouds of classical antiquity (it is easy to see why Freud had such fun with the story). Zoë, on the other hand, has come to Pompeii with her father and knows perfectly well that Norbert has been traveling to the same places. Under the clear light of Campania, with the evanescence of life evident along every Pompeian street and in every Pompeian building, Norbert gladly exchanges his fantasy Gradiva for the flesh-and-blood Zoë, with her life-giving Greek name and her thoroughly German practicality. Like so many tourists over so many centuries, he throws down his own challenge to death and kisses his beloved in the middle of Pompeii, and everyone lives happily ever after in Jensen's comic, bemused tale of longing, sublimation, and academic blindness.

Sigmund Freud analyzes the gently humorous novel as Norbert's initiation from repressed sexuality into adult love:

> There is no better analogy for repression, which at the same time makes inaccessible and conserves something psychic, than the burial which was the fate of Pompeii, and from which the city was able to rise again, through work with the spade. Therefore in his imagination the young archaeologist has had to transport the original figure of the relief which reminded him of the forgotten beloved of his youth. Jensen, however, had a good right to linger over the significant resemblance which his fine sense traced out between a bit of psychic occurrence in the individual and a single historical event in the history of man.[5]

Sigmund Freud wrote this essay on *Gradiva* in 1907, but he could just as easily be describing Rossellini's *Viaggio in Italia* in 1953. This short analysis of *Gradiva* also provides a suggestive prelude to the famous passage that begins his *Civilization and Its Discontents* of 1930, in which he compares the human psyche and its layers of experience to the overlapping strata of ancient Rome.

> Now let us make the fantastic supposition that Rome were not a human dwelling-place, but a mental entity with just as long and varied a past history: that is, in which nothing once constructed had perished, and all the earlier stages of development had survived alongside the latest. This would mean that in Rome the palaces of the Caesars were still standing on the Palatine and the Septizonium of Septimius Severus was still towering to its old height; that the beautiful statues were still standing in the colonnade of the Castle of St. Angelo, as they were up to its siege by the Goths, and so on.

But more still: where the Palazzo Caffarelli stands there would also be, without this being removed, the Temple of Jupiter Capitolinus, not merely in its latest form, moreover, as the Romans of the Caesars saw it, but also in its earliest shape, when it still wore an Etruscan design and was adorned with terra-cotta antifixae. Where the Coliseum stands now, we could at the same time admire Nero's Golden House; on the Piazza of the Pantheon we should find not only the Pantheon of today as bequeathed to us by Hadrian, but on the same site also Agrippa's original edifice; indeed, the same ground would support the church of Santa Maria sopra Minerva and the old temple over which it was built. And the observer would need merely to shift the focus of his eyes, perhaps, or change his position, in order to call up a view of either the one or the other.[6]

Freud must have been thinking of Edward Gibbon at that moment and of the journal entry about the autumn evening in 1764 when the historian claimed to have conceived *The Decline and Fall of the Roman Empire:* "It was at Rome, on the fifteenth of October 1764, as I sat musing amidst the ruins of the Capitol, while the barefooted fryars were singing Vespers in the temple of Jupiter, that the idea of writing the decline and fall of the City first started to my mind."[7]

However, as we have seen already, Emily Dickinson had explored this territory of psychic archaeology, too, if in a more volcanic vein. Something about these cities of the dead on the outskirts of Naples, from the Fontantelle to Herculaneum to Pompeii, haunts the imagination of nearly everyone who visits them. Women writers, however, unlike so many men, from the real Gautier to the fictitious Norbert Hanold, never seem to fantasize about meeting an ancient Pompeian swain in the ruins. Perhaps this is because there is no need to fantasize. There usually is a living, breathing

Pompeian swain on hand, ready to try his luck with the tourists as all those ancient phallic symbols silently urge him on to conquest.

For Roberto Rossellini and Ingrid Bergman, the filming of *Viaggio in Italia* in the cemetery of Fontanelle and the ruins of Pompeii produced a marvelous work of art and must have inspired profound thoughts about life and mortality. But unlike the cinematic couple, Alex and Katherine Joyce, the Italian director and the Swedish actress responded to the shortness of life by abandoning, not saving, their marriage. Three years after the film was released in 1957, their remarkable partnership was over in every possible sense.

19

Autobus Gran Turismo

By the end of "Don Amedeo" Maiuri's term as superintendent of Pompeii, two-thirds of the ancient walled city had been excavated, as well as suburban villas and the graveyards outside the gates. For his successors, the prime concerns have been to study and maintain what has already been cleared rather than conducting new excavations. Maintenance is Pompeii's most urgent problem, as it always is for archaeological sites.[1] The tight-packed volcanic lapilli are what have kept Pompeii standing all these centuries, and when they are removed from the city's buildings, these structures are no longer stable. The timber roofing that held the walls of Pompeian houses in balance was seared away in the pyroclastic phases of the eruption, and in the months after the eruption of 79, that sudden emptying of Vesuvius let loose a series of earthquakes as the ground settled to its new levels. The city that lay buried for seventeen hundred years was badly damaged before it began its long sleep..

For mysterious reasons, buildings truly thrive only when they are lived in. The buildings of Pompeii, roofless and derelict, begin to fall apart the moment they are brought to light, and although many have been supplied with new roofing and supporting structures, only a few of them have real inhabitants who use them as offices, storerooms, and a little onsite clinic. For the rest, the natural processes of decay automatically set in, accelerated because there is no one to live in these places and care for them as intently as people care for their own homes. There are simply too many buildings in Pompeii to watch over them all successfully. A former superintendent, Fausto Zevi, has openly admitted wishing that Don Amedeo had been just a little less efficient in uncovering new sections of the city because the vast extent of excavated ground only made his own task as superintendent so much more monumental.

Furthermore, Pompeii continues to exist in a seismic zone, not least because of the active volcano on its horizon. In September of 1980 San Gennaro's blood failed to liquefy, and in November of that year the region of Campania was struck with a devastating earthquake, so strong that we felt it in Rome, too. Areas of Naples and Pompeii sustained severe damage, including the famous House of the Vettii, where a painted wall buckled in one of the side rooms (alae) off the atrium and had to be propped up with metal tubing. This, the first large earthquake since the massive clearings of the mid-twentieth century, turned the focus of work onsite almost entirely to restoration and maintenance of what had already been exposed. Enough time has elapsed since Maiuri's teams put in their concrete and iron additions to the ancient structures for these to have deteriorated, and because the restorations were carried out in different materials from the structures themselves, they have decayed at different rates, with the result that the two kinds of construction, ancient and modern, tend to pull apart. Ancient Roman concrete was seasoned for two years before it was put to work and is nearly indestructible; modern concrete normally is left to season for only two weeks.

A walk through Pompeii today is also a walk through the archaeology of the more recent campaigns to keep the site on its feet. A few signs survive from the early twentieth century, like the metal exit signs at the amphitheater, hand painted in red letters on a white ground, works of craftsmanship in their own right and remarkably durable. The labels and signs printed on plastic sheets and glued to metal or fiberglass bases have proven far less reliable; they are almost all sun bleached and peeling away. The most recent material for maps and labels is a superhard ceramic that looks durable and relatively vandalproof; pottery was one of the materials that survived the eruption of Vesuvius without significant damage. Only time will tell how gracefully these ceramic panels will age, and when it time reveals its truths, as in the case of those Pompeians who built on the cheap and used cut-rate color for their wall paintings, it holds back nothing.

The Pompeian houses that archaeologists have explored are all closed off by iron gates, some dating from Maiuri's time, some from the early 2000s; these later barriers bear the legend "Pompei Viva"—Living Pompeii, a campaign that began in 2010 and ended in 2012. In 2009 an initiative led to putting up panels describing the plants and gardens of the site; these, though faded, still provide welcome information about a place that can be gloriously lush at certain times of year. One of the saddest projects to present an archaeological ruin in its own right was an attempt to help the stray dogs who populate the site. To draw up a census of the dogs, sterilize them, guarantee them veterinary care, and encourage their adoption, 132,000 euros were allocated to the "Project (C)Ave Canem."[2] Fifty-five dogs were listed on the census, twenty-six were adopted, a handful of doghouses were scattered around the site, and most of the money was pocketed by the man entrusted with the office of "special commissioner" for Pompeii, who is now under indictment for embezzlement. No one has the heart to take down the tattered sign that says "Adopt Melager," with the face of a winsome pup. Now Pompeii is filled with signs warning tourists not to touch the dogs, and the population of stray dogs has soared; people dump their dogs because they know that they will be cared for—but not as well as they should be. The cats, an exotic Egyptian rarity in ancient Roman times but common today, still need a guardian angel.[3]

The climate of Italy seems to be changing, too; it is becoming significantly hotter and wetter. Erosion caused by rain has been Pompeii's worst problem in recent years. Seepage softens the soil and enters the spaces between bricks and building blocks, corroding the mortar and undermining stability. Two buildings (one largely a modern reconstruction) and several walls have collapsed since 2010. Much of the site is now off limits to visitors for fear that tottering structures might fall on them.

Other structures have been erected over the years to spruce up entrances or host exhibitions, like the buildings at the Nolan gate, which were put up in 1914 to greet the new line of the Circumvesuviana railway, or the modernistic horseshoe-shaped twin pavilions that were installed in 2009 at the amphitheater entrance and now stand empty and fading on either side of an equally defunct drinking fountain. Most of the wine that has been made from the vineyards within Pompeii, a vintage called "Villa of the Mysteries," is lying stacked in a storeroom, used as diplomatic gifts or sold at eighty euros a bottle. Most of the plaster casts of the dead are also lying in a storeroom, turning into powder.

Neglect is not the only fate to threaten an archaeological site. Excessive use and excessive restoration can change it, too, and some archaeologists regard this kind of change as destruction. In 2010, for example, the theater of Pompeii was restored in order to turn it into a functional performance space, but this "restoration" turned out to be a massive, permanent reconstruction in concrete. Since 1964 the Venice Charter for the Conservation and Restoration of Monuments and Sites has prescribed that restorers' interventions at archaeological sites be reversible, but the definition of "reversible" can be extremely flexible, and not only in Pompeii or only in Italy.

From the mid-eighteenth century until the 1990s, workers at every level from the guards to the superintendent lived in a separate village near the amphitheater, on land that belonged first to the Crown and then to the Italian state. Until Bartolo Longo appeared on the scene, there was no town of Pompeii to house them. This pine-shaded excavators' village was finally evacuated by order of the superintendency in 1997, breaking a tradition built up over centuries. Up to then, the director of the excavations had always lived on site. Baldassare Conticello was the last superintendent of Pompeii and Herculaneum to live in the village (in the house where he suddenly found himself hosting the Clinton family in 1994). His wife, Marisa de' Spagnolis, was surprised at the intensity of her reaction when the order came for them to move out:[4]

> The eviction from the [village], even if legitimate, hit me so hard that I considered it an unjust act. It wiped out the last witnesses to a world that had, if only subconsciously, reflected the life of Pompeii under the Bourbons. It struck down the soul of unburied Pompeii, made up of workers, assistants, excavators, archaeologists, who lived on location, ready for every kind of intervention on behalf of the ancient city. One stroke obliterated an aspect of the past that should instead have been safeguarded, so that it could continue to bear witness to a bygone way of life, miraculously preserved by persons who transmitted a heritage without even thinking about it. . . . The population of the [village] no longer existed. It had been dispersed, annihilated, forced to opt for modern Pompeii, to live far away from that strip of land that constituted the border with ancient Pompeii, a threshold between reality and imagination, between present and

past. I felt myself a part of that ancient world and I was surprised to find myself contemplating a desolate future.

The little workers' village was where old Pompeii maintained its historical memory through the families that had lived there for generations. As we have already seen, these people had never been a part of New Pompeii, and the elderly villagers, especially, resisted their eviction desperately, if unsuccessfully. The buildings, evacuated with such trouble, have been turned from houses, the purpose for which they were built, into storerooms, a purpose for which they are at best a jerry-built solution. Most of them have been vandalized. Today they stand, lifeless and dilapidated, behind a parking lot, a wretched substitute for what was there before: an anchor of security and stability for the site and, as Dottoressa de' Spagnolis realized with rare insight, for its history.

The real problem with all of these interventions is a decades-long lack of coordination; they have been financed project by project, by money taken from different sources. Don Amedeo's twenty-seven-year reign as superintendent secured a consistent policy for the site that shorter-term directors cannot possibly match; fortunately, the proposal made early in 2013 to limit the terms of superintendents to three years was squelched shortly after it was introduced.

That venerable landmark, the Hotel Diomede, was sacrificed circa 1960 to the entrance booth of the autostrada, an extravagant 1960s fantasy that has itself been replaced by a taller, utterly anonymous structure that can admit double-decker tour buses. The Hotel Sole was bombed into nothingness in World War II but has been rebuilt on the same site. Of the earliest hostelries, only the Hotel Suisse survives, flanked by the venerable Hotel Vittoria (formerly the Hotel Pompei), which still has a bar and a cameo shop just as it did in 1962, though both bar and shop have been much remodeled since that more austere time. Since the 1960s,

Pompeii has adjusted, better than many historical places, to the motorization of Italy. And motorization has once again changed the way that visitors experience the buried city. Individuals still take the train or drive their own cars, but the great bulk of visitors come in gigantic buses that look like metallic insects with mirror antennae.

Today, the cheapest way to tour Pompeii, both site and sanctuary, is through a peculiar kind of Italian package tour (memorably satirized in the film *Bread and Tulips*). Leaflets advertising these low-cost adventures begin appearing in Italian mailboxes as soon as the spring flowers come out. The reason for this sudden bloom is eminently practical: daylight savings time lengthens the touring day, so, for example, a one-day jaunt from Rome to the south of Naples is logistically feasible. The itinerary is changeless regardless of the company or the destination, and it leaves little to the imagination: pickup between 6 and 6:30 a.m. at several different sites in Rome in an "autobus Gran Turismo" or simply "autobus G/T," where the "gran" no longer means grand but only big, not Grand Tourism, then, but Big Mass Tourism.

Once it has loaded its cargo, the Autobus Gran Turismo heaves its way onto the Autostrada del Sole somewhere near the New Appian Way and barrels the 150 kilometers to Pontecorvo in about two hours. Pontecorvo is a tiny medieval town that lies in the plain beneath the looming silhouette of Montecassino, the great Benedictine monastery obliterated by Allied bombs in World War II and lovingly reconstructed in the 1950s. At the Pontecorvo rest stop (either the official Autogrill or the private facility just off the off ramp), the Gran Turisti breakfast on their allotment of one brioche, one coffee or cappuccino, and one glass of juice. Back onto the bus and on to a demonstration of home appliances, which takes place either on a factory floor in the middle of a blasted Campanian heath or on the bus itself. Gifts are given to the participants to induce them to buy home appliances in gratitude. Now it is time

FROM POMPEII

for lunch, which consists of one pasta course, one meat, one vegetable, one fruit, half a liter of water, and one-quarter liter of vino. Then and only then do the Gran Turisti meet Pompeii and deepen the acquaintance for another hour or so. After the designated time for souvenirs, it is already time for a return to the Autobus Gran Turismo and the three and a half-hour ride back to Rome. Italian law prevents the driver of the Autobus Gran Turismo from working more than twelve hours a day, and every bus has a built-in recorder to register its movements with implacable impartiality. The low-cost trip to Pompeii provides an hour or two of Pompeii in exchange for a few euros, eight hours of travel time, and the home appliance show. Pompeii, in other words, can now be explored in isolation from the rest of the Bay of Naples, and what visitors bring back with them is likely to have little or nothing to do with Pompeii itself; it will be either a pan or a Chinese-made, two-euro refrigerator magnet or plastic "coral."

A slightly higher-end bus tour from Rome to Pompeii makes two stops in the course of a ride down the Autostrada del Sole. Pontecorvo figures, of course, for "coffee"; human physiology requires, on average, a stop every two hours. When the bus leaves the autostrada again, Vesuvius is directly in their view, and passengers can see another windswept monastery, this one Baroque and brilliant white, gleaming in splendid isolation over a solidified lava flow. Pompeii is almost close enough to touch, but the owners of the Torre del Greco cameo shops know that visitors will never be more alert and more attentive (and more grateful for the rest stop) than they are at midmorning. And so the bus pauses for half an hour as the passengers watch a demonstration of cameo carving, drink more coffee, and wander among the cases of cameos and corals in every size and shape, carved at every level of skill for every budget.

At quarter of twelve every day of the year but Christmas and New Year's, the forum of Pompeii is crammed with humanity.

The cruise ships that have landed at Naples, Salerno, or Gaeta gather their flocks behind guides armed with numbered paddles and shuffle toward the Temple of Venus and the exit; lunch is waiting, and nothing, absolutely nothing, is more important on these mass excursions than The Schedule. School groups are gathering, too, more rowdily though no less hungrily; they leave the most trash behind them, but as a rule they also take away the liveliest, sometimes most life-changing impressions.

The best way to explore Pompeii, of course, is to spend several days there, to walk around the city walls, explore every room and every pathway, and find the places where it is perfectly possible to forget what century it is (Figure 19.1).

Like the peripheral industries around Pompeii, the archaeological site itself has been an important source of employment in the area for two centuries. The guides who once took visitors around the site, the descendants of the original *ciceroni,* used to be local dynasts with varying degrees of expertise and a desperate need to feed their families. Today the guides are apt to be recent graduates of the University of Naples with degrees in archaeology—as are some of the vendors who work the souvenir stands outside the gates. Italy runs specialized "technical institutes," the equivalent of high schools, for hotels and tourism; in Pompeii itself, the Istituto Bartolo Longo offers this opportunity. At present, therefore, what travelers may expect from their Autobus Gran Turismo, from their learned companionship to their food to their experience on-site, is often professionalism at a very high level. That professional skill extends to the clinic inside the archaeological site in an ancient Pompeian house equipped to care for every visitor who faints, falls, or steps on a rusty pin (as one of my students once managed to do). Visitors are Pompeii's lifeline; news of bad service gets around. The guide for Carrani Tours, who was my sworn "enemy" in the early 1980s, was qualified and efficient; we were enemies because, as a very young professor, I tended to go

FROM POMPEII

19.1.   Pompeii, amphitheater at Porta Nolana, May 2013. Photo by author.

on much too long when I stood in the Stabian baths or the House of Vettii, and my endless disquisitions interfered with his well-honed, finely tuned schedule. In his youth, he was probably more like me; with experience, I, like him, have learned to pare down my presentations to the essentials. Our rivalry reached its climax one day in 1979, when he and his group stormed through my flock of students at the entrance to the House of the Vetti—leaving us to deal with the painting of Priapus while he and his group contemplated the atrium. Too late he realized what a gift he had left me: an opportunity to talk about macho men and phallic symbols with a prime exhibit fresh in everyone's memory. His suspicions were instantly confirmed by waves of laughter from the vestibule, and he was ready for me when we finally came into the atrium. "Do you try me again? Do you want a fight?" he asked and stalked off to the alcove with the sculpted Priapus (the one forbidden to Hillary Clinton) as my students and I went the other way, into the dining room. Bacchus, the god of drama, had been served his tribute for the day, and perhaps Priapus had as well.

Coda: Atomic Pizza

Pompeii, the living Roman city, ended in a cataclysm, but that same cataclysm is where the phenomenon we know as Pompeii began. Where will it end? Vesuvius has not erupted since 1944. Geologists warn that, with every passing year, the likelihood that a plug has formed becomes greater, and that means that when the plug is finally expelled, the explosion will undoubtedly be violent. Samuel Johnson's dear friend, Hester Lynch Piozzi, worried about the wrath of Vesuvius in 1789: "How dreadful are the thoughts which such a sight suggests! how *very* horrible the certainty, that such a scene might be all acted over again tomorrow; and that, who to-day are spectators, may become spectacles to travellers of a succeeding century, who mistaking our bones for those of the Neapolitans, may carry some of them to their native country back again perhaps."[1]

When Athanasius Kircher wrote *Mundus subterraneus,* Naples, with about 300,000 souls, was one of the world's most populous cities. Today the same region supports a population of 3.5 million. When Vesuvius erupts again, as it certainly will, between 550,000 and 600,000 people will be at extreme risk: those living on the mountain itself or in the cities of Pompeii, Ercolano, Torre del Greco, Castellamare di Stabia, the places downwind from the prevailing local breezes, the same places that have always suffered first. Responsibility for their evacuation will fall by law to the Italian state's Department of Civil Protection (Protezione civile). This agency maintains permanent monitoring stations for seven volcanic areas in Italy: Etna, Vesuvius, the volcanic islands of Stromboli, Vulcano, and Ischia, the Phlegraean Fields (the area of Monte Nuovo, Pozzuoli, and the Solfatara), and the volcanic fields under the Tyrrhenian Sea. As geologists keep reminding us, the volcano's lack of activity since 1944 suggests that it has once again built up a solid core of material that will explode in an eruption of the kind and on the scale of the ones that occurred in 79, 472, and 1631. The website of the Protezione civile pulls no punches for all its restrained bureaucratic language ("volcanic bombs" says it all):

> In light of [the volcano's] past behavior it is predicted that, if activity resumes within the next few decades, the next eruption will be of sub-Plinian type (that is, a massive explosion accompanied by pyroclastic surges without lava), similar to that of 1631 or of 472. In that case, the scenario of expected phenomena would include the formation of a sustained eruptive column several kilometers in height, the fall of volcanic bombs and blocks in the immediate vicinity of the crater and of smaller particles (ash and lapilli) to a distance of several dozen kilometers, along with the formation of pyroclastic flows that would run down the slopes of the volcano for several kilometers.[2]

The area has never been so carefully watched; there is an observation station on Vesuvius itself, and seismographs monitor every movement of the earth in the surrounding area. The study of volcanoes has become a science. Moreover, scientists, along with the Protezione civile, insist that the next eruption of Vesuvius will not occur overnight; warning signs will appear, just as they did in 79. The earthquake of 63 was one indication that the earth had begun to move, but, as we know, it was only a vague predictor of future events. The real signs of imminent eruption in 79 and again in 1631, for which we have the best documentation, seem to have shown themselves only the day before Vesuvius exploded. With the help of modern instruments that track movements within the volcano's cone and on its surface, the Protezione civile estimates that it will have several weeks' advance notice rather than a single day, enough time, the agency hopes, to evacuate the area safely. Needless to say, the archbishop of Naples and San Gennaro will also be on the alert.

Scientists are looking for several different signs of renewed activity: a change in ground level, small earthquakes, and changes in the gravitational field, in temperature, and in the gases the volcano emits. If any of these parameters should alter, the Protezione civile will put the whole Bay of Naples in a state of "pre-alert," especially the "Red Zone"—those communities at greatest risk. Police, firefighters, and rescue workers will take up the stations they have long been assigned by a national emergency plan, and residents who wish to evacuate may do so; their homes will be placed under surveillance to avoid looting. These future evacuees already know where they should go if friends or relatives cannot take them in; each of the eighteen towns at greatest risk has been "adopted" by a separate region (in Italy, the equivalent of states in the United States):

> If the phenomena should continue to increase, then a phase of alarm will be announced. This means that the experts agree that the eruption is almost certain to happen and may happen within the space of a few weeks. The alarm phase is

declared, in fact, a few weeks before the eruption. The entire Red Zone is evacuated, and the population of the 18 communities is transferred to secure areas . . . in this phase the removal of the whole population of the Red Zone is foreseen. The plan foresees that within 72 hours 600,000 residents of the Red Zone will be removed according to the specifications contained in the individual emergency plans for each community. The population may travel to [safety] using their own automobile or buses provided by the Protezione civile. They will use the streets and access points already established by the Emergency Plan. Trains and boats are used as strategic resources for possible critical situations in activating the plan and for possible transport of additional rescue workers.[3]

Will everyone escape? It is hard to know, but it seems unlikely. The Protezione civile, with its vast network of carefully prepared volunteers from the Red Cross and other organizations, has become an extremely efficient organization. But Naples is a special case among cities, a place so troubled by millennia of bad government, so dense and so complicated that the heretic Giordano Bruno, in one of his works, used the city as an image of the universe itself. Yet despite its appearance of chaos, Naples has a resilient spirit that has seen it through millennia of trouble. Neither total efficiency nor total disorder would be out of character; probably, as with most human tales, the story of the next eruption will amount to a bit of both.

Panic is the hardest factor to predict in any disaster, and panic in a society as theatrical as that of Naples is particularly hard to assess beforehand. A quiet evacuation does not seem conceivable. Furthermore, public transportation in the region is already packed, while the traffic from private cars is so dense that the autostrada has had to add a third lane to the route between Naples and

Salerno. What will happen when the earth is shaking, when overpasses and train tracks threaten to buckle?

After centuries of oppressive government, moreover, Neapolitans are born skeptics. They are also, necessarily, long accustomed to looking out for themselves by bending rules and evading supervision. But generations of experience in getting by as individuals, in providing ingenious, generous help to family, friends, or guests is nothing like participating in a great collective action, which an evacuation needs to be. It was probably easier for Pliny the Elder to manage his rescue operation in 79, under the strong arm of the Roman Empire, than it will be for his democratic successors in the Protezione civile two millennia later.

If the towns around Mount Etna provide any indication, some people will also refuse to leave their homes either for sentimental reasons, out of faith in San Gennaro, or for fear of looters. No matter how well the region may be prepared for it, the next eruption of Vesuvius, like the next big earthquake in Los Angeles, will obey the whims of the subterranean world rather than the desires of the creatures, animal or vegetable, dwelling on its surface.

Besides, no matter how dangerous Vesuvius may be, brooding within its ashen cone, statistical odds favor the people who have always lived out their lives on its slopes. For most people, plants, and animals, fertility within their limited lifespan is more important to their own survival than the long cycles of Earth's crust. Most of the living creatures that populate the mountain will never experience a terrible eruption, and among those that do eventually witness one, many, perhaps even most, will survive the experience. There is simply no way to escape the discrepancy of scale between Vesuvius and human beings; it is one of the reasons that Pompeii pulls so on our imagination. The eruption could happen again any time. It will happen. But it is a disaster only to the tiny creatures that cling to the earth's surface, not to the earth itself.

For Father Kircher, the specter of Vesuvius was a stimulus to religious faith as well as scientific curiosity:

> But the Conversions of the Terrestrial Globe are so large and so horrible that they lay bare both the infinite power of GOD and the uncertainty of human fortune, and warn the human inhabitants of this Earth to recognize that nothing is perpetual and stable, but that all things are fallible, subject to the varying fates of fortune and mortality, and that they should raise their thoughts, studies, soul and mind, which can be satisfied by no tangible object, toward the sublime and eternal Good, and long for GOD alone, in whose hands are all the laws of Kingdoms, and the boundaries of universal Nature.[4]

San Gennaro and Bartolo Longo, among others, would surely agree. However, regardless of our beliefs about God, San Gennaro, nature, and fate, Vesuvius inexorably confronts us with our own mortality. Pompeii, the volcano's ancient victim, seizes our imagination both because it was so alive up until the moment the mountain exploded and because that place, so intensely, so intricately living, could be gone in a flash.

But long before that flash erupts again, Pompeii may fall to pieces bit by bit, suffering gradual death by entropy and neglect. Archaeological sites are notoriously vulnerable places; the complex balances of load and support that keep buildings standing were destroyed when the city was buried, and when these damaged buildings are freed from their layers of volcanic detritus, they are exposed to gravity as well as the elements. Frescoes deteriorate in both rain and the presence of salt and carbon dioxide. So does stucco. The earthquake of November 1980 shook Pompeii badly, and heavy rains, which are one symptom of climate change in Italy, have undermined some Pompeian buildings to the point of collapse. It will all disappear someday, no matter what we do; astronomers tell us that we will all be incinerated one day by an expanding sun and geologists warn that every bit of dry land will one day be subducted under the earth's crust.

Often, however, change sneaks up on us with such tiny steps that we barely notice. Take the wild and crazy concrete buildings that sprang up in the 1960s alongside the autostrada from Naples to Pompeii, including the tollbooth that supplanted the Hotel Diomede: they once seemed as permanent as the Mediterranean landscape, and now they are gone. They heralded the future as confidently as the hot-peppery pizzas and pasta sauces named "Atomic," also a favorite in the 1960s. "Atomic" cuisine, sadly, is also largely a thing of the past, especially since the 1986 explosion of the nuclear reactor at Chernobyl showered Italy with poisonous fallout and gave the adjective "atomic" a different nuance. But once upon a time, the roadside constructions and the tollbooths of Campania were as excitingly modern as Giordano Robbiati's "Atomic" aluminum coffeemakers, those joyous stovetop espresso machines with lines as graceful as an Airstream camper or, as one admirer has suggested, a sculpture by Henry Moore.

Because these "atomic" extravaganzas stood so close to the new modern roadway that provided them with their customers, the construction of the third lane of the A3 autostrada has swept them all away in the space of a few years, together, sad to say, with the spirit of optimism that created them. Today Pompeii looks out on a different world from the one it knew when I first visited in 1962; it is an internationally recognized UNESCO World Heritage Site managed, however haphazardly, by an infinitely more prosperous, a healthier, more broadly educated, and in many ways a kinder Italy. But these improvements have come at the price of environmental degradation, the persistence of organized crime, and a global network that stocks the souvenir stands at Porta Marina with Chinese-made souvenirs rather than the work of local artists

C.1.   Pompeii, juice vendor's stand. May 2013. Photo by author.

FROM POMPEII

and artisans (plastic cameos and "corals" are legion). Prosperity has brought a cynicism that the sincere "atomic" age lacked. Nonetheless, the juice sellers at Porta Marina still serve lemonade made from fat Amalfi lemons (Figure C.1), just as they have ever since the eighteenth century; the Hotel Suisse, still serves a creditable lunch to the masses with a stoic smile and the patience of centuries; and the sun still smiles down on Pompeii through the umbrella pines.

Notes

1. Pompeii, May 2013

1. Giacomo Leopardi, *Canti,* 39, "La ginestra o il fiore del deserto." My translation. Written in 1836, published posthumously in 1845.

2. See the official website of the Pompeii excavations for the connection the superintendent's department has made between Settembrini's letter and the casts: http://www.pompeiisites.org/Sezione.jsp?titolo=L%27+inven zione+dei+Calchi&idSezione=1220.

3. Luca Mercalli, weather columnist for *La Stampa* and president of the Italian Meteorological Association, is an authority on climate change in Italy; in addition to his column in *La Stampa,* see *Prepariamoci* (Milan: Chiarelettere, 2011).

4. The Pompeii Viva project was launched in 2010 by Marcello Fiori, then commissioner of Pompeii, now under indictment for corruption; see Andrea Guerrini, "Gli ultimi giorni di Pompei?," http://tropismi.altervista .org/wordpress/gli-ultimi-giorni-di-pompei/ (accessed August 25, 2013).

2. The Blood of San Gennaro and the Eruption of Vesuvius

1. Bruno Brillante, *Sebeto: Storia e mito di un fiume* (Naples: Massa Editore, 2000). A Roman mile, from which the English mile derives, consisted of a thousand steps.

2. Alwyn Scarth, *Vesuvius: A Biography* (Princeton, NJ: Princeton University Press, 2009), 36–37.

3. Vitruvius, *Ten Books on Architecture,* trans. Ingrid D. Rowland, illustrated by Thomas Noble Howe, commentary by Michael J. Dewar, Thomas Noble Howe, and Ingrid D. Rowland (Cambridge: Cambridge University Press, 1999), II.6.2.

4. Scarth, *Vesuvius,* 36–37.

5. Vitruvius, *Ten Books on Architecture,* I.praef.2.

6. Martial, *Epigrams*, ed. D. R. Shackleton Bailey, 3 vols. (Cambridge, MA: Loeb Classical Library, 1995), IV.44: "Haec iuga quam Nysae colles plus Bacchus amavit." The exact location of Nysa, whether in Ethiopia, India, Asia Minor, or Central Asia, is uncertain.

7. For the discussion that follows, see Scarth, *Vesuvius,* 38–85.

8. Ibid., 44.

9. Ibid., 44–82.

10. Ibid.

11. In addition to ibid., see Sean Cocco, *Watching Vesuvius: A History of Science and Culture in Early Modern Italy* (Chicago: University of Chicago Press, 2013); Gillian Darley, *Vesuvius: The Most Famous Volcano in the World* (New York: Profile Books, 2011); Haraldur Sigurdsson, *Melting the Earth: The History of Ideas on Volcanic Eruptions* (New York: Oxford University Press, 1999).

12. Giordano Bruno, *De Immenso,* quoted in Ingrid D. Rowland, *Giordano Bruno, Philosopher/Heretic* (New York: Farrar, Straus, and Giroux, 2008), 20–21.

13. Ibid.

14. Scarth, *Vesuvius,* 115–134; Cocco, *Watching Vesuvius,* 40–43.

15. The famous popular revolt led by the fisherman Masaniello broke out in 1648. For social tensions in Naples in 1631, see Cocco, *Watching Vesuvius,* and Nino Leone, *Napoli ai tempi di Masaniello* (Milan: Biblioteca Universale Rizzoli, 2001).

16. Joan Molina Figueras, "Un emblema arturiano per Alfonso d'Aragona: Storia, mito, propaganda," *Bullettino dell'Istituto Storico Italiano per il Medioevo* 114 (2012): 231–269.

17. For Ferdinand and Isabella, see Felipe Fernandez-Armesto, *Ferdinand and Isabella* (London: Dorset, 1992). For Juana, see Bethany Aram,

Juana the Mad: Sovereignty and Dynasty in Renaissance Europe (Baltimore: Johns Hopkins University Press, 2005). For Philip II and Charles V, see Henry Kamen, *The Escorial: Art and Power in the Renaissance* (New Haven, CT: Yale University Press, 2010).

18. Gino Fornaciari, "Le mummie aragonesi in San Domenico Maggiore a Napoli," http://www.paleopatologia.it/articoli/aticolo.php?record ID=49 (accessed August 26, 2013).

19. Catholic Church, *The Roman Martyrology*, rev. ed. (Baltimore: John Murphy, 1916), 289 (September 19).

20. Diana Norman, "The Succorpo in the Cathedral of Naples: 'Empress of All Chapels,'" *Zeitschrift für Kunstgeschichte* 49, no. 3 (1986): 323–355.

21. See Maria Ann Conelli, "The *Guglie* of Naples: Religious and Political Machinations of the Festival *Macchine*," *Memoirs of the American Academy in Rome* 45 (2000): 153–183, esp. 154–160.

22. Hershel Shanks, "The Destruction of Pompeii: God's Revenge?," *Biblical Archaeology Review* 36, no. 4 (July/August 2010): 60–69.

3. Before Pompeii

1. Scarth, *Vesuvius,* 29–35. See also the website for the Comune di Nola: http://www.comune.nola.na.it/index.php?option=com_content&view =article&id=168&Itemid=218 (accessed August 20, 2013).

2. Cocco, *Watching Vesuvius,* 26–39.

3. Jacopo Sannazaro, *Arcadia* (Venice: Aldus Manutius, 1534), 77–78.

4. Carlo Bonucci, *Pompei descritta da Carlo Bonucci, architetto, terza edizione, contenente tutte le scoverte sino alla fine di Aprile del 1827* (Naples: Da' Torchi di Raffaele Miranda, 1827), 33, 221; Count Egon Caesar Corti, *The Destruction and Resurrection of Pompeii and Herculaneum* (London: Taylor and Francis, 1944), 98. See also Andrew Wallace-Hadrill, *Herculaneum: Past and Future* (London: Frances Lincoln, 2011). Judith Harris, *Pompeii Reawakened: A Story of Rediscovery* (London: I. B. Tauris, 2009), 269, misidentifies Bonucci's citation from Sannazaro's *Arcadia* as a diary entry for Fontana.

5. Giulio Cesare Capaccio, *Il forastiero: Dialogi di Giulio Cesare Capaccio, accademico otioso* (Naples: Giovanni Domenico Roncagliolo, 1634), 1008, 1014.

6. Vincenzo Noghera (Vincente Nogueira), [Letters to Cardinal Francesco Barberini], MS Barb. Lat. 6472, 23v.

7. MS Barb. Lat. 6488, 6r–41v.

8. Ibid., 36r.

9. Philippus Cluverius, *Italia antiqua* (Leiden: Ex officina Elsiviriana, 1624).

10. Lucas Holste [Holstenius], *Letters*, Vatican Library, MS Barb. Lat. 6488, 36v–37r.

11. Ibid., 53r.

12. Lucas Holstenius [Lucas Holste], *Commentaria in Cluverii Italiam,* in Holste, *Annotationes in geographiam sacram Caroli à S. Paulo; Italiam antiquam Cluverii; et thesaurum geographicum Ortelii* (Rome: Typis Iacobi Dragondelli, 1666), 243: "Quinimò certissimum est Pompeios fuisse ubi nunc maxima visuntur rudera, loco, qui Civita vulgo dicitur, ut Ambr. Nolanus Stabias olim fuisse existimavit. Sed lapides nuper hic effossi, et Stabias translati Pompeiios fuisse certo ostendunt. Tum nomen ipsum Civita hoc confirmat, ut Cluverius non semel in aliis locis observat. Tum etiam intervallum inter Pompeios et Nuceriam XII m. p. ostendi citra Scafati ponendam esse."

13. Otto Hein, *Athanasius Kircher in Malta: Ein Beitrag zur Geschichte* (Weinheim: Wiley–VCH Verlag, 1996).

14. Athanasius Kircher, *Vita Admodum Reverendi Athanasii Kircheri, Societatis Jesu, viri toto orbe celebratissimi* (Augsburg: Utschneider, 1684). Paula Findlen provides a good biographical sketch of Kircher in "The Last Man Who Knew Everything . . . or Did He? Athanasius Kircher, S.J. (1602–1680) and His World," in Paula Findlen, ed., *Athanasius Kircher: The Last Man Who Knew Everything* (New York: Routledge, 2004), 1–50. For an occasionally overt theosophist's standpoint, see Joscelyn Godwin, *Athanasius Kircher's Theatre of the World: The Life and Work of the Last Man to Search for Universal Knowledge* (Rochester, VT: Inner Traditions, 2009).

15. Athanasius Kircher, *Mundus subterraneus,* in *XII Libros digestos* (Amsterdam: Apud Joannem Janssonium et Elizaeum Weyerstraten, 1665; third ed. 1678), ***v.

16. As in *Mundus Subterraneus,* ** 2r.

17. Harald Siebert, *Die große kosmologische Kontroverse: Rekonstruktionsversuche anhand des Itinerarium exstaticum von Athanasius Kircher SJ (1602–1680)* (Stuttgart: Franz Steiner Verlag, 2006).

18. The first edition of this work was called *Itinerarium Extaticum Coeleste* (Rome: Typis Vitalis Mascardi, 1656); in 1660 it was republished, with annotations and revision, by his fellow Jesuit Gaspar Schott as *Iter Exstaticum Coeleste* (Würzburg: Sumptibus Joh. Andr. & Wolffg. Jun. Endterorum Haeredibus).

19. Cocco, *Watching Vesuvius*, 154–155.

20. Athanasius Kircher, *Scrutinium physico-medicum perniciosae lues sive pestis* (Rome: Typis Mascardi, 1658).

21. Kircher was already touting the *Mundus subterraneus* in the *Obeliscus pamphilius* of 1650 and *Itinerarium extaticum* of 1656.

22. Athanasius Kircher, *Athanasii Kircheri Diatribe de prodigiosis Crucibus, quae tam supra vestes hominum, quam res alias, non pridem post ultimum incendium Vesuvii montis Neapoli comparuerunt* (Rome: Sumptibus Blasii Deversin, 1661), 30–31.

23. Ibid. 31–32.

24. Ibid., 42.

25. Rome, Archivum Societatis Iesu 663, *Censurae librorum 1626–1663*, 306r–306v.

26. Kircher, *Diatribe de prodigiosis crucibus.* 44.

27. Pope Alexander's copy is Vatican Library, Chigi S.81.

28. Kircher, *Iter Exstaticum Coeleste*, 141 (cited from 1671 edition).

29. Ingrid D. Rowland, "A Catholic Reader of Giordano Bruno in Counter-Reformation Rome: Athanasius Kircher, SJ, and *Panspermia Rerum*," in Henning Hufnagel and Anne Eusterschulte, eds., *Turning Tradition Upside Down: Rethinking Giordano Bruno's Enlightenment* (Berlin: Max-Planck-Institut für Wissenschaftsgeschichte, 2013), 221–236.

30. Richard J. Blackwell, *Behind the Scenes at Galileo's Trial: Including the First English Translation of Melchior Inchofer's* Tractatus syllepticus (Notre Dame, IN: University of Notre Dame Press, 2008).

31. Cocco, *Watching Vesuvius*.

32. See Ingrid D. Rowland, "Athanasius Kircher, Giordano Bruno, and the *Panspermia* of the Infinite Universe," in Paula Findlen, ed., *Athanasius Kircher, the Last Man Who Knew Everything* (New York: Routledge, 2004), 191–206; Rowland, "Catholic Reader."

33. Svante Arrhenius, "Die Verbreitung des Lebens im Weltraum," *Die Umschau*, 1903.

34. Wolf-Dieter Barz, "Landgraf Friedrich von Hessen und zu Goletta, eine markante Persönlichkeit und ein markanter Ort in der Geschichte des Malteser-Ordens," *Zeitschrift des Vereins für Hessische Geschichte und Landeskunde,* 93 (1988): 73–94; Anton Ph. Brück, "Friedrich, Landgraf von Hessen-Darmstadt," in Historische Kommission bei der Bayerischen Akademie der Wissenschaften, *Neue Deutsche Biographie,* vol. 5 (Berlin: Duncker und Humblot, 1961), 504; Ulrich Köchli, "Friedrich von Hessen-Darmstadt," in Friedrich Wilhelm Bautz, ed., *Biographisch-Bibliographisches Kirchenlexikon,* vol. 23 (Nordhausen: Bautz, 2004), 424–433.

35. Christopher C. Parslow, *Rediscovering Antiquity: Karl Weber and the Excavation of Herculaneum, Pompeii, and Stabiae* (Cambridge: Cambridge University Press, 1995), 23–24.

36. Ibid., 23.

37. http://www.corteappello.napoli.it/astegiudiziarie/Secondasel.aspx?id =606779&ida=133700&idp=353253&m=&t= (accessed October 20, 2013).

38. Maria Luisa Margiotta, "Asta per Villa d'Elboeuf un' occasione di riscatto," *La Repubblica,* February 21, 2012, refers to the third auction. For the appalling state of the property, see Andrea Scala, "Villa d'Elboeuf all'asta: C'è il pericolo camorra," *Portici Press,* April 4, 2013, http://www .porticipress.it/home/leggiNotizia.asp?ID=6221 (accessed August 18, 2013); Andrea Scala, "Portici, in fiamme villa d'Elboeuf, la denuncia dell'associazione Borgo Antico," *Il Gazzettino Vesuviano,* August 20, 2011; Maurizio Vitale, "La rovina di Villa d'Elboeuf," *Lo Speaker,* March 12, 2013, http://www .lospeaker.it/la-rovina-di-villa-delbeouf/[*sic*], with photographs; "Portici, le macerie della villa reale," *Napoli Città Sociale,* February 25, 2013, http:// www.napolicittasociale.it/portal/reportage/2975-portici (all accessed August 18, 2013). A beautiful but shocking photo essay published in April 2013 by Aniello Langella, "Il Palazzo D'Elbeuf a Portici—reportage fotografico," appears at http://www.vesuvioweb.com/it/2012/01/aniello-langella-il-palazzo-delbeuf -a-portici-reportage-fotografico/ (accessed August 18, 2013). Langella, notably, spells the duke's name correctly.

39. "Villa d'Elboeuf [*sic*] venduta per quattro milioni," *La Repubblica,* April 26, 2013; Fabio Di Bitonto, "È stata venduta Villa D'Elboeuf," *Il Brigante,* April 12, 2013, http://www.ilbrigante.it/attualita/e-stata-venduta-villa -delboeuf (both accessed August 18, 2013).

4. Mr. Freeman Goes to Herculaneum

1. Jacopo Sannazaro, *Arcadia* (Venice: Aldus Manutius, 1534), 78.

2. Many of the texts I cite here and in the following chapters have unusual spellings, sometimes occurring in rapid succession.

3. "Extract of a Letter from Mr. George Knapton to Mr. Charles Knapton, concerning the same Subject" (sc. Herculaneum), *Philosophical Transactions of the Royal Society* 41 (1739–1741): 490–491.

4. William Hammond, letter published in "An Account of the Discovery of the Remains of a City under-ground, near Naples, communicated to the Royal Society by William Sloane, Esq., F.R.S.," *Philosophical Transactions of the Royal Society* 41 (1739–1741): 345.

5. Sergio Brancaccio, *L'ambiente delle ville vesuviane* (Naples: Società editrice napoletana, 1983).

6. John H. D'Arms, *Romans on the Bay of Naples and Other Essays on Romans in Campania,* ed. Fausto Zevi (Bari: Edipuglia, 2003).

7. Maria Luisa Margiotta, Pasquale Belfiore, and Ornella Zerlenga, *Giardini storici napoletani* (Naples: Electa Napoli, 2000).

8. David Marshall, "A View of Poggioreale by Viviano Codazzi and Domenico Gargiulo," *Journal of the Society of Architectural Historians* 45, no. 1 (1986): 32–46.

9. Frank Snowden, *Naples in the Time of Cholera, 1884–1911* (Cambridge: Cambridge University Press, 2010).

10. Maria Corti, "Sannazaro, Iacobo," in Vittore Branca, ed., *Dizionario critico della letteratura italiana,* vol. 3 (Turin: UTET, 1973), 299–305.

11. Shulamit Furstenberg-Levi, "The Fifteenth-Century Accademia pontaniana: An Analysis of Its Institutional Elements," *History of Universities* 21 (2006): 33–70.

12. Ippolita di Maio, "Vittoria Colonna, il Castello di Ischia e la cultura delle corti," in P. Ragionieri, ed., *Vittoria Colonna e Michelangelo: Catalogo della mostra a Casa Buonarroti, 24 maggio–12 settembre 2005* (Florence: Mandragora 2005), 19–32.

13. John A. Marino, "Constructing the Past of Early Modern Naples," in Tommaso Astarita, ed., *The Brill Companion to Naples* (Leiden: Brill, 2013), 11–34; John A. Marino, *Becoming Neapolitan: Citizen Culture in*

Baroque Naples (Baltimore: Johns Hopkins University Press, 2010); Cocco, *Watching Vesuvius.*

14. Dawson W. Carr, *Velazquez* (London: National Gallery, 2006), 226.

15. Carlo Gasparri, ed., *Le gemme farnese: Museo Archeologico Nazionale* (Naples: Electa Napoli, 1994, 2006); Marina Belozerskaya, *Medusa's Gaze: The Extraordinary Journey of the* Tazza Farnese (Oxford: Oxford University Press, 2012).

16. "Extract of a Letter from Naples, concerning Herculaneum, Containing a Description of the Place, and What Has Been Found in It," *Philosophical Transactions of the Royal Society* 47 (1751–1752): 157.

17. Nicole Dacos, *La découverte de la Domus Aurea et la formation des grotesques à la Renaissance* (London: Warburg Institute, 1969).

18. Paolo Enrico Arias, "Mosaico ellenistico dalla Via Ardeatina," *Rivista del R. Istituto Nazionale d'Archeologia e Storia dell'arte,* ser. 1, 8, no. 1 (1940): 16–24.

19. This section owes a great debt to Paul Zanker, *Roman Art,* trans. Henry Heitmann-Gordon (Los Angeles: Getty Publications, 2010), 21–32.

20. Ada Cohen, *The Alexander Mosaic: Stories of Victory and Defeat* (Cambridge: Cambridge University Press, 2000). My thanks to Kenneth Lapatin for this reference.

21. John C. Clarke, *Looking at Lovemaking: Constructions of Sexuality in Roman Art, 100 B.C.–A.D. 250* (Berkeley: University of California Press, 2001); Mary Beard, "Dirty Little Secrets: Changing Displays of Pompeian 'Erotica,'" in Victoria C. Gardner Coates, Kenneth Lapatin, and Jon L. Seydl, *The Last Days of Pompeii: Decadence, Apocalypse, Resurrection* (Los Angeles: Getty Publications, 2013), 60–69.

22. *De rerum natura: The Nature of Things: A Poetic Translation,* trans. David R. Slavitt (Berkeley: University of California Press, 2008), 1.

23. "Extract of a letter, dated May 2, 1750, from Mr. Freeman at Naples, to the Right Noble the Lady Mary Capel, Relating to the Ruins of Herculaneum," *Philosophical Transactions of the Royal Society* 47 (1751–1752): 132.

24. Christopher C. Parslow, *Rediscovering Antiquity: Karl Weber and the Excavation of Herculaneum, Pompeii, and Stabiae* (Cambridge: Cambridge University Press, 1995), 77–106.

25. "Extract of a letter, dated May 2, 1750," 132.

26. Richard Broxton Onians, *The Origins of European Thought about the Mind, the Body, the World, Time and Fate* (Cambridge: Cambridge University Press, 1951), 97–173.

27. This information is taken from a trip to the catacombs of the Rione Sanità; for this remarkable initiative, see http://www.catacombedinapoli.it (accessed October 20, 2013).

28. Parslow, *Rediscovering Antiquity.*

5. The Rediscovery of Pompeii

1. Antonio d'Ambrosio, ed., *Pompei, gli scavi dal 1748 al 1860* (Naples: Electa Napoli, 2002).

2. Mariano Vasi, revised by Venanzio Monaldini, revised in turn by Antonio Nibby, *Guide of Naples and its Environs, containing a description of the antiquities and interesting curiosities preceded by the Journey from Rome to Naples by the Pontine marshes and Montecassino from the Italian of Vasi* (Rome: Sold by Monaldini English Library and Reading Room, Piazza di Spagna, no. 79, 1841), 33.

3. D'Ambrosio, *Pompei, gli scavi,* 95–114.

4. Rome: Paolo Giunchi, 1775.

5. Giovanni Longobardi, *Pompei sostenibile* (Rome: "L'Erma" di Bretschneider, 2002), 41.

6. Wolfgang Amadeus Mozart

1. Leopold Mozart to Maria Anna Mozart, May 19, 1770, in Cliff Eisen et al., *In Mozart's Words,* letter 184, http://letters.mozartways.com, version 1.0, published by HRI Online, 2011 (accessed August 2013).

2. Evelyne Lever, *Marie Antoinette: The Last Queen of France* (New York: Farrar, Straus, and Giroux, 2000, 8n4).

3. Leopold Mozart to Maria Anna Mozart, Rome, March 13, 1770, in Eisen et al., *In Mozart's Words,* letter 165.

4. Leopold Mozart to Maria Anna Mozart, Rome, April 14, 1770: "On Monday we'll make a start delivering our *20* letters of recommendation." In Eisen et al., *In Mozart's Words,* letter 176.

5. Leopold Mozart to Maria Anna Mozart, Rome, May 19, 1770, in Eisen et al., *In Mozart's Words,* letter 184.

6. Leopold Mozart to Maria Anna Mozart, Rome, April 14, 1770, in Eisen et al., *In Mozart's Words,* letter 176.

7. See Scarth, *Vesuvius,* 187–223.

8. Leopold Mozart to Maria Anna Mozart, April 14, 1770, in Eisen et al., *In Mozart's Words,* letter 184; emphasis in the original.

9. Leopold Mozart to Maria Anna Mozart, May 19, 1770, in Eisen et al., *In Mozart's Words,* letter 184.

10. Percy Alfred Scholes, ed., *Dr. Burney's Musical Tours in Europe,* vol. 1 (Oxford: Oxford University Press, 1957), 247.

11. Leopold Mozart to Maria Anna Mozart, March 27–28, 1770, in Eisen et al., *In Mozart's Words,* letter 171.

12. J. S. Jenkins, "The Voice of the Castrato," *Lancet* 351 (1998): 1877–1880.

13. Eisen et al., *In Mozart's Words,* "Exsultate, jubilate K.165 K6 158a." The singer for whom Mozart composed this motet, Venenzio Rauzzini, was sometimes rumored to have been a natural soprano rather than a castrato, given the number of mistresses he amassed in his brilliant career; see Mark Brown, "Bath Celebrates the Life of the Bedhopping Singing Star of the 1700s," *Guardian,* April 11, 2010, http://www.guardian.co.uk/music/2010 /apr/12/bath-castrato-bicentenary (accessed June 29, 2013). My thanks to Dermot O'Connell for this reference.

14. The conservatory's website gives its history: http://www.sanpietro amajella.it/ (accessed August 26, 2013).

15. David Constantine, *Fields of Fire: A Life of Sir William Hamilton* (London: Weidenfeld and Nicholson, 2001); Ian Jenkins and Kim Sloan, *Vases and Volcanoes: William Hamilton and His Collection* (London: British Museum Press, 1996); Cocco, *Watching Vesuvius.*

16. Jenkins and Sloan, *Vases and Volcanoes.*

17. Scarth, *Vesuvius,* 197–200.

18. Cocco, *Watching Vesuvius,* 206–231; Scarth, *Vesuvius,* 185–266.

19. Jenkins and Sloan, *Vases and Volcanoes.*

20. Leopold Mozart to Maria Anna Mozart, May 19, 1770, in Eisen et al., *In Mozart's Words,* letter 184.

21. Jill H. Casid, *Sowing Empire: Landscape and Colonization* (Minneapolis: University of Minnesota Press, 2005), 60.

22. Leopold Mozart to Maria Anna Mozart, June 9, 1770, in Eisen et al., *In Mozart's Words,* letter 190.

23. See Rosaria Ciardiello, "Le antichità di Ercolano esposte: Contributi per la ricomposizione dei contesti pittorici antichi," *Papyrologica lupiensia* 15 (2006): 87–106.

24. Leopold Mozart to Maria Anna Mozart, June 9, 1770, in Eisen et al., *In Mozart's Words,* June 16, 1770, letter 191.

25. Ibid.

26. Antonio Baldi, "Grotta del cane: Antico tesoro nascosto," *Il Denaro* 98 (May 21, 2003): 15.

27. Mark Twain, *The Innocents Abroad, or, the New Pilgrims' Progress, Being Some Account of the Steamship* Quaker City's *Pleasure Excursion to Europe and the Holy Land: With Descriptions of Countries, Nations, Incidents and Adventures, as They Appeared to the Author* (Hartford, CT: American Publishing, 1870), 322.

28. Arthur H. Norway, *Naples Past and Present* (London: Methuen, 1901; 3rd ed. 1909), 28–29.

29. Cited from Laurence Goldstein, "The Impact of Pompeii on the Literary Imagination," *Centennial Review* 23 (1979): 232.

30. William Beckford, *Dreams, Waking Thoughts, and Incidents* (London: Printed for J. Johnston, 1783), letter XXIV.

31. Ibid.

32. Ibid.

33. Ibid.

34. Leopold Mozart to Maria Anna Mozart, June 9, 1770, in Eisen et al., *In Mozart's Words,* letter 190.

35. Brian Curran, *The Egyptian Renaissance: The Afterlife of Egypt in Early Modern Italy* (Chicago: University of Chicago Press, 2007); Eugenio Lo Sardo, ed., *The She-Wolf and the Sphinx: Rome and Egypt from History to Myth,* exhibition catalogue (Milan: Electa Editrice, 2008); Daniel Stoltzenberg, *Egyptian Oedipus: Athanasius Kircher and the Secrets of Egyptian Antiquity* (Chicago: University of Chicago Press, 2013).

36. Antonio Emanuele Piedimonte, *Raimondo di Sangro, Principe di Sansevero: La vita, le invenzioni, le opere, i libri, la Cappella, le leggende, i misteri,* with an essay by Sigfrido Höbel (1903) (Naples: Edizioni Intra Moenia, 2010).

37. Glenn Watkins, *Gesualdo: The Man and His Music,* 2nd ed. (Oxford: Oxford University Press, 1991).

38. Lucia Dacome and Renata Peters, "Fabricating the Body: The Anatomical Machines of the Prince of Sansevero," in Virginia Greene, ed., *Objects Specialty Group Postprints,* vol. 14 (Washington, DC: Objects Specialty Group of the AIC, 2007), 161–177. Since then a contract for the purchase of the models from a Sicilian natural philosopher has emerged: Antonio Emanuele Piedimonte, "Gli 'scheletri' di Sansevero? Il principe li aveva solo comprati," *Il Corriere del Mezzogiorno,* August 11, 2011, http:// corrieredelmezzogiorno.corriere.it/napoli/notizie/arte_e_cultura/2011/11 -agosto-2011/gli-scheletri-sansevero-principe-li-aveva-solo-comprati -1901280322627.shtml (accessed August 26, 2013).

Günther Hagens, the creator of the embalmed bodies on display worldwide as "Bodyworlds," says, without hands-on contact, that the models are real: "I modelli sono corpi umani lo dimostra il 'Dottor Morte,'" *La Repubblica,* April 13, 2012, http://ricerca.repubblica.it/repubblica/archivio/re pubblica/2012/04/13/modelli-sono-corpi-umani-la-mostra.html (accessed August 26, 2013).

39. Agnese Travaglione, "Il 'Lavoratorio de' Papiri' di Padre Antonio Piaggio," in Renata Cantilena and Annalisa Porzio, eds., *Herculanense Museum: Laboratorio sull'antico nella Reggia di Portici* (Naples: Electa Napoli, 2008), 147–172.

40. Mario Capasso, "L'Accademia Ercolanese la papirologia," *Papyrologica Lupiensia* 15 (2006): 49–64; Don Raimondo appears on p. 50.

41. Travaglione, "Il Lavoratorio."

42. Fabrizio Pesando, "Shadows of Light: Cinema, Peplum, and Pompeii," in Pier Giovanni Guzzo, ed., *Pompeii: Stories from an Eruption: Pompeii, Herculaneum, Oplontis: A Guide to the Exhibition* (Milan: Electa, 2006), 36. My thanks to Kenneth Lapatin for this reference.

7. Further Excavations

1. Cited in Luciana Jacobelli, "Arria Marcella e il *Gothic Novel* pompeiano," in Renzo Cremante, Maurizio Harari, Stefano Rocchi, and Elisa Romano, eds., *I misteri di Pompei: Antichità pompeiane nell'immaginario della modernità* (Pompeii: Flavius, 2008), 55.

2. Luciana Jacobelli, "Il viaggio di Madame de Staël: Uno sguardo femminile su Napoli," in Luciana Jacobelli, ed., *Pompei, la costruzione di un mito: Arte letteratura, aneddotica di un'icona turistica* (Rome: Bardi Editore, 2008), 59–72.

3. Felicia Dorothea Hemans, "The Image of Lava," in *The Poetical Works of Mrs. Felicia Hemans*, vol. 2, Fourth American Edition (New York: Evert Duykinck, 1828), 157–158.

4. Jacobelli, *Arria Marcella.*

5. Madame de Staël, *Corinne, or Italy* [1807], trans. Sylvia Raphael (Oxford: Oxford University Press, 1998), 198–199.

6. Ibid., 225.

7. Longobardi, *Pompei sostenibile,* 42.

8. Parslow, *Rediscovering Antiquity,* 107–122, 282–295 passim.

9. Gaetano Navarro, *Le biografie dei più celebri scrittori che han trattato delle catacombe* (Naples: Stabilimento Tipografico dell'Ancora, 1855), 121–157.

10. Adam Kendon, "Andrea De Jorio, the First Ethnographer of Gesture?," *Visual Anthropology* 7 (1995): 375–394. See also Adam Kendon, ed., *Andrea de Jorio: Gesture in Naples and Gesture in Classical Antiquity* (Bloomington: Indiana University Press, 2000).

11. "Abbicì dei gesti," De Jorio, *La mimica,* 1.

12. De Jorio, *La mimica,* 218. Author's translation. Kendon's translation is excellent, but De Jorio's florid Italian is fun to translate.

13. Ibid., 219–220.

14. Alexandre Dumas tells of King Ferdinand dying the day after an audience with the canon in *Le corricolo,* in *Oeuvres de Alex. Dumas,* vol. 7 (Brussels: Société belge de la librairie, 1844; reprint, Montreal: Le Joyeux Roger, 2006), 80.

8. Karl Bryullov

1. See Kenneth Lapatin's entry for this painting in Gardner Coates, Lapatin, and Seydl, *Last Days of Pompeii,* 140–142. I have also benefited from his comments as a reader.

2. Rosalind P. Gray, *Russian Genre Painting in the Nineteenth Century* (Oxford: Oxford University Press, 2000), 101–107.

3. See the biography of Bryullov at http://russiapedia.rt.com/prominent -russians/art/karl-bryullov/ (accessed October 20, 2013).

4. Kirsten Regina, "Love Letter to a Goddess," *Apollo* 165 (June 2007): 64–69.

5. Cocco, *Watching Vesuvius*, 24.

6. The Bulwer-Lytton Fiction Contest is sponsored by San Jose State University; see the official website at http://www.bulwer-lytton.com/ (accessed August 26, 2013).

7. Sumner Lincoln Fairfield, "The Last Night of Pompeii versus The Last Days of Pompeii," excerpted in the *Southern Literary Messenger* 1 (1834–1835): 246–247, ed. T. W. White.

8. Sumner Lincoln Fairfield, *The Last Night of Pompeii: A Poem* (New York: Elliott and Palmer, 1832), canto II, 119.

9. Ibid., canto III, 195.

10. Edward Bulwer, later Baronet Lytton, *The Last Days of Pompeii* (Philadelphia: J. B. Lippincott, 1867), 289.

11. Ibid., 303.

12. Ibid., 321.

13. Wilhelmina Jashemski and Frederick G. Meyer, eds., *The Natural History of Pompeii* (Cambridge: Cambridge University Press, 2002), 426–427.

9. Railway Tourism

1. Serena G. Federico, "Le stazioni ferroviarie," in Marco Iuliano and Serena G. Federico, eds., *Bartolo Longo "urbanista" a Valle di Pompei, 1876–1926* (Naples: Edizioni Scientifiche Italiane, 2000), 93–106.

2. Theophile Gautier, *Arria Marcella,* translated from the annotated Italian version of Luciana Jacobelli, *Arria Marcella, ricordo di Pompei* (Pompeii: Flavius, 2007), 15–16. See also Luciana Jacobelli, *"Arria Marcella e il Gothic Novel* pompeiano," in Renzo Cremante, Maurizio Harari, Stefano Rocchi, and Elisa Romano, eds., *I misteri di Pompei: Antichità pompeiane nell'immaginario della modernità* (Pompeii: Flavius, 2008).

3. Gérard de Nerval, "Isis," from *Les filles du feu* (Paris: Michel Lévy Frères, 1856), 215. My translation. My thanks to Eugenio Lo Sardo for this reference.

4. Stefano de Caro, ed., *Museo archeologico nazionale di Napoli: Guida alle collezioni* (Naples: Electa Napoli, 1999). A brief history of the museum

is also available at its website: http://cir.campania.beniculturali.it/museoar
cheologiconazionale/storia-del-museo (accessed August 26, 2013).

5. Vasi, *Guide of Naples*, 33.

10. Charles Dickens and Mark Twain

1. Twain, *Innocents Abroad*, 120 (chapter 13).

2. Charles Dickens, *Pictures of Italy* (1846), ed. Kate Flint (London: Penguin, 1998), 169.

3. Ibid., 166.

4. Ibid., 166–167.

5. Ibid., 168.

6. Ibid., 187.

7. Andrew C. A. Jampoler, *The Last Lincoln Conspirator: John Surratt's Flight from the Gallows* (Annapolis, MD: Naval Institute Press, 2009); Charles A. Coulombe, *The Pope's Legion: The Multinational Fighting Force That Defended the Vatican* (Basingstoke: Palgrave Macmillan, 2009).

8. Twain, *Innocents Abroad*, 311 (chapter 30).

9. Ibid., 319 (chapter 31).

10. Ibid., 309 (chapter 30).

11. Ibid., 261 (chapter 25).

12. Ibid., 329 (chapter 31).

13. William Gell and John P. Gandy, *Pompeiana: The Topography, Edifices, and Ornaments of Pompeii* (London: Rodwell and Martin, 1819), 94. For Poynter's painting, see Alexandra Sofroniew, in Gardner Coates, Lapatin, and Seydl, *Last Days of Pompeii*, 150–152.

14. Marisa de' Spagnolis, *The Grotto of Tiberius and the Homeric Sculptures* (Montalto Ligure: Edizioni Phoenix, 2013).

15. Twain, *Innocents Abroad*, 335 (chapter 31).

16. Eric Moorman, "Una città mummificata: Qualche aspetto della fortuna di Pompei nella letteratura europea e moderna," in Pier Giovanni Guzzo, ed., *Pompei: Scienza e società, 250° anniversario degli scavi di Pompei, Convegno internazionale Napoli, 25–27 Novembre 1998* (Milan: Electa, 2001), 11–13.

17. Emily Dickinson, Poem 175, ca. 1860, in Thomas H. Johnson, ed., *The Complete Poems of Emily Dickinson* (London: Faber and Faber, 1975), 83.

18. Twain, *Innocents Abroad*, 335 (chapter 31).

19. Hamlin Hill, *Mark Twain: God's Fool* (Chicago: University of Chicago Press, 2010), 71–90.

11. Giuseppe Fiorelli, the "Pope" of Pompeii

1. Mr. Freeman, "Extract of a letter," 140.

2. Estelle Lazer, *Resurrecting Pompeii* (Abingdon, UK: Routledge, 2009), 28–35.

3. Luciana Jacobelli, *Pompei nell'Unità d'Italia* (Pompeii: Flavius, 2011).

4. Laura Ambrosini, "G. F. Gamurrini and the Great Renewal of Italian Archaeology in the Second Half of the Nineteenth and Early Twentieth Centuries," paper presented at the conference "Classical Archaeology in the Late Nineteenth Century," Swedish Institute of Classical Studies, Rome, April 6, 2013.

5. Lazer, *Resurrecting Pompeii*.

12. Bartolo Longo

1. The Pompei Scavi station on the national rail line, the one used by Gautier and Bartolo Longo and so many others, was closed in 1960. The present-day Pompei Scavi station belongs to the private Circumvesuviana railroad and dates from 1932. It has come to be called "Pompei Scavi" only in the past few years; before that it was known as "Villa dei Misteri." Another Pompei Scavi station on the northern (Sarno) branch of the Circumvesuviana was inaugurated in 1914 and continued in use until 2004. Serena G. Federico, "Le stazioni ferroviarie," in Iuliano and Federico, *Bartolo Longo "urbanista,"* 93–106.

2. Bartolo Longo, quoted in Eufrasio M. Spreafico, *Il servo di dio Bartolo Longo,* vol. 1: *La preparazione, 1841–1872* (Pompeii: Scuola tipografica pontificia pei figli dei carcerati fondata da Bartolo Longo, 1944), 286–287.

3. Spreafico, *Bartolo Longo,* 56.

4. Ibid., 73.

5. Ibid., 290. The Sixth Commandment in the Catholic tradition is "thou shalt not commit adultery."

6. Quoted from Maria Carolina Campone, "L'immagine della beata Vergine del Rosario di Pompei," in Iuliano and Federico, *Bartolo Longo "urbanista,"* 173–174.

7. Campone, "L'immagine," 173–178.

8. Marco Iuliano, "La Gestazione," in Iuliano and Federico, *Bartolo Longo "urbanista,"* 35.

9. Bartolo Longo, *La Civiltà e la religione nelle feste della nuova Pompei,* pamphlet for festivities 6–9 May 1887 (Pompeii: Scuola Tipografica, 1888), 1.

10. Ibid., 4.

11. Ibid., 14.

12. Giancarlo Alesio, *Napoli e il risanamento: Ricupero di una struttura urbana* (Naples: Edizioni Banco di Napoli, 1980); Frank Snowden, *Naples in the Time of Cholera, 1884–1911* (Cambridge: Cambridge University Press, 2010).

13. Iuliano and Federico, *Bartolo Longo "urbanista."*

14. Mariapina Frisini, "Le case operaie," in Iuliano and Federico, *Bartolo Longo "urbanista,"* 107–115; Serena G. Federico, "L'osservatorio," in ibid., 116–122.

15. Ewa Kawamura, "Alberghi e albergatori svizzeri in Italia tra Ottocento e Novecento," *Annale di Storia del Turismo* 4 (2003): 28.

16. Wilhelm Jensen, *Gradiva: A Pompeiian Fantasy,* from Sigmund Freud, *Delusion and Dream in Wilhelm Jensen's Gradiva, Which Is Here Translated by Helen M. Downey* (New York: Moffatt, Yard, & Co., 1917), 44.

17. Quoted in Giovanni Longobardi, *Pompei Sostenibile* (Rome: "L'Erma" di Bretschneider, 2002), 45.

18. Frisini, "Le case operaie," 107–115.

19. Serena G. Federico, "La Fonte Salutare e il Palazzo De Fusco," in Iuliano and Federico, *Bartolo Longo "urbanista,"* 140–145; Sonia Uliano and Agnese Serrapica, "Pompei ed il culto dell'acqua: dalle Terme del Foro alla Fonte Salutare," http://www.iststudiatell.org/rsc/art_9n\Pompei _culto_acqua.htm (accessed August 8, 2013).

13. The Social Role of Tourist Cameos

1. Nino d'Antonio, "Cammei e coralli," for ARCA, the consortium of cameo and coral artists in Torre del Greco, http://www.na.camcom.it/on

-line-sa/Home/Pubblicazioni/ArtigianatoArtisticoNapoletano/Cammeie
Coralli.html (accessed August 25, 2013).

2. David Gentilcore, *Pomodoro! A History of the Tomato in Italy* (New York: Columbia University Press, 2010), 69–98.

3. There is remarkably little published on this subject aside from pamphlets issued by the various cameo firms in Torre del Greco and their Internet sites, which change frequently. Anna M. Miller, *Cameos Old and New* (Woodstock, VT: Gemstone, 2002), is useful as a general introduction to the subject of cameos. The Istituto Statale d'Arte di Torre del Greco, founded in 1878, became the Regia Scuola d'Incisione sul Corallo e di Arti Decorative e Industriali in 1887. In 1969 it became an *istituto statale dell'arte,* a fine arts high school. In 2009 this institute was absorbed into the Istituto Francesco Degni of Torre del Greco, an *istituto tecnico* with courses in economics, social sciences, and tourism as well as art: http://www.isdegni.it/ (accessed August 25, 2013). The school maintains a museum of coral and cameo carving.

4. Mr. Freeman, "Extract of a letter dated May 2, 1750," 136.

5. Anonymous, "Extract of a Letter from Naples, concerning Herculaneum," 158.

6. Amy C. Smith, "Queens and Empresses as Goddesses: The Public Role of the Personal Tyche in the Graeco-Roman World," in Susan B. Matheson, ed., *An Obsession with Fortune: Tyche in Greek and Roman Art. Yale University Art Gallery Bulletin* (1994): 86–105, 93.

7. Jensen, *Gradiva,* 91.

14. Pierre-Auguste Renoir

1. See Barbara Ehrlich White, "Renoir's Trip to Italy," *Art Bulletin* 51, no. 4 (1969): 333–351; Richard Covington, "Renoir's Controversial Second Act," *Smithsonian Magazine,* February 2010, http://www.smithsonianmag.com /arts-culture/Renoirs-Controversial-Second-Act.html (accessed April 2013); Sterling and Francine Clark Art Institute, *Great French Paintings from the Clark: Barbizon through Impressionism* (New York: Rizzoli, 2011), 184–191.

2. Antonio Canova, *Letter from the Chevalier Antonio Canova on the Sculptures in the British Museum and Two Memoirs Read to the Gentlemen of the Academy of France* (London: John Murray, 1816), xxii.

3. Letter to Paul Durand-Reuel from Naples, 21 November 1881, cited in White, "Renoir's Trip," 347 (Letter 3); my translation.

4. Letter to Mme. Georges Charpentier from L'Estaque, January or February 1882, cited in White, "Renoir's Trip," 350 (Letter 11); my translation.

5. Fronia E. Wissman, "Renoir's Onions," *Gastronomica: The Journal of Food and Culture* 9, no. 2 (Spring 2009): 7–9.

6. Jean Renoir maintained that the sitter was his mother, Aline, and that she had joined Renoir in Italy, but White notes that there is no other clear indication that she actually did so; White, "Renoir's Trip," 334. On the other hand, who would know better than Jean Renoir and the sitter herself?

7. Zanker, *Roman Art*, 21–32.

15. The Legacy of August Mau

1. John Murray, Octavian Blewett, and George Dennis, *Murray's Handbook for Travellers in Southern Italy*, 9th ed. (London: John Murray, 1892), 17.

2. Ibid., 296.

3. Ibid., 299.

4. Vitruvius, *Ten Books on Architecture,* VII.5.3.

5. Ibid., I.praef. 2.

6. Ibid., VII.5.3–4.

7. August Mau, *Geschichte der decorativen Wandmalerei in Pompeji* (Berlin: Reimer, 1882).

8. Vitruvius, *Ten Books on Architecture,* VII. 5.1.

9. Ibid., VII.5.2.

16. Crown Prince Hirohito of Japan

1. Herbert P. Bix, *Hirohito and the Making of Modern Japan* (New York: HarperCollins, 2000), 104.

2. Ibid., 103–109.

3. Leonard Mosley, *Hirohito, Emperor of Japan* (Englewood Cliffs, NJ: Prentice-Hall, 1966), 65.

4. See footage from United States Memorial Holocaust Museum, possibly October 1942, http://collections.ushmm.org/search/catalog/fv3351 (accessed September 20, 2013).

5. Katsuyuki Okamura and Akira Matsuda, eds., *New Perspectives in Global Public Archaeology* (New York: Springer 2011), 177.

6. Marisa de' Spagnolis, *Dieci anni a Pompei e nella Valle del Sarno: Esperienze ed emozioni di una archeologa* (Nocera Inferiore: Franco Alfano, 2006), 100.

17. Don Amedeo Maiuri

1. Wilhelmina Jashemski and Frederick G. Meyer, eds., *The Natural History of Pompeii* (Cambridge: Cambridge University Press, 2002).

2. Fausto Zevi, "Aspetti dell'archeologia pompeiana nel Novecento: Gli scavi del Maiuri a Pompei," in Guzzo, *Pompei: Scienza e società,* 182–206.

3. Amedeo Maiuri, *Pompeii,* 15th ed. English translation revised by W. F. McCormick. (Rome: Istituto Poligrafico dello Stato, 1978), 71.

4. My thanks to Sean Cocco for this information.

5. Norman Lewis, *Naples '44: A World War II Diary of Occupied Italy* (New York: Carroll and Graf, 2005), 93, letter of March 19, 1944.

18. Roberto Rossellini and Ingrid Bergman

1. Ingrid Bergman with Alan Burgess, *My Story* (New York: Dell, 1981), 17–18.

2. Peter Brunette, *Roberto Rossellini* (Berkeley: University of California Press, 1996), 156.

3. Isabella Rossellini, interview at the British Film Institute, *The Guardian,* May 6, 2007, http://www.theguardian.com/film/2007/may/06/guardianinterviewsatbfisouthbank (accessed October 20, 2013).

4. Wilhelm Jensen, *Gradiva,* from Sigmund Freud, *Delusion and Dream in Wilhelm Jensen's* Gradiva, *Which Is Here Translated by Helen M. Downey* (New York: Moffatt, Yard, & Co., 1917), 77–78.

5. Sigmund Freud, *Delusion and Dream in WIlhelm Jensen's* Gradiva, 178.

6. Sigmund Freud, *Civilization and Its Discontents, Newly Edited from the German and Translated by James Strachey* (New York: W. W. Norton, 1961), 17. See also Gardner Coates, Lapatin, and Seydl, *Last Days of Pompeii,* 26, 70–77, 116.

7. *Edward Gibbon*, Journal, in John Murray, ed., *The Autobiographies of Edward Gibbon, Printed verbatim from hitherto unpublished mss., with an introduction by Earl of Sheffield. Edited by John Murray. With portrait*, 2nd ed. (London: John Murray, 1897), 302.

19. Autobus Gran Turismo

1. Eliane Patriarca, "Pompei, l'histoire tombe en ruines," *Le Monde*, February 18, 2013.

2. The (C)Ave Canem project, which began in 2009 with high hopes, is officially sponsored by the Archaeological Superintendency of Pompeii, the Ente Nazionale Protezione Animali, the Lega Italiana Antivivisezione, and the Lega Italian per la Difesa del Cane: http://www.icanidipompei.com /english/progetto_cave_canem.html (accessed September 22, 2013). For its scandalous mismanagement, see, for example, Gian Antonio Stella, "Cemento e sprechi: Il 'sacco' di Pompei," *Corriere della Sera*, February 6, 2013; Alessandra Arachi, "Cemento e mattoni, così il teatro antico diventò l'arena di un villaggio vacanze," *Corriere della Sera*, February 6, 2013, and the irreverent website Dagospia: http://www.dagospia.com/rubrica-3/polit ica/piu-dannosi-del-vesuvio-inchiesta-sul-restauro-del-teatro-grande-di -pompei-avviso-a-50475.htm (accessed August 25, 2013).

3. Roman cats fare considerably better because of the sanctuaries established for them in the ruins at Largo di Torre Argentina and the Pyramid of Gaius Cestius; see www.romancats.com and www.igattidellapiramide.it. See also Massimo Gatto, "A Roman Cat Fight," http://www.nybooks.com /blogs/nyrblog/2012/nov/16/roman-cat-fight/ (accessed September 22, 2013).

4. Marisa de' Spagnolis, *Dieci anni a Pompei e nella Valle del Sarno: Esperienze ed emozioni di una archeologa* (Nocera Inferiore: Franco Alfano, 2006), 114–116. The passage cited is on page 114.

Coda

1. Hester Lynch Piozzi, *Observations and Reflections made in the Course of a Journey through France, Italy, and Germany*, vol. 2 (London: A. Strahan and T. Cadell, 1789), 35.

2. The current website is http://www.protezionecivile.gov.it/jcms/it /vesuvio.wp;jsessionid=BCEAA9A0B7514DC6E5755484B51025D6 (accessed October 20, 2013). The volcanic bombs are discussed at http://www .protezionecivile.gov.it/jcms/it/rischio_vulcanico_vesuvio.wp (accessed October 20, 2013).

3. Evacuation plans are detailed at http://www.protezionecivile.gov.it /jcms/it/view_pde.wp?contentId=PDE12771 (accessed October 20, 2013).

4. Kircher, *Mundus Subterraneus*, vol. 1, 83.

Bibliography

Alesio, Giancarlo. *Napoli e il Risanamento: ricupero di una struttura urbana*. Naples: Edizioni Banco di Napoli, [1980].

Ambrosini, Laura. "G.F. Gamurrini and the Great Renewal of Italian Archaeology in the Second Half of the Nineteenth and Early Twentieth Centuries." Paper presented at the conference "Classical Archaeology in the Late Nineteenth Century," Swedish Institute of Classical Studies, Rome, April 6, 2013.

Anonymous. "Extract of a Letter from Naples, concerning Herculaneum, Containing a Description of the Place, and What Has Been Found in It." *Philosophical Transactions [of the Royal Society]* 47 (1751–1752): 150–159.

Aram, Bethany. *Juana the Mad: Sovereignty and Dynasty in Renaissance Europe*. Baltimore: Johns Hopkins University Press, 2005.

Arias, Paolo Enrico. "Mosaico ellenistico dalla Via Ardeatina." *Rivista del R. Istituto Nazionale d' Archeologia e Storia dell'arte*, ser. 1, 8, no. 1 (1940): 16–24.

Arrhenius, Svante. "Die Verbreitung des Lebens im Weltenraum." *Die Umschau*, 1903.

Baldi, Antonio. "Grotta del Cane: Antico tesoro nascosto." *Il Denaro* 98 (May 21, 2003): 15.

Barz, Wolf-Dieter. "Landgraf Friedrich von Hessen und zu Goletta, eine markante Persönlichkeit und ein markanter Ort in der Geschichte des Malteser-Ordens." *Zeitschrift des Vereins für Hessische Geschichte und Landeskunde* 93 (1988): 73–94.

Beard, Mary. "Dirty Little Secrets: Changing Displays of Pompeiian 'Erotica.'" In Victoria C. Gardner Coates, Kenneth Lapatin, and Jon L. Seydl, *The Last Days of Pompeii: Decadence, Apocalypse, Resurrection*. Los Angeles: Getty Publications, 2013, 60–69.

Beckford, William. *Dreams, Waking Thoughts, and Incidents*. London: Printed for J. Johnston, 1783.

Belozerskaya, Marina. *Medusa's Gaze: The Extraordinary Journey of the Tazza Farnese*. New York: Oxford University Press, 2012.

Bergman, Ingrid, with Alan Burgess. *My Story*. New York: Dell, 1981.

Bix, Herbert P. *Hirohito and the Making of Modern Japan*. New York: HarperCollins, 2000.

Blackwell, Richard, J. *Behind the Scenes at Galileo's Trial: Including the First English Translation of Melchior Inchofer's* Tractatus Syllepticus. Notre Dame, IN: University of Notre Dame Press, 2008.

Bonucci, Carlo. *Pompei descritta da Carlo Bonucci, architetto, terza edizione, contente tutte le scoverte sino alla fine di Aprile del 1827*. Naples: Da' Torchi di Raffaele Miranda, 1827.

Brancaccio, Sergio. *L'ambiente delle ville vesuviane*. Naples: Società editrice napoletana, 1983.

Brillante, Bruno. *Sebeto: Storia e mito di un fiume*. Naples: Massa Editore, 2000.

Bruck, Anton Ph. "Friedrich, Landgraf von Hessen-Darmstadt." *Neue Deutsche Biographie*, vol. 5. Berlin: Duncker & Humblot, 1961, 504.

Brunette, Peter. *Roberto Rossellini*. Berkeley: University of California Press, 1996.

Bulwer, Edward, later Baronet Lytton. *The Last Days of Pompeii*. Philadelphia: J. B. Lippincott, 1867.

Buranelli, Francesco, ed. *Palazzo Farnèse: Dalle collezioni rinascimentali ad Ambasciata di Francia*. Florence: Giunti, 2010.

Campone, Maria Carolina. "L'Immagine della Beata Vergine del Rosario di Pompei." In Marco Iuliano and Serena G. Federico, eds., *Bartolo Longo "urbanista" a Valle di Pompei, 1876–1926*. Naples: Edizioni Scientifiche Italiane, 2000, 173–178.

Canova, Antonio. *Letter from the Chevalier Antonio Canova on the Sculptures in the British Museum and Two Memoirs Read to the Gentlemen of the Academy of France*. London: John Murray, 1816, xxii.

Cantilena, Renata, and Annalisa Porzio. *Herculanense Museum, Laboratorio sull'antico nella Reggia di Portici*. Naples: Electa Napoli, 2008.

Capaccio, Giulio Cesare. *Il forastiero, Dialogi di Giulio Cesare Capaccio Academico Otioso*. Naples: Giovanni Domenico Roncagliolo, 1634.

Capasso, Mario. "L'Accademia Ercolanense e la papirologia." *Papyrologica Lupiensia* 15 (2006): 49–64.

Carr, Dawson W. *Velazquez*. London: National Gallery, 2006.

Casid, Jill H. *Sowing Empire: Landscape and Colonization*. Minneapolis: University of Minnesota Press, 2005.

Catholic Church. *Roman Martyrology*. Revised Edition. Baltimore: John Murphy, 1916.

Ciarallo, Annamaria. *Pompei romantica: Percorsi letterari dell'Ottocento*. Naples: Electa Napoli, 2005.

Ciardiello, Rosaria. "Le Antichità Esposte: Contributi per la ricomposizione dei contesti pittorici antichi." *Papyrologica lupiensia* 15 (2006): 87–106.

Clarke, John C. *Looking at Lovemaking: Constructions of Sexuality in Roman Art, 100 B.C.–A.D. 250*. Berkeley: University of California Press, 2001.

Cluverius, Philippus. *Italia Antiqua*. Leiden: Ex officina Elsiviriana, 1624.

Coates, Victoria C. Gardner, Kenneth Lapatin, and Jon L. Seydl. *The Last Days of Pompeii: Decadence, Apocalypse, Resurrection*. Los Angeles: Getty Publications, 2013.

Coates, Victoria C. Gardner, and Jon L. Seydl. *Antiquity Recovered: The Legacy of Pompeii and Herculaneum*. Los Angeles: Getty Publications, 2007.

Cocco, Sean. "Natural Marvels and Ancient Rome: Volcanoes and the Recovery of Antiquity in Early Modern Naples." In Victoria C.

Gardner Coates and Jon L. Seydl, *Antiquity Recovered: The Legacy of Pompeii and Herculaneum*. Los Angeles: Getty Publications, 2007, 15–36.

————. *Watching Vesuvius: A History of Science and Culture in Early Modern Italy*. Chicago: University of Chicago Press, 2013.

Cohen, Ada. *The Alexander Mosaic: Stories of Victory and Defeat*. Cambridge: Cambridge University Press, 2000.

Conelli, Maria Ann. "The '*Guglie*' of Naples: Religious and Political Machinations of the Festival '*Macchine.*'" *l* 45 (2000): 153–183.

Constantine, David. *Fields of Fire: A life of Sir William Hamilton*. London: Weidenfeld and Nicholson, 2001.

Corti, Count Egon Caesar. *The Destruction and Resurrection of Pompeii and Herculaneum*. London: Taylor and Francis, 1944.

Corti, Maria. *Sannazaro, Iacobo*. In Vittore Branca, ed., *Dizionario critico della letteratura italiana*, vol. 3. Torino: UTET, 1973, 299–305.

Coulombe, Charles A. *The Pope's Legion: The Multinational Fighting Force that Defended the Vatican*. Basingstoke: Palgrave Macmillan, 2009.

Covington, Richard. "Renoir's Controversial Second Act." *Smithsonian Magazine*, February 2010. http://www.smithsonianmag.com/arts-culture/Renoirs-Controversial-Second-Act.html (accessed April 2013).

Cremante, Renzo, Maurizio Harari, Stefano Rocchi, and Elisa Romano, eds. *I misteri di Pompei: Antichità pompeiane nell'immaginario della modernità*. Pompeii: Flavius, 2008.

Curran, Brian. *The Egyptian Renaissance: The Afterlife of Egypt in Early Modern Italy*. Chicago: University of Chicago Press, 2007.

Dacome, Lucia, and Renata Peters. "Fabricating the Body: The Anatomical Machines of the Prince of Sansevero." In V. Greene, ed., *Objects Specialty Group Postprints*, vol. 14. Washington, DC: Objects Specialty Group of the AIC, 2007, 161–177.

Dacos, Nicole. *La découverte de la Domus Aurea et la formation des grotesques à la Renaissance*. London: Warburg Institute, 1969.

d'Ambrosio, Antonio, ed. *Pompei, gli scavi dal 1748 al 1860*. Naples: Electa Napoli 2002.

d'Antonio, Nino. "Cammei e coralli." For ARCA, the consortium of cameo and coral artists in Torre del Greco: http://www.na.camcom.it/on

-line-sa/Home/Pubblicazioni/ArtigianatoArtisticoNapoletano
/CammeieCoralli.html (accessed August 25, 2013).

Darley, Gillian. *Vesuvius: The Most Famous Volcano in the World*. New
York: Profile Books, 2011.

D'Arms, John H. *Romans on the Bay of Naples and Other Essays on Romans
in Campania*. Ed. Fausto Zevi. Bari: Edipuglia, 2003.

De Caro, Stefano, ed. *Museo Archeologico Nazionale di Napoli: Guida alle
Collezioni*. Naples: Electa Napoli, 1999.

De Jorio, Andrea. *La mimica degli antichi investigata nel gestire napoletano*.
Naples: Dalla Stamperia e Carteria Del Fibreno, 1832.

De' Spagnolis, Marisa. *Dieci anni a Pompei e nella Valle del Sarno:
Esperienze ed emozioni di una archeologa*. Nocera Inferiore: Franco
Alfano, 2006.

———. *The Grotto of Tiberius and the Homeric Sculptures*. Montalto
Ligure: Edizioni Phoenix, 2013.

De Staël, Madame. *Corinne, or Italy* [1807]. Trans. Sylvia Raphael.
Oxford: Oxford University Press, 1998.

Dickens, Charles. *Pictures of Italy* [1846]. Ed. Kate Flint. London:
Penguin, 1998.

Dickinson, Emily. *The Complete Poems of Emily Dickinson*. Ed. Thomas
H. Johnson. London: Faber & Faber, 1975.

Di Maio, Ippolita. "Vittoria Colonna, il Castello di Ischia e la cultura
delle corti." In Pina Ragionieri, ed., *Vittoria Colonna e Michelangelo,
Catalogo della mostra a Casa Buonarroti, 24 maggio–12 settembre 2005*.
Florence: Mandragora 2005, 19–32.

Dumas, Alexandre. *Le Corricolo*. In *Oeuvres de Alex. Dumas*, vol. 7
Brussels: Société belge de la librairie, 1844. Reprint, Montreal: Le
Joyeux Roger, 2006.

Eisen, Cliff, et al. *In Mozart's Words*. http://letters.mozartways.com.
Version 1.0, published by HRI Online, 2011 (accessed August 2013).

Fairfield, Sumner Lincoln. *The Last Night of Pompeii: A Poem*. New York:
Elliott and Palmer, 1832.

———. "The Last Night of Pompeii versus The Last Days of Pompeii."
Excerpted in the *Southern Literary Messenger* 1 (1834–1835): 246–247.
Ed. T. W. White.

Federico, Serena G. "La Fonte Salutare e il Palazzo De Fusco." In Marco Iuliano and Serena G. Federico, eds., *Bartolo Longo "urbanista" a Valle di Pompei, 1876–1926*. Naples: Edizioni Scientifiche Italiane, 2000, 140–145.

———. "Le stazioni ferroviarie." In Marco Iuliano and Serena G. Federico, eds., *Bartolo Longo "urbanista" a Valle di Pompei, 1876–1926*. Naples: Edizioni Scientifiche Italiane, 2000, 93–106.

———. "L'osservatorio." In Marco Iuliano and Serena G. Federico, eds., *Bartolo Longo "urbanista" a Valle di Pompei, 1876–1926*. Naples: Edizioni Scientifiche Italiane, 2000, 116–122.

Fernandez-Armesto, Felipe. *Ferdinand and Isabella*. London: Dorset, 1992.

Findlen, Paula, ed. *Athanasius Kircher, S.J.: The Last Man Who Knew Everything*, New York: Routledge, 2004.

———. "The Last Man Who Knew Everything . . . Or Did He? Athanasius Kircher, S.J. (1602–1680) and His World." In Paula Findlen, ed., *Athanasius Kircher, S.J.: The Last Man Who Knew Everything*, New York: Routledge, 2004, 1–50.

Fornaciari, Gino. "Le mummie aragonesi in San Domenico Maggiore a Napoli." http://www.paleopatologia.it/articoli/aticolo.php?recordID=49 (accessed August 26, 2013).

Freeman, Mr. "Extract of a letter, dated May 2, 1750, from Mr. Freeman at Naples, to the Right Noble the Lady Mary Capel, Relating to the Ruins of Herculaneum." *Philosophical Transactions of the Royal Society* 47 (1751–1752): 131–142.

Freud, Sigmund. *Civilization and Its Discontents, Newly Edited from the German and Translated by James Strachey*. New York: W. W. Norton, 1961.

———. *Delusion and Dream in Wilhelm Jensen's* Gradiva, *Which Is Here Translated by Helen M. Downey*. New York: Moffatt, Yard, & Co., 1917.

Frisini, Mariapina. "Le Case Operaie." In Marco Iuliano and Serena G. Federico, eds., *Bartolo Longo "urbanista" a Valle di Pompei, 1876–1926*. Naples: Edizioni Scientifiche Italiane, 2000, 107–115.

Furstenberg-Levi, Shulamit. "The Fifteenth Century Accademia Pontaniana: An Analysis of Its Institutional Elements." *History of Universities* 21 (2006): 33–70.

Garcia y Garcia, Laurentino. *Danni di guerra a Pompei: una dolorosa vicenda quasi dimenticata.* Rome: "L'Erma" di Bretschneider, 2006.

Gardner Coates, Victoria C., Kenneth Lapatin, and Jon L. Seydl. *The Last Days of Pompeii: Decadence, Apocalypse, Resurrection.* Los Angeles: Getty Publications, 2013.

Gasparri, Carlo, ed. *Le Gemme Farnese.* Naples: Electa Napoli, 1994, 2006.

Gatto, Massimo. "A Roman Cat Fight." http://www.nybooks.com/blogs /nyrblog/2012/nov/16/roman-cat-fight/ (accessed September 22, 2013).

Gell, William, and John Gandy. *Pompeiana: The Topography, Ornaments and Edifices of Pompeii.* London: Rodwell and Martin, 1819.

Gentilcore, David. *Pomodoro! A History of the Tomato in Italy.* New York: Columbia University Press, 2010.

Gibbon, Edward. *Journal.* In John Murray, ed., *The Autobiographies of Edward Gibbon, Printed verbatim from hitherto unpublished mss., with an introduction by Earl of Sheffield. Edited by John Murray. With portrait.* 2nd ed. London: John Murray, 1897.

Godwin, Joscelyn. *Athanasius Kircher's Theatre of the World: The Life and Work of the Last Man to Search for Universal Knowledge.* Rochester, VT: Inner Traditions, 2009.

Goldstein, Laurence. "The Impact of Pompeii on the Literary Imagination." *The Centennial Review* 23 (1979): 227–241.

Gray, Rosalind P. *Russian Genre Painting in the Nineteenth Century.* Oxford: Oxford University Press, 2000.

Guide d'Italie pour faire agréablement le voyage de Rome, Naples, et autres lieux. Rome: Paolo Giunchi, 1775.

Guzzo, Pier Giovanni, ed. *Pompei Scienza e Società, 250.o Anniversario degli Scavi di Pompei Convegno Internazionale Napoli, 25–27 Novembre 1998.* Milan: Electa, 2001.

Hammond, William. Letter published in "An Account of the Discovery of the Remains of a City under-ground, near Naples, communicated to the Royal Society by William Sloane, Esq., F.R.S." *Philosophical Transactions of the Royal Society* 41 (1739–1741): 345.

Harris, Judith. *Pompeii Reawakened: A Story of Rediscovery.* London: I. B. Tauris, 2009.

Hein, Otto. *Athanasius Kircher in Malta: Ein Beitrag zur Geschichte.* Weinheim: Wiley–VCH Verlag, 1996.

Hemans, Felicia Dorothea. "Casabianca." In *The Poetical Works of Mrs. Felicia Hemans*, Fourth American Edition, vol. 2. New-York: Evert Duykinck, 1828, 135–136.

———. "The Image of Lava." In *The Poetical Works of Mrs. Felicia Hemans*, Fourth American Edition, vol. 2. New-York: Evert Duykinck, 1828, 157–158.

Hill, Hamlin. *Mark Twain: God's Fool.* Chicago: University of Chicago Press, 2010.

Holste [Holstenius], Lucas. *Letters.* Vatican Library, MS Barb. Lat. 6488.

Holstenius, Lucas [Lucas Holste]. *Annotationes in geographiam sacram Caroli à S. Paulo; Italiam antiquam Cluverii; et thesaurum geographicum Ortelii.* Rome: Typis Iacobi Dragondelli, 1666.

Iuliano, Marco. "La Gestazione." In Marco Iuliano and Serena G. Federico, eds., *Bartolo Longo "urbanista" a Valle di Pompei, 1876–1926.* Naples: Edizioni Scientifiche Italiane, 2000.

Iuliano, Marco, and Serena G. Federico, eds. *Bartolo Longo "urbanista" a Valle di Pompei, 1876–1926.* Naples: Edizioni Scientifiche Italiane, 2000.

Jacobelli, Luciana. *Arria Marcella, ricordo di Pompei.* Pompeii: Flavius, 2007.

———. "*Arria Marcella* e il *Gothic Novel* pompeiano." In Renzo Cremante, Maurizio Harari, Stefano Rocchi, and Elisa Romano, eds., *I misteri di Pompei: Antichità pompeiane nell'immaginario della modernità.* Pompeii: Flavius, 2008.

———. "Il viaggio di Madame de Staël: Uno sguardo femminile su Napoli." In Luciana Jacobelli, ed., *Pompei, la costruzione di un mito: Arte letteratura, aneddotica di un'icona turistica.* Rome: Bardi Editore, 2008, 59–72.

———, ed. *Pompei, la costruzione di un mito: Arte letteratura, aneddotica di un'icona turistica.* Rome: Bardi Editore, 2008.

———. *Pompei nell'Unità d'Italia*, Pompeii: Flavius, 2011.

Jampoler, Andrew C. A. *The Last Lincoln Conspirator: John Surratt's Flight from the Gallows.* Annapolis, MD: Naval Institute Press, 2009.

Jashemski, Wilhelmina, and Frederick G. Meyer, eds. *The Natural History of Pompeii*. Cambridge: Cambridge University Press, 2002.

Jenkins, Ian, and Kim Sloan. *Vases and Volcanoes: William Hamilton and his Collection*. London: British Museum Press, 1996.

Jenkins, J. S. "The Voice of the Castrato." *Lancet* 351 (1998): 1877–1880.

Jensen, Wilhelm. *Gradiva, A Pompeiian Fantasy*. In Sigmund Freud, *Delusion and Dream in Wilhelm Jensen's* Gradiva, *Which Is Here Translated by Helen M. Downey*. New York: Moffatt, Yard, & Co., 1917.

Kamen, Henry. *The Escorial: Art and Power in the Renaissance*. New Haven, CT: Yale University Press, 2010.

Kawamura, Ewa. "Alberghi e albergatori svizzeri in Italia tra Ottocento e Novecento." *Annale di Storia del Turismo* 4 (2003): 11–41.

Kendon, Adam. *Andrea de Jorio: Gesture in Naples and Gesture in Classical Antiquity*. Bloomington: Indiana University Press, 2000.

———, ed. "Andrea De Jorio, the First Ethnographer of Gesture?" *Visual Anthropology* 7 (1995): 375–394.

Kircher, Athanasius. *Athanasii Kircheri Diatribe de prodigiosis Crucibus, quae tam supra vestes hominum, quam res alias, non pridem post ultimum incendium Vesuvii montis Neapoli comparuerunt*. Rome: Sumptibus Blasij Deversin, 1661.

———. *Athanasij Kircheri e Soc. Iesu Itinerarium exstaticum quo mundi opificium id est coelestis expansi, siderumque tam errantium, quam fixorum natura, vires, proprietates, singulorumque compositio & structura, ab infimo telluris globo, vsque ad vltima mundi confinia, . . . noua hypothesi exponitur ad veritatem interlocutoribus Cosmiele et Theodidacto*. Rome: Typis Vitalis Mascardi, 1656.

———. *Mundus subterraneus*. In *XII Libros digestos*. Amsterdam: Apud Joannem Janssonium et Elizaeum Weyerstraten, 1665; third ed. 1678.

———. *Scrutinium physico-medicum perniciosae lues sive pestis*. Rome: Typis Mascardi, 1658.

———. *Vita Admodum Reverendi Athanasii Kircheri, Societatis Jesu Viri toto orbe celebratissimi*. Augsburg: Utschneider, 1684.

Kircher, Athanasius, and Gaspar Schott. *Athanasii Kircheri iter extaticum coeleste: Quo mundi opificium, id est, coelestis expansi. . . . Accessit eiusdem auctoris iter exstaticum terrestre, et synopsis mundi subterranei*.

Würzburg: Sumptibus Joh[annis] Andr[eae] & Wolffg[angi] Jun[ioris] Endterorum Haeredibus, 1660; reprinted 1671.

Knapton, George. "Extract of a Letter from Mr. George Knapton to Mr. Charles Knapton, concerning the same Subject" [sc. Herculaneum]. *Philosophical Transactions of the Royal Society* 41 (1739–1741): 490–491.

Köchli, Ulrich. "Friedrich von Hessen-Darmstadt: *Biographisch-Bibliographisches Kirchenlexikon*," vol. 23. Nordhausen: Bautz, 2004, 424–433.

Lazer, Estelle. *Resurrecting Pompeii.* Abingdon: Routledge, 2009.

Leone, Nino. *Napoli ai tempi di Masaniello.* Milan: Biblioteca Universale Rizzoli, 2001.

Lever, Evelyne. *Marie Antoinette: The Last Queen of France.* New York: Farrar, Straus, and Giroux, 2000.

Lewis, Norman. *Naples '44: A World War II Diary of Occupied Italy.* New York: Carroll and Graf, 2005.

Longo, Bartolo. *La Civiltà e la religione nelle feste della nuova Pompei.* Pamphlet for festivities 6–9 May 1887. Pompeii: Scuola Tipografica, 1888.

Longobardi, Giovanni. *Pompei Sostenibile.* Rome: "L'Erma" di Bretschneider, 2002.

Lo Sardo, Eugenio, ed. *The She-Wolf and the Sphinx: Rome and Egypt from History to Myth.* Exhibition catalogue. Milan: Electa Editrice, 2008.

Lucretius. *De Rerum Natura, Lucretius, The Nature of Things: A Poetic Translation.* David R. Slavitt. Berkeley: University of California Press, 2008.

Margiotta, Maria Luisa, Pasquale Belfiore, and Ornella Zerlenga. *Giardini Storici Napoletani.* Naples: Electa Napoli, 2000.

Marino, John. *Becoming Neapolitan: Citizen Culture in Baroque Naples.* Baltimore: Johns Hopkins University Press, 2010.

———. "Constructing the Past of Early Modern Naples." In Tommaso Astarita, ed., *The Brill Companion to Naples.* Leiden: Brill, 2013, 11–34.

Marshall, David. "A View of Poggioreale by Viviano Codazzi and Domenico Gargiulo." *Journal of the Society of Architectural Historians* 45, no. 1 (1986): 32–46.

Martial. *Epigrams*. Ed. D. R. Shackleton Bailey. 3 vols. Cambridge, MA: Loeb Classical Library, 1995.

Mau, August. *Führer durch Pompeji auf Veranlassung des Kaiserlich Deutschen Archäologischen Instituts*. Leipzig: W. Engelmann, 1896.

———. *Geschichte der decorativen Wandmalerei in Pompeji*. Berlin: Reimer, 1882.

———. *Pompeji in Leben und Kunst*. 2nd ed. Leipzig: W. Engelmann, 1908.

Miller, Anna M. *Cameos Old and New*. Woodstock, VT: Gemstone Press, 2002.

Molina Figueras, Joan. "Un emblema arturiano per Alfonso d'Aragona: Storia, mito, propaganda." *Bullettino dell'Istituto Storio Italiano per il Medioevo* 114 (2012): 231–269.

Moorman, Eric. "Una città mummificata: Qualche aspetto della fortuna di Pompei nella letteratura europea e moderna." In Pier Giovanni Guzzo, ed., *Pompei Scienza e Società, 250.0 Anniversario degli Scavi di Pompei Convegno Internazionale Napoli, 25–27 Novembre 1998*. Milan: Electa, 2001, 11–13.

Mosley, Leonard. *Hirohito, Emperor of Japan*. Englewood Cliffs, NJ: Prentice-Hall, 1966.

Murray, John, Octavian Blewett, and George Dennis. *Handbook for Travellers in Southern Italy and Sicily*. London: John Murray, 1892.

Navarro, Gaetano. *Le biografie dei più celebri scrittori che han trattato delle catacombe*. Naples: Stabilimento Tipografico dell'Ancora, 1855.

Nerval, Gérard de. "Isis." In *Les Filles du feu*. Paris: Michel Lévy frères, 1856, 215–230.

Noghera, Vincenzo (Vincente Nogueira). *Letters*. Vatican Library, MS Barb. Lat. 6472.

Norman, Diana. "The Succorpo in the Cathedral of Naples: 'Empress of All Chapels.'" *Zeitschrift für Kunstgeschichte* 49, no. 3 (1986): 323–355.

Norway, Arthur H. *Naples Past and Present*. London: Methuen, 1901; 3rd ed. 1909.

Okamura, Katsuyuki, and Akira Matsuda, eds. *New Perspectives in Global Public Archaeology*. New York: Springer, 2011.

Onians, Richard Broxton. *The Origins of European Thought about the Mind, the Body, the World, Time and Fate.* Cambridge: Cambridge University Press, 1951.

Parslow, Christopher C. *Rediscovering Antiquity: Karl Weber and the Excavation of Herculaneum, Pompeii, and Stabiae.* Cambridge: Cambridge University Press, 1995.

Pesando, Fabrizio. "Shadows of Light: Cinema, Peplum, and Pompeii." In Pier Giovanni Guzzo, ed., *Stories from an Eruption: Pompeii, Herculaneum, Oplontis: A Guide to the Exhibition.* Milan: Electa, 2006, 34–43.

Piedimonte, Antonio Emanuele. "Gli 'scheletri' di Sansevero? Il principe li aveva solo comprati." *Il Corriere del Mezzogiorno*, August 11, 2011, http://corrieredelmezzogiorno.corriere.it/napoli/notizie/arte_e _cultura/2011/11-agosto-2011/gli-scheletri-sansevero-principe-li-aveva -solo-comprati-1901280322627.shtml (accessed August 26, 2013).

———. *Raimondo di Sangro, Principe di Sansevero: La vita, le invenzioni, le opere, i libri, la Cappella, le leggende, i misteri.* With an essay by Sigfrido Höbel [1903]. Naples: Edizioni Intra Moenia, 2010.

Piozzi, Hester Lynch. *Observations and Reflections made in the Course of a Journey through France, Italy, and Germany*, vol. 2. London: A. Strahan and T. Cadell, 1789.

Regina, Kristen. "Love Letter to a Goddess." *Apollo* 165, no. 544 (June 2007): 64–66.

Rowland, Ingrid D. "Athanasius Kircher, Giordano Bruno, and the *Panspermia* of the Infinite Universe." In Paula Findlen, ed., *Athanasius Kircher, the Last Man who Knew Everything.* New York: Routledge, 2004, 191–206.

———. "A Catholic Reader of Giordano Bruno in Counter-Reformation Rome: Athanasius Kircher, SJ, and *Panspermia Rerum.*" In Henning Hufnagel and Anne Eusterschulte, eds., *Turning Tradition Upside Down: Giordano Bruno's Enlightenment.* Berlin: Max-Planck-Institut für Wissenschaftsgeschichte, 2013, 221–236.

———. *Giordano Bruno, Philosopher/Heretic.* New York: Farrar, Straus, and Giroux, 2008.

Sannazaro, Jacopo. *Arcadia.* Venice: Aldus Manutius, 1534.

Santa Maria della Sanità. Naples: Cooperativa Sociale "La Paranza," [2012].

Scarth, Alwyn. *Vesuvius: A Biography*. Princeton, NJ: Princeton University Press, 2009.

Scholes, Percy Alfred, ed. *Dr. Burney's Musical Tours in Europe*. Oxford: Oxford University Press, 1957.

Serrapica, Agnese. " Pompei ed il culto dell'acqua: dalle Terme del Foro alla Fonte Salutare." http://www.iststudiatell.org/rsc/art_9n\Pompei _culto_acqua.htm (accessed August 8, 2013).

Shanks, Hershel. "The Destruction of Pompeii—God's Revenge?" *Biblical Archaeological Review* 36, no. 4 (July/August 2010): 60–69.

Siebert, Harald. *Die große kosmologische Kontroverse: Rekonstruktionsversuche anhand des Itinerarium exstaticum von Athanasius Kircher SJ (1602–1680)*. Stuttgart: Franz Steiner Verlag, 2006.

Sigurdsson, Haraldur. *Melting the Earth: The History of Ideas on Volcanic Eruptions*. New York: Oxford University Press, 1999.

Smith, Amy C. "Queens and Empresses as Goddesses: The Public Role of the Personal Tyche in the Graeco-Roman World." *Yale University Art Gallery Bulletin, An Obsession with Fortune: Tyche in Greek and Roman Art* (1994): 86–105.

Snowden, Frank. *Naples in the Time of Cholera, 1884–1911*. Cambridge: Cambridge University Press, 2010.

Spreafico, Eufrasio M. *Bartolo Longo, Servo di Dio*, vol. 1: *La Preparazione, 1841–1872*. Pompeii: Scuola tipografica pontificia pei figli dei carcerati fondata da Bartolo Longo, 1944.

Sterling and Francine Clark Art Institute. *Great French Paintings from the Clark: Barbizon through Impressionism*. New York: Rizzoli, 2011.

Stoltzenberg, Daniel. *Egyptian Oedipus: Athanasius Kircher and the Secrets of Egyptian Antiquity*. Chicago: University of Chicago Press, 2013.

Travaglione, Agnese. "Il Lavoratorio de' papiri di Padre Antonio Piaggio." In Renata Cantilena and Annalisa Porzio, eds., *Herculanense Museum, Laboratorio sull'antico nella Reggia di Portici*. Naples: Electa Napoli, 2008, 147–172.

Twain, Mark. *The Innocents Abroad, or, the New Pilgrims' Progress, Being Some Account of the Steamship Quaker City's Pleasure Excursion to Europe and the Holy Land: with Descriptions of Countries, Nations,*

Incidents and Adventures, as They Appeared to the Author. Hartford, CT: American Publishing Company, 1870.

Vasi, Mariano, rev. Venanzio Monaldini, rev. Antonio Nibby. *Guide of Naples and its Environs, containing a description of the antiquities and interesting curiosities preceded by the Journey from Rome to Naples by the Pontine marches and Montecassino from the Italian of Vasi.* Rome, 1841, sold by Monaldini English Library and Reading Room, Piazza di Spagna no. 79.

Vitruvius. *Ten Books on Architecture*, trans. Ingrid D. Rowland, illustrated by Thomas Noble Howe, commentary by Michael J. Dewar, Thomas Noble Howe, and Ingrid D. Rowland. Cambridge: Cambridge University Press, 1999.

Volpe, Francesco, ed. *Bartolo Longo e il suo tempo: Atti del convegno storico promosso dalla Delegazione pontificia per il Santuario di Pompei (Pompei 24–28 maggio 1982).* Rome: Edizioni di Storia e Letteratura, 1983.

Wallace-Hadrill, Andrew. *Herculaneum Past and Future.* London: Frances Lincoln, 2011.

Watkins, Glenn. *Gesualdo: The Man and His Music.* 2nd ed. Oxford: Oxford University Press, 1991.

White, Barbara Ehrlich. "Renoir's Trip to Italy." *The Art Bulletin* 51, no. 4 (1969): 333–351.

Wissman, Fronia E. "Renoir's Onions." *Gastronomica, the Journal of Food and Culture* 9, no. 2 (Spring 2009): 7–9.

Zanker, Paul. *Roman Art*, trans. Henry Heitmann-Gordon. Los Angeles: Getty Publications, 2010.

Zevi, Fausto. "Aspetti dell'archeologia pompeiana nel Novecento: Gli scavi del Maiuri a Pompei." In Pier Giovanni Guzzo, ed., *Pompei Scienza e Società, 250.0 Anniversario degli Scavi di Pompei Convegno Internazionale Napoli, 25–27 Novembre 1998.* Milan: Electa, 2001, 182–206.

Acknowledgments

The true credit for this book belongs to Sharmila Sen, an editor extraordinary. Kenneth Lapatin and Sean Cocco read the manuscript and provided a wealth of suggestions as well as inspiration with their comments.

Dario Ianneci and Teresa Rettino have always made me feel at home in Campania. Eugenio Canone, Eugenio Lo Sardo, John Marino, Livio Pestilli, and Thomas Howe have ensured that my life in Rome always has a bit of Naples in it. As students at the University of Chicago in the far-off 1990s, Crispin Corrado, Mario Pereira, Marina Belozerskaya, and Eric Poehler broadened my knowledge of Pompeii and Naples.

I owe much to Maria Ann Conelli and Kim Hartswick, but in this context special thanks for taking me to the Sanctuary of Pompeii to meet Maria's late uncle, Archbishop Francesco Saverio Toppi, and for first drawing my attention to Bartolo Longo.

Thanks to Liz at Art Resource, Alessandro at Bridgeman Fine Arts, and Ivana and the staff at Getty Images for their help with securing the illustrations. Princeton University Press kindly granted permission to reprint the poetry of George Seferis, in *George Seferis,* ed. Edmund Keeley (© 1967 Princeton University Press, 1995 renewed, revised edition). John

Donohue and Carol Hoke have saved me from a multitude of errors and infelicities.

Dermot O'Connell has supplied me with a wealth of books and conversation. Edoardo Schina put me in touch with Marisa de' Spagnolis and her memoir. Portia Prebys provided an amazing library of mid-twentieth-century literature on Pompeii, as well as memorable company on my very first student trips, including those dramatic interludes with my "enemy" from Carrani Tours. It is only appropriate to dedicate the book to her.

The best part of writing this book was the chance to return to Pompeii, old and new. It has never seemed so welcoming, or so beautiful.

Index